The Environmental Optimism of Elinor Ostrom

Edited by: Megan E. Jenkins,
Randy T Simmons, and Camille H. Wardle

The Center for
Growth and **Opportunity**
at Utah State University

Paperback ISBN 978-1-7348561-0-1

eISBN 978-1-7348561-1-8

Cover design and typesetting by Brooke Jacques

The Center for Growth and Opportunity at Utah State University
3525 Old Main Hill
Logan, UT 84322
www. thecgo.org

"As an institutionalist studying empirical phenomena, I
presume that individuals try to solve problems as effectively
as they can. . . . It is my responsibility as a scientist to
ascertain what problem individuals are trying to solve and
what factors help or hinder them in these efforts."

–*Elinor Ostrom, 2009 Nobel Laureate in Economic Sciences*

Contents

Introduction

Megan E. Jenkins and Randy T Simmons

U TAH STATE UNIVERSITY HAS HAD a long-term involvement in water resources management in the Dominican Republic. A few
years ago one of us (Randy Simmons) visited the Dominican Republic's National Institute for Water Resources. Behind a counter
on the main floor of their offices, an entire wall was taken up by a
map of the country, showing its nearly five thousand kilometers
of irrigation canals and fourteen major dams. When asked how
this system was managed, one of the water managers answered
with a question: "Have you ever heard of Elinor Ostrom?" They
were implementing her framework as they transferred management authority from the central government to local water-user
associations.

The Dominican experiment in irrigation management illustrates a key point in the Ostromian approach, because the management system is neither purely public nor purely private. It is
polycentric—that is, there are overlapping jurisdictions with multiple decision-making centers.[1] As Elinor Ostrom said in her Nobel
prize lecture, "The humans we study have complex motivational
structures and establish diverse private-for-profit, governmental,
and community institutional arrangements that operate at mul-

tiple scales to generate productive and innovative as well as destructive and perverse outcomes."[2] Social scientists use the term *social dilemma* to label situations in which there is conflict between individual and collective interests. Historically, there have been two basic ways of looking at such situations: a pessimistic point of view and an optimistic point of view. The pessimistic view—that individuals are helplessly trapped—was dominant in the past, and often still seems so. Ostrom's approach is so much more optimistic than this.

The most influential statement of pessimism about social dilemmas was Garrett Hardin's 1968 article, "The Tragedy of the Commons." Hardin claimed, "The inherent logic of the commons remorselessly generates tragedy. . . . Ruin is the destination toward which all men rush, each pursuing his own best interest in a society that believes in the freedom of the commons. Freedom in a commons brings ruin to all."[3] Many reacted to Hardin by proposing either government management or privatization of commons and commons-like resources. Ostrom and her colleagues helped researchers understand that there is a broad array of potential management schemes for resources held in common; the choice is not limited to purely public or purely private solutions.

As Ostrom explained in her Nobel lecture, "What have we learned? We now know that the earlier theories of rational, but helpless, individuals who are trapped in social dilemmas are not supported by a large number of studies using diverse methods."[4] Toward the end of her lecture, Ostrom summarized the key policy implications of her work: "The most important lesson for public policy analysis derived from the intellectual journey I have outlined here is that humans have a more complex motivational structure and more capability to solve social dilemmas than posited in earlier rational-choice theory."[5]

The essays in this volume are in the Ostromian tradition of exploring and attempting to understand complex institutional forms. Each chapter explores a particular issue in environmental policy by carefully analyzing how institutions impact the incentive to "help or hinder the innovativeness, learning, adapting, trustworthiness, levels of cooperation of participants, and the achievement of more effective, equitable, and sustainable outcomes at multiple scales."[6]

The diversity of topics studied in this volume serves as a tribute to the wide applicability of the foundational research Elinor Ostrom conducted. The volume begins with an examination of resource governance in the American West, looking at how top-down institutions developed to govern a complex and demanding landscape that new settlers were unaccustomed to. It then explores another example from the western United States: that of the largely successful polycentric management of the greater sage-grouse. The third chapter explores the role of American and Canadian indigenous groups in governing Pacific salmon fisheries. Chapter 4 moves on to an examination of Garrett Hardin's classic, "The Tragedy of the Commons," and of Ostrom's response to Hardin's claim that unchecked human population growth is a recipe for tragedy. The fifth chapter bridges the gap between the work of natural resources scholar and University of California Santa Barbara professor Gary Libecap on property rights and Ostrom's work on polycentric governance. And the sixth and final chapter explores the importance of long-distance trade in developing markets for industrial by-products, and thus in cleaning up the commons.

Although the chapters included here span diverse areas of study, several common themes emerge. The first is Elinor Ostrom's core finding that one-size-fits-all solutions cannot adequately address complex local conditions. Environmental issues tend to be complex, and solving them requires robust local knowledge and cooperation among on-the-ground actors. The chapters in this volume explore this theme by examining how settlers in the American West decided to allocate water and grazing rights as well as how indigenous groups work with national and international organizations to effectively manage salmon in the Pacific.

Another common theme is that human ingenuity and creativity are limitless. Garrett Hardin predicted that population growth would inevitably result in environmental catastrophe as human beings outstripped the earth's ability to keep them alive. But, as the authors of this volume point out, population growth has led to exponential increases in wealth, an increasing ability to produce greater amounts of food, and the development of life-saving and life-improving technologies. The case studies explored throughout this volume, from managing sage-grouse to developing markets that turn waste products into valuable by-products, demonstrate humans' limitless ability to work together to find creative solutions to environmental problems.

If we have learned anything about how to get better environmental outcomes, it is that institutions truly matter. The chapters here all shed light on how institutional design impacts whether local actors will cooperate to find mutually beneficial outcomes, or whether they will resort to conflict to get their desired outcome at the expense of someone else. Property rights, the enforcement of contracts, and cultural factors like trust all play an important role, and each of these institutions is explored in this volume.

Taken together, the work in this volume suggests that Elinor Ostrom was right—we don't have to choose between purely private or purely public responses to environmental problems. In fact, many problems will be best addressed by a solution that combines the best of both types of responses by allowing for polycentric governance at multiple levels. Environmental issues will continue to be complex and ever-changing, and may only increase in scale. Addressing these issues will require harnessing the limitless ingenuity of humankind to find innovative solutions to new problems. And the only way to fully harness that ingenuity will be to allow human beings to experiment, to try new approaches, to fail, to learn from that failure, and to work together.

Resource Governance in the American West: Institutions, Information, and Incentives

Peter J. Hill and Shawn Regan

T HE AMERICAN WEST IS A peculiar place. Depending on the location, the West can be drier, wetter, hotter, colder, or more
rugged than the eastern United States. Much of the West receives
only five to fifteen inches of precipitation each year, compared to
thirty to fifty inches in eastern states. Regional variation is also
much greater in the West. For example, while eastern Washington
and Oregon receive about ten inches of annual precipitation, the
western parts of those states receive more than one hundred inches per year. In addition to differences in precipitation patterns, the
overall climate, soil types, and topography of the West are strikingly different from those of the East.

Not only are the climates and landscapes of the West vastly
different from those of the eastern United States, the formal institutions that have been developed to govern the West's natural resources differ as well. In particular, top-down institutional
governance of land and natural resources has prevailed to a far
greater extent in the West than in the East. This trend includes
the Homestead Acts and other nineteenth-century land disposal
laws, which imposed strict limits on the size of land settlement
claims, as well as various policies in the early twentieth century

that placed large amounts of western land and natural resources under federal control. The legacies of these policies are evident in many ways today. The federal government owns 46.4 percent of the land in the eleven coterminous western states, compared to only 4.2 percent of the land outside the West.[1] As a result of this large-scale federal ownership, the management of timber, rangelands, minerals, water, and other natural resources throughout much of the West is controlled by centralized government policies and mandates.

This top-down institutional governance presents challenges for efficient management of the West's natural resources for two primary reasons. First, adjusting management methods to the region's varied landscapes and climates requires the use of local knowledge and continual adaptation to new realities, but both of these practices are often anathema to centralized control. Second, top-down institutions are often less adaptable to changing circumstances and new values than bottom-up solutions. In recent years, for example, federal and use regulations are based on consumptive uses, particularly timber harvest and cattle grazing. In the meantime, amenity values and other environmental demands have increased pressure for changes in use, yet the existing institutions don't allow for these new demands and have often contributed to rigidity and inefficiency. The result is that disputes over resource use are often resolved through top-down political means such as regulation and government mandates or through litigation, if they are resolved at all.

Elinor Ostrom's influential work provides useful insights into the various institutional frameworks for resource governance in the American West. In particular, her work demonstrates the importance of locally responsive institutions that are well adapted to circumstances of time and place. When such institutions are unable to emerge—whether because of institutional rigidity, top-down control by external authorities, or other reasons—resource governance is often inefficient, costly, and conflict-ridden. However, when such institutions do emerge, conflicts over resource use in the West can be resolved more efficiently and cooperatively.

Drawing from the insights of Ostrom and others, this chapter explores the emergence of various institutions governing the management of natural resources in the American West, both past and present, and discusses modern challenges associated with natural resource governance. It concludes by exploring policy reforms that would enable more cooperative, bottom-up solutions to today's resource management challenges in the American West.

1. Polycentric Governance

Much of Ostrom's work refutes the notion that there is "a single solution to a single problem."[2] She argues instead that "many solutions exist to cope with many different problems."[3] Specifically, much of her work has explored the conditions under which local resource users can develop bottom-up, self-governing institutional arrangements to manage resources — but a broader critique of top-down control is embedded in much of her work as well. "Instead of presuming that optimal institutional solutions can be designed easily and imposed at low cost by external authorities," she wrote in 1990, "'getting the institutions right' is a difficult, time-consuming, conflict-invoking process," one that "requires reliable information about time and place variables as well as a broad repertoire of culturally acceptable rules."[4] Ostrom's work suggests that the different formulations of governance structures to manage natural resources are best discovered through a process of experimentation driven by people who have localized control—in other words, through bottom-up institutional evolution.[5]

Ostrom also describes well the problems with centralized solutions to resource governance issues:

When analysts perceive the human beings they model as being trapped inside perverse situations, they then assume that other human beings external to those involved—scholars and public officials—are able to analyze the situation, ascertain why counterproductive outcomes are reached, and posit what changes in the rules-in-use will enable participants to improve outcomes. Then, external officials are expected to impose an optimal set of rules on those individuals involved. It is assumed that the momentum for change must come from outside the situation rather than from the self-reflection and creativity of those within a situation to restructure their own patterns of interaction.[6]

Ostrom's work is useful for understanding resource governance challenges in the West, both in the past and in the present. A historical perspective of resource governance in the American West reveals that many western resource-governance institutions were initially developed in a bottom-up manner that was responsive to local conditions and local knowledge, similar to those institutions described by Ostrom. Before the establishment of formal government control in the American West, Euro-American settlers developed locally responsive institutional innovations that were well adapted to the region's unique and varied landscapes. This system required a process of learning about and adapting production to a largely unknown resource base, including new climates and landscapes. In some cases, governance of these natural resources remains relatively decentralized today. In other cases, the political institutions developed in the nineteenth and early twentieth centuries to govern western natural resource use were top-down in nature and have continued to be so throughout the past century, contributing to rent dissipation, high transaction costs, and political conflict.

2. The West: A Different World

The region of the United States west of the 100th meridian is strikingly different from the rest of the country.[7] Not only is much of it arid, but the variation in rainfall is much greater than in the region east of the Mississippi. Droughts and extended periods of low precipitation are common. Detailed precipitation records only go back to around 1900, but tree-ring studies suggest that drought has been a recurring phenomenon over long periods of time. For instance, one study of western Nebraska found an extended thirty-six-year drought from 1631 to 1667.[8] Reconstructions of California's drought history reveal frequent "mega-droughts" throughout history that were severe and long-lasting.[9]

Economic historians Gary Libecap and Zeynep Hansen capture well the West's weather conditions and the challenges therein: "The Great Plains could either be wet and lush or dry and barren, with no particular pattern," they write. "These conditions presented unusual learning and adaptation challenges for all parties on the frontier in ways not fully appreciated in the existing literature."[10] Historian Warren Beck and cartographer Ynez Haase also describe the very different terrain explorers and settlers encountered: "Americans moving westward may have been ill prepared for the strange conditions of Great Plains; they were totally unprepared for their encounter with the mountain ranges and desert terrain. In fact, some considered the Rockies to be an impassable barrier."[11]

Throughout the nineteenth century, both settlement and transportation became issues of much experimentation as Euro-Americans struggled to deal with the West's strange new environments.[12] Agricultural practices that were successful in one portion of the West were not readily transferable to other areas.

The twenty-inch rainfall line, an approximate north-south boundary beyond which there is not enough precipitation to grow crops without irrigation, lies fairly close to the 100th meridian. Even using that as a dividing line, however, is misleading because of the large variations in yearly rainfall: rainfall statistics can vary widely over short distances in the western United States.

Historian Walter Prescott Webb aptly describes the necessity of experimentation and adaption of new institutions and techniques in the West:

> For two centuries American pioneers had been working out a technique for the utilization of the humid regions east of the Mississippi River. They had found solutions for their problems and were conquering the frontier at a steadily accelerating rate. Then in the early nineteenth century they crossed the Mississippi and came out on the Great Plains, an environment with which they had no experience. The result was a complete though temporary breakdown of the machinery and ways of pioneering.
>
> As one contrasts the civilization of the Great Plains with that of the eastern timberland, one sees what may be called an institutional *fault* (comparable to a geological fault) running from middle Texas to Illinois or Dakota, roughly following the ninety-eighth meridian. At this *fault* the ways of life and living changed. Practically every institution that was carried across it was either broken and remade or else greatly altered. The ways of travel, the weapons, the method of tilling the soil, plows and other agricultural

implements, and even the laws themselves were modified.[13]

Given the wide variation in topography in the American West and the necessity of experimentation and local knowledge, it is somewhat surprising that resource governance in the West today is generally more top-down than bottom-up. One can argue, in fact, that the West is characterized by more top-down resource governance institutions than the eastern United States.[14] Moreover, the perception of the highest and best use of the West has also changed dramatically over time. In the face of such changes, one would again expect bottom-up institutional evolution to be appropriate to allow resources to be allocated to their highest-valued uses. Top-down governance, however, has hampered much of the adjustment process, especially the move from commercial agriculture to amenity values and other environmental demands.

3. Institutions, Information, and Incentives

Ostrom developed a framework that helps one understand the importance of institutions and institutional change in the context of natural resource management.[15] People make decisions on the basis of the information available to them, the incentives they face, and the belief framework they use for processing and judging information flows. The institutions—or the rules of the game governing resources—play an important role in the decision-making process.[16] Institutions, both formal and informal, also determine the locus of decision making and the process by which decisions by one person are coordinated with the choices of others.[17]

In much of her work, Ostrom used detailed case studies to demonstrate how resource users can often develop self-governing institutions to effectively manage common-pool natural resources. Whether such institutions emerge, however, depends on certain conditions. Ostrom outlines several "design principles" that help explain the success of existing self-governance arrangements for common-pool resources. They include clearly defined resource boundaries, locally tailored rules that reflect the specific attributes of a particular resource, sufficient monitoring and sanctions undertaken by participants, conflict-resolution mechanisms, and the ability to devise locally adapted institutions without interference from external governmental authorities.[18]

Such bottom-up institutional arrangements rely extensively on what F. A. Hayek describes as "the knowledge of the particular circumstances of time and place" that is of primary importance for effective decision making.[19] In the context of natural resource management, the physical environment is important for determining the value of such local knowledge. If one compares two environments, an environment in which there exists unknown or contradictory knowledge about appropriate production decisions and another environment with more uniform circumstances, one would expect that the varied environment would require more decentralized decision making. Moreover, if environmental conditions are dynamic, or if human demands on natural resources are evolving over time, centralized control will tend to impose rigidities on natural resource use that are inefficient and difficult to modify.

It is an obvious anomaly, then, that as Euro-American settlers moved into the western half of the United States, the institutions governing decisions about natural resource use largely became more centralized. Compared to the East, far more aspects of resource management in the West are under federal control.[20] Government involvement in agricultural investment through massive irrigation projects is primarily a western phenomenon. Federal management of rangelands for livestock grazing is unique to the West. National forest management is largely a western issue. Public ownership of vast stores of energy and mineral wealth such as oil, gas, and coal is limited to the western half of the United States. This pattern of large-scale, centralized control means that questions of natural resource governance in the American West are fundamentally political questions decided by federal decision makers rather than by local decision makers responding to local knowledge.

Such centralized control would perhaps make sense if expert knowledge were superior to local knowledge. Yet whether this is true in the context of natural resource management has been a matter of extensive debate dating back to the Progressive Era.[21] Hayek discusses the relative importance of technical knowledge, or the knowledge of experts versus the knowledge of individuals on the ground. He argues that if expert knowledge is of more importance, the institutional order does not have to be exclusively centered on bottom-up, local knowledge. Expert knowledge, however, is "frequently contradictory knowledge,"[22] and if the knowledge of experts is incorrect and institutions favor that knowledge over local knowledge, then greater errors will occur than would in a more decentralize decision-making setting. In a setting with many unknowns, the discovery process is important, and the rule of experts is often mistaken.

Three examples in the settlement of the West illustrate this point: the theory that the "rain follows the plow," the theory that forestation would increase rainfall in the arid West, and the dry farming doctrine.

The aridity of much of the West was a primary concern for settlers who wanted to establish agricultural operations. The notion that the "rain follows the plow" was an oft-repeated theme among early settlers and was based on expert advice. Samuel Aughey Jr., appointed the first professor of natural science at the University of Nebraska in 1871, published articles, pamphlets, and a book arguing that rain did indeed follow the plow: that is, once the soil was broken by a plow, it would absorb more moisture. This moisture would be given back slowly to the atmosphere through evaporation, causing rainfall to increase. He predicted that as more and more of the Great Plains was plowed, rainfall would increase to the point that crops could be grown on a regular basis without irrigation.[23] Others publicized the argument through books and public lectures. "Rain follows the plow" was the major thesis of a popular book by Charles Dana Wilber, *The Great Valleys and Prairies of Nebraska and the Northwest*, published in 1881. Orange Judd, publisher of the *Prairie Farmer*, and Frank Snow, chancellor the University of Kansas, were other prominent exponents of the idea.[24] The theory was a primary justification for the original Homestead Act of 1862, which limited settlers to 160-acre land claims that were later viewed as too small for the arid conditions of the West. At the time, it was thought that acreage limitations would be overcome by intensive plowing.

Another theory, later discredited, suggested that increasing forestation would increase rainfall through increased humidity. Again, the aridity of much of the West meant that there were extensive efforts to discover what worked and what did not work in terms of rainfall and agriculture. Among the prominent advocates of planting trees to increase precipitation were Frederick Olmsted, the famous landscape architect, and Ferdinand Hayden, one of the foremost explorers and surveyors of the West. Professors at land-grant universities and forestry officials lent additional support to the idea.[25] In 1873, tree planting became official federal policy with the passage of the Timber Culture Act, which modified the original Homestead Act to allow claimants to receive an extra 160 acres of land if they planted 40 acres of trees.

Another expert-driven solution to aridity was the dry farming doctrine that dominated discussion of appropriate farming techniques from 1905 until 1917.[26] Deep cultivation, packing the subsurface soil, and harrowing after every rain were techniques that supposedly would allow farming to succeed in areas of low rainfall. Agricultural experiment stations, created by Congress in 1887 and attached to land-grant colleges, were major advocates of dry farming techniques. Years with higher-than-normal rainfall gave credence to the theory, but the 1917–1921 drought in eastern Montana was the death knell of the idea that dry farming techniques could compensate for low and variable precipitation.

These varied attempts to discover how to interact with the aridity of the American West provide ample evidence for Ostrom's insights about the importance of communication among those with local knowledge and those directly involved in a particular resource issue. Walter Prescott Webb, for example, describes how such local knowledge and trial-and-error experimentation radically transformed many of the longstanding institutions and practices that were familiar to Euro-Americans as they advanced across the western frontier. Webb describes the frontier as "a modifier of institutions" on the basis of local adaptation and innovation.[27] The frontier, he writes, "acted as a force in modifying old institutions or displacing them with new ones better fitted to the needs of a frontier culture."[28] These modifications took on many forms in response to local conditions on the frontier, such as changes in the way water rights were allocated, the development of new fence-building techniques, and even the adoption of new weaponry.

In the context of the American West, Gary Libecap explains how assigning property rights to western resources required adaptation from established eastern practices. He notes that "property rights allocations that were based on local conditions and prior use and were unconstrained by outside government mandates were most effective in addressing not only the immediate threat of open-access, but in providing a longer-term basis for production, investment, and trade."[29] Yet Libecap also notes that some of the property institutions developed to govern natural resources were poorly constructed—the result of what he calls "initial faulty property allocations"—and, to the extent that such institutions were formalized by governments, they created path dependencies today that are difficult to modify. In particular, Libecap explains that the political transaction costs of reforming faulty property institutions are high, and political constituencies that benefit from the status quo often emerge and create significant barriers to change.

4. Top-Down Governance in the American West

The history of resource governance in the American West is replete with examples of top-down control ill-suited to the physical realities and local knowledge requirements of the western landscape. These institutions created obstacles for appropriate adjustments to the unique conditions of the region.

4.1 Western Settlement

The Land Ordinance of 1785 set in motion the mechanisms for dealing with the vast areas of land that later became part of the United States. One of the most important elements in the ordinance was the relinquishment to the national government of the original thirteen colonies' land claims beyond their borders. Originally, land policy was driven by two primary tenets: first, that federal lands should be transferred to private ownership, and second, that the mechanism of transfer would be sale of land to the highest bidder.[30]

Early land sales focused on the minimum acres that could be sold at auction, which varied over time from 40 to 640 acres. Many sales were for blocks of land much larger than the minimum; a land speculator would buy a large segment and then divide it over time into appropriate farm-sized units or town sites for subsequent sale. This process was well designed to take account of local knowledge since the purchaser had strong incentives to create parcels that reflected the existing farming technology and local climate conditions. Legal historian Robert Ellickson makes the case for individual land ownership of a size that takes into account the productive potential of land and the interactions of individuals in using the land.[31] US land policy before 1862 fit quite well Ellickson's prescription of the optimal design of a land ownership regime.

Since land sales were designed to maximize revenue for the federal government, a minimum price was set that specified the process of land sales. Often, however, settlers pushed into lands available for purchase and settled without following the formal legal process. Congress was reluctant to use force to evict the squatters, and gradually legal rights of preemption were recognized. Again, however, settlers relied heavily on local knowledge in choosing where to settle. Economic rents were dissipated through people racing for the most productive lands, but rent dissipation was mitigated through land claims clubs. These extralegal organizations would claim an area for a group of settlers through preemption and hold it until it became profitable to settle, and then those settlers would bring the land into production.[32]

Land privatization changed dramatically with the 1862 Homestead Act. Instead of codifying minimum size allocations, the act specified 160 acres as the maximum homestead size. And rather than being distributed via cash sales, the land was to be "free" to homesteaders who lived on a plot for five years and made appropriate improvements.[33] In reality, however, the land was never free. Settlers dissipated any rents available from land ownership through racing to claim property rights.[34] For example, if a 160-acre claim in Wyoming would generate rents in 1900—in other words, if it would generate some return above the opportunity cost of settlement—settlers would not wait until 1900 to move to the land and bring it into production. Instead, they would compete for the rents by settling the land as soon as the discounted present value of the stream of future rents was positive.

The move from allowing privatization to occur gradually through preemption and land purchases to forcing races for maximum-size units was especially inappropriate because the Homestead Act applied primarily to poorly understood western lands. A farm of 160 acres was quite feasible in Ohio, but was poorly suited to the semi-arid conditions in Kansas. And for land that was not suitable for tillage but instead was used for livestock grazing, acreage limits were even more constraining.

The costs were large, both in terms of loss of production and in terms of human suffering as settlers tried to claim land too early and in plots that were too small for them to set up a profitable operation. Dan Fulton, a Montana cattle rancher and historian, reports that, by 1922, 88 percent of homesteaders who entered claims in Montana between 1909 and 1918 "had starved out or given up."[35] Fewer than half of the homestead claims in Wyoming between 1910 and 1934 were completed.[36] By 1905, there were still 450,000 acres that had yet to be claimed,[37] further evidence of the difficulty of establishing viable agricultural operations on 160 acres. Zeynep Hansen and Gary Libecap argue that homesteading was a major contributor to the dust bowl conditions of the 1930s.[38] Small farm size meant it was more difficult to use fallow methods that limited soil erosion.

Given that such small homestead sizes were decidedly unworkable for agricultural operations in the West, why did the policy persist for as long as it did?[39] Two forces were at work. The idea of free land continued to have political appeal in the US Congress, but there was also a strong desire for that land to go to small-scale yeoman farmers. Despite numerous attempts to revise the Homestead Acts, Congress refused to budge from granting supposed privileges to small farmers. Also, as discussed above, there was scientific evidence (although it turned out to be flawed) that plowing the land and planting trees would increase precipitation and make small farms economically viable.[40]

Texas provides an interesting contrast to federal homestead policy. Because Texas entered the United States as a sovereign nation, the Homestead Acts did not apply there. As a result, land disposition policy there was much more rational and led to a wide variety of farm sizes. The Texas Constitution of 1836 granted a league of land (4,428 acres) to household heads, and single men received one-third of a league (1,476 acres).[41] Over time more such "headright" grants were made, and as the arid lands of the Texas Panhandle were settled, the state used land trades to fund projects.[42] Throughout the nineteenth century, state lands were available for purchase, leading to ownership of property for cattle raising on a more appropriate economic scale. As a result of these land disposal policies, most of the land in Texas was privatized, and only a small portion of the state (just 1.8 percent) remains in public ownership today. This stands in sharp contrast to most of the American West, where large amounts of land were ultimately retained by the federal government—a topic we turn to next.

4.2 Federal Land Retention and Management

The other major change in land policy was the move away from privatization to retention by the federal government. Even though the Homestead Acts imposed high transaction costs on establishing private rights, those rights could later be organized into efficiently sized units. The costs of top-down governance became even higher, however, once policy changes cemented the federal government as a permanent, large-scale landowner in the West. Today, nearly half of the land in western states is owned and managed by federal agencies, primarily the US Forest Service and the Bureau of Land Management.

The move to retention rather than sale began with the General Revision Act of 1891, which allowed the president to set aside, or reserve, public lands bearing forests. President Benjamin Harrison made the first such withdrawal, setting aside fourteen million acres.[43] In 1897, Congress passed the Forest Service Organic Administration Act, which strengthened the federal government's ability to reserve and manage forest lands.

The move from privatization to retention was driven by the dominant Progressive Era ideology of the late nineteenth and early twentieth centuries. The Progressive Era embodied a strong commitment to the idea that scientific management could replace market forces. Progressives at the time favored centralized control of the nation's natural resources on the basis that management by experts would be superior to management by local communities left to the whims of the market. President Theodore Roosevelt, along with Gifford Pinchot, the first chief of the US Forest Service, advocated what historian Samuel Hays calls "the gospel of efficiency," which Hays describes as the belief that "experts, using technical and scientific methods, should decide all matters of development and utilization of resources."[44] This Progressive Era ideology favors large-scale federal ownership of natural resources, federal bureaus devoted to efficient management, and formal comprehensive land-use planning, all of which remain hallmarks of federal land policy today.

This Progressive Era thinking, which has been widely criticized for its failures,[45] captures well Ostrom's concern that centralized control will often be seen as a panacea for resource governance problems. Such top-down solutions may well crowd out more responsive and incentive-compatible local institutional innovations.

As forest lands were being set aside for government management, and with homestead claims limited to small sizes, massive amounts of arid land not suitable for farming were not being claimed by homesteaders. Congress eventually attempted to create better incentives for stock raising with the Enlarged Homestead Act of 1909 and the Stock-Raising Homestead Act of 1916. The 1909 act doubled the maximum size of a land claim, bringing it to 320 acres, and the 1916 act increased it again, to 640 acres.

Yet both acts still imposed size limitations that made cattle ranching unprofitable in much of the West. On the Great Plains' prairie land, stocking rates are between 20 and 30 acres per cow per year, so—even with the increases—the herd size enabled by a single land claim was far below what was necessary for a sustainable grazing operation.

With much of the arid western land unclaimed, ranchers knew there was little chance for complete privatization, so they argued for leasing arrangements that would give them legal use and management opportunities on the unclaimed open range. In 1934, the Taylor Grazing Act was passed, which allowed the Department of the Interior to actively manage unclaimed rangelands. The legislation specified that 80 million acres could be withdrawn from the unreserved public land and placed in grazing districts. Such a designation closed those lands to homesteading. The 80-million-acre limitation was subsequently removed, and 162 million acres were eventually allocated for federally managed livestock grazing. These lands are now administered by the Bureau of Land Management.

4.3 Irrigation

Another major top-down institutional structure in the West is the provision of irrigation water through the Bureau of Reclamation. Rather than relying on the private provision of irrigation or Ostrom-style local collective action, the federal government has enabled the bureau to be a dominant force in bringing western lands under irrigation. Federal irrigation was promoted starting in the 1870s, but it was not until 1902, when Congress passed the Reclamation Act with the enthusiastic support of Theodore Roosevelt, that irrigation became a function of the federal government. Since financing was originally predicated on the sale of federal lands, thirteen western states were covered, with Texas excluded because it had no federal lands.

Despite the claims that federal support of irrigation was necessary to foster the development of western land for agriculture, there were already 8.9 million acres of private irrigated land when the Reclamation Act passed in 1902.[46] Thus, it was not the case that federal involvement was necessary for irrigation to occur. Once the federal government got involved, the necessity of carefully calculating benefits and costs ended, and the Bureau of Reclamation became a source of massive subsidies and unnecessary projects. The bureau has aggressively attempted to dam every major river at multiple locations. Furthermore, the requirement that irrigation project costs should be repaid by users went by the wayside, and soon most projects suffered from cost overruns and little attention was given to payback obligations. On the whole, less than 15 percent of project costs were paid back by 1980. Since present payments from users focus on operating costs, the large-scale subsidies continue.[47]

Reclamation projects have continued to the present day, with political considerations overriding efficiency concerns. The Central Arizona Project was authorized in 1968 and was completed in 1987 with a loss of $1 billion.[48] The official in charge of providing benefit-cost analysis for that project has been quoted as saying, "I had to fly all the way out to Denver and jerk around the benefit-cost numbers to make the thing look sound."[49]

5. Institutional Evolution from the Bottom

Despite the top-down institutions discussed above, in some cases settlers developed bottom-up institutions for natural resource governance similar to those Ostrom described in her numerous works. The process of land privatization was slow and incomplete, but there were several situations that afforded opportunities for institutional innovation. Settlers sought to find ways to allow resources to be claimed and moved to their highest-valued uses, as well as to develop rules that reduced waste and minimized conflict. Many of these innovations were extralegal, and some were eventually incorporated into state law, while others were negated by state or federal action.

5.1 Varying Forms of Agriculture

An early issue that required entrepreneurial insight and innovation was the challenge of putting western land to its highest and best use.[50] Many settlers tried growing row crops, and dry farming was successful in certain areas. In other places, settlers quickly developed irrigation. Often, however, cattle grazing was more economical. The search for optimal use was an ongoing process, in which local information was vital. Family farms dominated agricultural production, but those farms used a wide variety of contractual forms to organize inputs and to sell outputs.[51] There was substantial leasing of land between farmers and from outside owners, and there was a wide range of lease contracts. In many cases, crop type and risk preferences led to crop-share arrangements, but in others cash leases dominated.[52]

As with any attempt to adapt to new conditions, there were costly mistakes. Early cattle grazing on the Northern Plains was done by absentee owners who turned livestock loose to graze with minimal supervision. It was thought that cattle could survive without extra care or feeding. The winter of 1886/87 was disastrous, with immense livestock loss. Owner-operators who put up hay for the winter and who provided much more supervision eventually became the main livestock producers.[53]

5.2 Water Rights

For allocating water, the common law historically relied on the riparian doctrine, which gave streambank landowners a right to undiminished quantity and quality of water. In the mining camps of the American West, it became clear that diversion of water from streams was important for sluicing gravel to find gold. But since the riparian doctrine did not provide for any diversion, a brand-new doctrine known as prior appropriation emerged as an alternative rights structure. The prior appropriation doctrine granted exclusive rights to the first person to divert water. The timing of the appropriation became a determinant of the quality of the right, because subsequent diverters held their rights conditional on the use of the prior appropriator. The quantity of the diversion was limited to the amount of water that could be put to beneficial use, defined as use in mining claims or to irrigate farm lands. Water could be diverted to nonriparian lands, and the rights to water could be transferred.

The prior appropriation doctrine was crucial to mining and the development of agricultural production in the American West. It was adopted in its purest form in the most arid states, with some modifications in western states that had higher rainfall.[54] The benefits of the new rights structure were large. Economists Bryan Leonard and Gary Libecap estimate that by 1930 the benefits of irrigated agriculture were 3.5 percent to 20 percent of state income, and that most of these benefits existed thanks to the prior appropriation doctrine.[55]

5.3 Irrigation

There was rapid development of irrigation in many areas in the West. By the time of the Reclamation Act in 1902, there were 8.9 million acres of land irrigated by private water.[56] Some stream diversion was carried out by individual operators, but most irrigation involved collective action. Many mutual ditch companies were created, with farmer-users owning the corporations that provided irrigation infrastructure. These companies were effective in organizing capital for irrigation development, and farmer ownership avoided the monopoly problem.[57]

States also created the opportunity for local groups to form a legal organization that could tax land to support diversion structures, pumping facilities, and canals. In 1887 California became the first state to pass such enabling legislation. It allowed a group of fifty or more farmers to petition the county board of supervisors to create a taxation district. A two-thirds majority of voters in the designated area was required for approval.[58] California irrigation districts received a 90 percent approval rate, a strong indication that these small-scale collective organizations had widespread community approval.[59] Other states followed California's lead: Washington's legislature passed enabling legislation in 1890; Kansas and Nevada in 1891; Idaho, Nebraska, and Oregon in 1895; and Colorado in 1901.[60]

Irrigation projects depended heavily on trust relationships. Mormons arrived in the Salt Lake Valley in 1847, and by 1848 they had irrigated 5,000 acres. Irrigation spread rapidly, with 150,000 acres growing irrigated crops by 1865.[61] The church provided the infrastructure for building canals and diverting water. Canal governance was also carried out by community religious-based organizations.[62]

5.4 Mining

The discovery of gold at Sutter's Mill in California in 1848 and silver in the Comstock Lode in Nevada in 1859 led to a rapid evolution of rights to mining claims. There was almost no federal presence in those areas and no clear rules for establishing mining claims. Therefore, the rules for mining claims grew organically and were time- and place-specific. Mining camps developed clear rules for establishing and maintaining claims, and those rules differed depending on the value of the claims and whether the precious metals were located in surface gravel, streams, or underground veins.

The rapid influx of miners from different backgrounds to claim a valuable resource would seem to be a sure recipe for violence. The mining camps were surprisingly orderly, however, because the miners found violence to be negative-sum in nature. Settling on rules provided prospectors with the opportunity to produce wealth rather than fight over ownership.[63] States gradually codified the rules that had evolved in mining camps, and the federal government accepted the principle of entry and patenting of claims in 1866.

Gold mining was based on the alluvial deposits in stream beds, and early prospectors were able to pan to extract the precious mineral. It became evident that using water in sluice boxes was more efficient, and this required different forms of organization in order to divert water and to provide labor for the sluices. Some efforts required new forms of ownership, and others involved the collective efforts of owners and nonowners.[64]

5.5 Grazing

By limiting the size of land claims, the Homestead Acts severely constrained cattle ranching on the frontier, but there were still strong incentives to develop rules to solve coordination problems on the open range. Since much of the range was unappropriated, there was potential for a tragedy of the commons to develop. Yet ranchers discovered innovative ways to establish extralegal rights to the open range by the rule of first possession and to limit new entrants through local norms and through restricting access to bi-annual community roundups. With the invention of barbed wire in 1873, fencing was used to prevent overgrazing on the common pastures. The fences, which followed locally-agreed-upon boundaries, did interfere with legal claims under the Homestead Acts, so in 1885, Congress passed an anti-fencing act that forced the removal of fences from more than a million acres.[65]

Local norms continued to dominate the legal framework for much of the cattle industry. The rules for claiming maverick calves and for organizing roundups were enforced by cattleman associations.[66] Likewise, Robert Ellickson finds that in Shasta County, California, the rules governing grazing land were bottom-up norms that ignored the top-down legal rules.[67]

6. Changing Demands in a Top-Down World

The institutional innovations discussed above provide a helpful case study in the use of time- and place-specific information to solve coordination issues. The bottom-up evolution of norms and rules ameliorated some of the heavy-handed, top-down governance of land and water during the first century and a half of western settlement. Another problem with top-down rules, however, emerged in the twentieth century: some resources became more valuable for producing nonconsumptive amenity and environmental goods than for commercial production of timber, crops, and cattle. Over the past half-century, these new amenity and environmental demands have often encountered natural resource governance institutions that were designed for the extraction-based demands of an earlier era. In many cases, these institutions have proved ill equipped to address these new resource demands.[68] Many of the top-down institutions governing natural resources in the West are rigid and favor traditional extraction-based demands, resulting in high transaction costs, legal disputes, and political controversy in the face of new conservation-oriented demands. Several examples illustrate these challenges.

These examples illustrate the challenges of institutional path dependence,[69] which tends to lock in suboptimal institutional arrangements, and also demonstrate the importance of the initial allocations of property rights in the presence of transaction costs, a point emphasized in the work of Ronald Coase.[70] Once a certain institution is established to allocate natural resources, it tends to prevail even in the face of changing demands. This helps explain why institutional reform has been so challenging in the American West. Because of the "stickiness" of top-down western resource institutions, new environmental and amenity demands have often resulted in the creation of even more top-down regulatory policies or political mandates. That is, because the existing governance institutions are unable to reconcile new demands with traditional resource uses, separate laws, regulations, and mandates are often created to address environmental and amenity concerns.

The dispute between the "Old West" and the "New West" is illustrative of these challenges. The Old West is characterized by traditional extractive uses of the western landscape, such as agricultural development, grazing, timber harvesting, and mining. The New West represents the emerging recreational, conservation, and environmental interests on the western landscape. These two visions are often incompatible. That is, the emerging demands for recreation and conservation often conflict with the demands of traditional extractive resources users. How these competing demands can be reconciled is one of the central challenges of western natural resource management today, and it is the source of much modern political debate.

6.1 Environmental Water Markets

The evolution of western water law demonstrates these challenges. As described above, the traditional rules established to govern water in the West, which were codified in the nineteenth century by state legislatures, were created for the unique needs of the arid West's agricultural economy. The prior appropriation doctrine provided usage rights on a first-come, first-served basis for settlers who put the water to "beneficial use."[71] This beneficial-use requirement was incorporated into state law, meaning that water rights were valid as long as the water was physically diverted from a stream and used in a manner determined to be "beneficial" by the state, primarily for crop irrigation.

Yet as new environmental and conservation demands emerged in the latter part of the twentieth century, the prior appropriation doctrine was unable to resolve conflicts over these new, competing demands for water use. The beneficial-use requirement precluded the possibility of water rights being acquired and used for instream flows to improve fish and wildlife habitat or for recreational or amenity purposes. Initially, courts denied voluntary trades to transfer water rights from an agricultural use to an environmental use, such as for instream flows, on the basis that such uses (or non-uses, as it were) were not a legally accepted form of "beneficial use."[72] The institutions governing water, which were conceived in an earlier era, simply did not allow for such voluntary transactions to occur. As a result, early efforts to promote instream flows relied on state regulations and restrictions on water use.

Over the past three decades, however, many western states have begun to gradually expand the legal systems governing water rights to recognize instream flows as a beneficial use and to allow voluntary trades to occur for the purpose of enhancing such flows.[73] This change has required amending the definition of a beneficial use. Today, as a result of this institutional change, a considerable number of water trades result in the transfer of water from agricultural uses to environmental purposes such as instream flows.[74] Nonetheless, despite these recent developments, considerable legal and institutional barriers still exist that complicate environmental water markets and make it difficult for new environmental demands to be expressed through the prior appropriation system of western water allocation. Reforms that lower the transaction costs of market exchanges and clarify rights to instream environmental flows could further enhance environmental water markets.[75]

6.2 Conflicts over Public Land Use

Other western resource governance institutions, however, have not been as flexible as state water law in accommodating new environmental and amenity demands. Consider livestock grazing on federal rangelands in the West. The Taylor Grazing Act of 1934 established federal control over grazing on the unclaimed public domain lands that composed the open range. The act created grazing districts on unclaimed public lands, established a permit system to manage grazing on these lands, and allowed grazing fees to be charged for use of the public rangeland. Under this system, ranchers were eligible to receive grazing permits if they owned a nearby qualifying "base property," which could serve as a base for the rancher's livestock operation, and if they could demonstrate a recent history of grazing on the open range. This system remains in place today. Grazing permits cannot be transferred to groups or individuals that do not hold a qualifying base property. Permits are issued for ten-year periods, and permit holders have priority over others to renew the permit for additional ten-year periods without competition.

The Taylor Grazing Act also gives preference to ranchers who operate within or near a grazing district and who are "engaged in the livestock business, bona fide occupants or settlers, or owners of water or water rights." Moreover, it establishes a use-it-or-lose-it permit requirement to ensure that federal grazing permits are actively used for grazing purposes: if they are not being used, they can be revoked and transferred to other ranchers. This requirement, like the traditional beneficial-use requirement in western water law, poses important challenges in the face of new environmental and recreational demands over the western rangelands.[76] The use-it-or-lose-it requirement, in addition to the base property requirement, significantly raises the costs of acquiring grazing permits for "non-use" conservation, environmental, or recreational purposes—and in some cases entirely precludes the possibility of acquiring grazing permits for such purposes. In short, permittees are required to graze livestock on their public grazing allotments, or the federal government could transfer the grazing privileges to another rancher who will use them.[77]

Unlike western water law, however, no meaningful institutional reforms have been implemented to modify these rigid grazing provisions, which complicate the ways in which federal rangeland policy can accommodate new environmental demands. In other words, no evolution has occurred in federal rangeland management whereby environmental use (or non-use) is recognized as a legally valid or "beneficial" use that could facilitate voluntary transactions of rangeland usage rights from grazing uses to environmental, recreational, or amenity uses.

The inability of federal rangeland policy to accommodate these new, competing environmental demands has important implications. In particular, one significant result is that federal rangelands are the source of immense political and legal controversy in the American West, as evidenced by several near-violent, high-profile conflicts over grazing rights in recent years.[78] Because there are significant obstacles to resolving competing demands through voluntary transactions, competing groups have instead resorted to political or legal channels to influence the management of federal rangelands. Over the years, this has resulted in various federal environmental regulations and mandates that restrict grazing through political means. Litigation is also often used by environmental groups in an attempt to force federal agencies to reduce grazing on certain public lands for the purposes of endangered species protection, water quality conservation, and mitigation of other environmental concerns.[79]

Federal rangeland policies have largely proved incapable of resolving new conflicting demands through negotiation rather than conflict. This institutional path dependence has thwarted mutually beneficial exchanges of grazing rights and contributed to political and legal disputes over western land use.[80] As a result, the western range is more often the subject of conflict, litigation, and regulation rather than of exchange and cooperation.

The story is much the same for other federally managed natural resources in the American West.[81] The top-down institutions governing resource use are largely ill equipped to effectively resolve new conflicting demands over resource use, resulting in the creation of other political or legal strategies to influence resource use. For example, the institutions governing timber management on federal lands do not allow use (or non-use) rights to be directly allocated to environmental or recreational groups.[82] Rather, the interests of such groups are expressed through a myriad of environmental laws and regulations that require, among other things, environmental assessments, lengthy public comment periods on proposed agency actions, or endangered species habitat protections, or that impose top-down restrictions on where certain management actions can and cannot occur.

Likewise, public land policies restrict market-based approaches to resolving disputes over energy development on federal lands.[83] For instance, the institutions governing oil and gas leasing prevent recreational, environmental, or conservation interests from holding leases. Lease terms require that leaseholders must intend to develop their energy leases.[84] This "diligent development requirement" dates back to the Mineral Leasing Act of 1920 and states that "lessees must exercise reasonable diligence in developing and producing" leased energy resources. The predictable result is that, to the extent that environmental or amenity values are represented in the political process governing federal energy development, they are expressed through regulations, mandates, and moratoriums, rather than directly through the institutions allocating the use of energy resources on federal lands.[85]

7. Conclusion

The settlement of the American West is a strange chapter in the history of institutions and institutional change in the United States that in some ways has ignored many of the insights of Elinor Ostrom's work on appropriate governance institutions. As settlement increased in the West, where the climate and topography varied much more than in the East, one might expect that a greater reliance on local knowledge would produce a variety of bottom-up institutional forms to govern resource use. Initially, for some resource uses such as water allocation, mining, and grazing on the open range, this was indeed the case. But over time top-down governance became the dominant theme of natural resource policy in the West. While in some cases there was enough latitude under government policy for bottom-up innovations to ameliorate the problems of top-down governance, the changing resource demands of the twentieth century have imposed additional burdens and politicized the adaptation process. Therefore, resource management in the American West has been more conflict-ridden than necessary, and inefficiencies in resource use have been a significant part of the region's history.

CHAPTER 2

Self-Governance, Polycentricity, and Environmental Policy

Jordan K. Lofthouse

B OTH ELINOR AND VINCENT OSTROM were leading scholars in economics and political science, and, as a married couple, they complemented and built on one another's research about overcoming social problems. Their research program focused on using self-governance to solve social problems. When people are self-governing, they develop their own institutions to resolve conflict and facilitate cooperation, rather than having institutions forced on them.[1] The Ostroms' research on self-governance incorporated both normative and analytical claims. A *normative claim* is a value judgment that something ought to be the case, and the Ostroms argued that societies ought to be self-governing.[2] An *analytical claim* is an assertion that something is the case, based on theory and evidence, and the Ostroms' analytical research found that self-governing societies can and have developed diverse institutional arrangements for solving social problems.[3]

This chapter explores the Ostroms' normative and analytical arguments regarding self-governance and how self-governing systems can resolve environmental problems without the need for top-down, centralized policies. On the normative side, the Ostroms argued that citizens should be free to develop their own rules and strategies for solving environmental problems. The Ostroms, in their conception of self-governance, push back against the practice of far-removed politicians and bureaucrats manipulating citizens like pieces on a chessboard. On the analytical side, self-governance can solve environmental problems because the people who are nearest to an environmental problem often have more knowledge and stronger incentives to solve it.

As the scale and scope of national environmental policies have increased, those policies have in many cases displaced the activities of civic associations and lower levels of government. In the 1970s, the federal government created the Environmental Protection Agency (EPA) and passed landmark legislation, such as the Clean Air Act, the Clean Water Act, and the Endangered Species Act. Although these actions have had many benefits, all public policies, including federal environmental policies, have trade-offs. One of the trade-offs has been the aggregation of decision-making power in the highest levels of federal bureaucracies. The shift to more centralized decision making is worrisome because the institutions that can most effectively solve environmental problems are most likely to be developed by the people closest to the problems.

Much of the Ostroms' research found that polycentric systems, which have multiple, overlapping decision-making centers, allow societies to both achieve self-governance and effectively solve environmental problems. A polycentric approach allows lower levels of government and private associations to find solutions that are tailored to local conditions, take advantage of local knowledge, and have more direct involvement of local populations. People in polycentric systems have more freedom to develop their own rules and strategies that conform to their unique circumstances and preferences. If taking advantage of the potential of polycentric systems is the goal, policymakers should look for ways to facilitate local communities, private associations, and lower levels of government to experiment with alternative institutional arrangements that fit those unique circumstances and preferences. This chapter will examine a case study of sage-grouse conservation in the American West that shows how polycentric and community-oriented institutions can solve environmental problems and uphold self-governance.

This chapter proceeds as follows. The following section explores the Ostroms' normative proposition that self-governance is desirable, and then it describes their analytical framework for understanding why self-governance is an effective tool for solving social problems. Section 2 examines how polycentric systems are a means to achieve self-governance while also effectively solving social problems. Section 3 analyzes the example of sage-grouse management in the western United States as a generally successful attempt at polycentric self-governance. Finally, the conclusion shows how those examples can be applied to other areas of environmental policy.

1. Self-Governance and Democracy

Both Elinor and Vincent Ostrom drew a distinction between governing *over* others and governing *with* others. Governing *with* others is one of the fundamental features of a democratic society. Democracy, in the Ostroms' view, is not just a system of voting; it is a system of how people relate to, tolerate, and associate with one another as equals.[4] The purpose of a self-governing, democratic society is to allow free and responsible individuals to find ways of avoiding conflict and facilitating cooperation. Self-governance is rooted in the classical liberal positions of individual liberty, constrained government, and the rule of law.[5] One of the Ostroms' main conclusions was that self-governing systems could address problems without the need for top-down, centralized policies.[6]

Elinor Ostrom argued that the overarching goal of governance is to "facilitate the development of institutions that bring out the best in humans."[7] Different societies will likely focus on different aspects of this goal, such as how efficiently resources are used, how equitably resources are shared, or how sustainably resources are managed. Each of these objectives might be best achieved by different institutional arrangements, and the Ostroms argued that citizens in a self-governing society have the ability and responsibility to set up their own institutions to solve their unique social problems to fit their unique preferences.[8]

The Ostroms' research was based on the normative assertion that self-governing democracies are desirable, which is rooted in the ideals of Alexis de Tocqueville. Tocqueville was a French political scientist who began his research on the United States in 1831. As he traveled across the young republic, he marveled at the robustness of American civic life. People formed associations that provided their communities with *governance*, especially when local, state, and federal officials could not provide sufficient *government*. One of Tocqueville's conclusions was a warning about the potential collapse of democracies owing to the gradual loss of civic virtues and increased reliance on a centralized government.

The Ostroms, like Tocqueville, were especially concerned with declining public participation in civic life. The national government's growing scale and scope have increasingly displaced activities that had previously been the responsibility of voluntary civic associations or state and local governments.[9] The Ostroms defined the mission of their work in terms of a direct contribution to an "art and science of association" to be used by citizens in the exercise of democracy.[10] Elinor Ostrom argued, "Self-governing, democratic systems are always fragile enterprises. Future citizens need to understand that they participate in the constitution and reconstitution of rules-governed politics."[11]

Vincent Ostrom argued that "democratic societies are necessarily placed at risk when people conceive of their relationship as being grounded on principles of command and control rather than on principles of self-responsibility and self-governing communities of relationships."[12] Paul Dragos Aligica, who studied under the Ostroms at their Workshop in Political Theory and Policy Analysis, reformulates the Ostroms' view on governance and places different forms of governance on a spectrum: at one end is a citizen-centered approach to governance and at the other end is an expert-centered approach.[13] A citizen-centered approach to governance means members of a community are actively and directly engaged in making the rules that govern them. In a citizen-centered society, the governance is centered on the primacy of citizen's values, interests, and preferences. Many different groups hold power simultaneously, and there is not necessarily a strict hierarchy of power. Citizen-centered approaches are based on voluntary action and allow people to govern *with* one another to solve social problems.[14]

At the expert-centered end of the spectrum, government officials become guardians and overseers for a society because citizens are viewed as being incapable of solving their own problems. As the Ostroms framed it, rule by expert is governing *over* others. An expert-centered approach divides a society into two groups: a small group that consists of ruling elites and a large group that consists of the obeying masses. Politicians and bureaucrats, as experts, solve social problems by manipulating others and forcing them to comply with the experts' "enlightened" desires. Another term for the expert-centered approach is *epistocracy*, a paternalistic form of social engineering that pushes the masses into the "correct" behaviors.[15] An expert-centered approach can devolve into tyranny because government officials enforce their desires and views, which may not align with the views of the citizens being ruled. As Vincent Ostrom argued, members of society should know how to govern themselves—otherwise self-governance is not sustainable and will devolve.[16]

Of course, this spectrum is stylized, and without some critical reflection, a casual observer might draw a false dichotomy between an expert-centered approach and a citizen-centered one. In the real world, there are many examples of government actors working collaboratively alongside citizens, private associations, nonprofit organizations, and other public-sector actors. Government is not a separate entity from citizens; governments are made up of citizens. In a citizen-centered system, governments are responsive to citizens, and citizens are involved directly in systems of governance. Not all *governance* takes place in *government*, however. Governance can take place in civic associations, clubs, and churches, as well as in various levels of formal government. A citizen-centered, democratic system of governance places voluntary action and association at the forefront, while political hierarchies of power and social control fall to the background.[17]

The Ostroms' normative project was meant to persuade people to adopt a citizen-centered model of public administration, but perhaps more importantly, their analytical project was meant to show how real-world people can successfully solve social problems with self-governance, negating the need for a small group of elites to rule over the rest of society.[18] Their work contributes to a scientific theory of self-governance that uses theoretical concepts from economics and political science and corroborates these theories with empirical and experimental evidence.[19]

On both theoretical and empirical grounds, the Ostroms firmly rejected the presupposition that centralized government control was the only viable means for solving environmental problems. Many of the most pressing environmental problems today take the form of a tragedy of the commons. A tragedy of the commons occurs when a common-pool resource is overexploited because that resource is either unowned or owned commonly by a large group. In technical terms, a common-pool resource is both subtractable, meaning that one person's use of a resource reduces the amount available for other users, and nonexcludable, meaning that is not possible to exclude a person from using the resource. Absent some sort of governance structure, a tragedy will result because no one can be excluded from using the resource, so it will be depleted as all individuals act rationally to use it before others do.[20] For example, no government has jurisdiction over the open oceans, meaning that fishers can take as many fish as they want. Thus, many fisheries are collapsing because they lack an effective governance structure to prevent the overexploitation of the common-pool resource.[21]

Elinor Ostrom wrote, "The presumption that an external Leviathan is necessary to avoid tragedies of the commons leads to recommendations that central governments control most natural resource systems."[22] If current public policies are rooted in the idea that people are incapable of escaping social dilemmas, then the only option for solving those problems is regulations or sanctions from a centralized government. From this perspective, only a Leviathan-like government can direct a society away from the tragedy of the commons.

However, constructing rules in a society to avoid or overcome the tragedy of the commons does not necessarily require top-down commands. As Vincent Ostrom argued,

> The command of the sovereign is not the only way to achieve an ordered way of life. Most societies, most of the time, have relied upon some combination of command structures and consensual arrangements. If we are to create alternatives to imperial orders, we must grapple with the problem of constituting systems of government that operate with the consent of the governed.[23]

Individuals are innovative and entrepreneurial, and they can create new rules and institutions to overcome social dilemmas. Because of the real effects of creativity, innovation, and entrepreneurship, centralized government action is likely not the most efficient or effective option for averting the tragedy of the commons.[24]

The Ostroms realized that there are many potential ways to avoid a tragedy of the commons. In addition to top-down, Leviathan-like approaches, a society could better define private property rights, or it could organize a community-oriented approach whereby community members engage in rule formation, monitoring, and enforcement. One of the Ostroms' main contributions to tragedy-of-the-commons research was demonstrating that successfully solving social problems usually requires a mix of private, community, and government efforts that overlap with one another at various levels.

Institutions that can best solve environmental problems are most likely to be developed by local communities in self-governing contexts. The Ostroms found that all across the world, local people have been able to devise rules and institutions that have solved environmental problems in a self-sustaining and self-enforcing way. Elinor Ostrom's field research in Switzerland, Japan, Spain, and the Philippines found evidence of successful management of common-pool resources that avoided the tragedy of the commons. Other places that they studied, such as communities in Turkey and Sri Lanka, had fragile institutions that did not always successfully manage common-pool resources. Those fragile institutions lacked some of the characteristics, which Elinor Ostrom called "design principles," of the more successful communities.[25]

Institutions developed by local, self-governing communities can solve tragedy problems, but there are limited conditions under which this is likely to be true. More complex environmental problems often require a mix of private, community, and government strategies. However, if government decision-making is partially decentralized to lower levels of governance, local people with on-the-ground experience and knowledge can make policies that fit their own priorities. Thus, societies are better equipped to solve environmental problems when they can use their local knowledge and see the policies as legitimate. When far-removed "outsiders" try to force environmental policies on local communities, even with the best of intentions, those policies are likely to have poor outcomes and to be oppressive. "Outsider" policies are less likely to solve problems because the people most familiar with a problem have unique and tacit knowledge that other people may not have.[26] Elinor Ostrom argued,

> Officials and policy analysts who presume that they have the right design can be dangerous. . . . Somehow, the officials and policy analysts assume that they have different motivations and can find optimal policy because they are not directly involved in the problem. . . . They are indeed isolated from the problems. This leaves them with little capability to adapt and learn in light of information about outcomes resulting from their policies. All too often, these "optimal" policies have Leviathan-like characteristics to them.[27]

2. Polycentric Systems and Their Social Function

Polycentric systems have multiple and overlapping decision-making centers at different scales and scopes, "without one central authority dominating all of the others."[28] Some familiar polycentric systems are federal systems of government, economic markets, and the scientific community. For example, in a federal system of government, decision-making centers are split horizontally into different branches, such as the executive, legislative, and judicial branches of the US government. Federal systems of government are also split vertically into national, state, county, and city governments. In the federated system of the United States, public policies are made independently at different levels, but they are interdependent because they can influence one another.

In terms of environmental policy, polycentric systems facilitate self-governance because they disperse decision-making power among a wide range of policymakers. Polycentric systems often devolve day-to-day decision-making power to lower levels of government where public administration can more effectively take into account the diversity and dynamism of environments, preferences, and values. Polycentric systems also leave space for private associations and community organizations to participate in the solutions to environmental problems. Different people in different places may have different cultures and values, which means that a public policy designed for one area may not function in the same way if it is imposed on another area.[29] Additionally, top-down policies are often ineffective because local people do not see the high-level policymakers or their policies as legitimate. Public policies need to be legitimized by the people if they are to govern effectively.[30] One of Elinor Ostrom's main research questions was how "diverse polycentric institutions help or hinder the innovativeness, learning, adapting, trustworthiness, levels of cooperation of participants, and the achievements of more effective, equitable, and sustainable outcomes at multiple scales."[31]

It is important to differentiate polycentricity from simple decentralization because polycentricity is a much more complex idea.[32] In a polycentric system, the interconnected and interrelated spheres of power make sure that there are multiple forms of checks and balances. Simple decentralization would mean devolving decision-making power to the lowest levels possible, and without proper checks and balances, each decentralized jurisdiction could become its own small tyranny. A polycentric system will have significant amounts of decentralization, but the lowest levels of decision making are nested within higher levels. The nested nature of power and decision making allows different spheres to interact when necessary and to provide a robust system of checks and balances. In the real world, federal and state governments offer a critical backstop to local policymaking and to private and associational action. Local decision-making works alongside and in collaboration with higher levels of governance.

In an analytical sense, polycentric systems often allow people to solve social problems effectively and efficiently. There are several ways in which polycentric systems lead to more effective and efficient outcomes. First, multiple spheres of policymaking allow for a larger set of opportunities for people to find innovative or entrepreneurial solutions to problems.[33] With multiple levels of governance, the diverse set of policymakers can engage in simultaneous experimentation within separate jurisdictions. The use of different approaches to solve similar problems is helpful because it allows policymakers to borrow knowledge gained from others and manipulate it to fit local circumstances. In contrast, monocentric systems only have one sphere of decision making, meaning that there are inherently fewer opportunities for innovation and experimentation regarding collective action problems.[34] It is important to note that real-world governance systems are not divided strictly into polycentric and monocentric. Some systems are more or less polycentric than others, and the least polycentric might reasonably be categorized as monocentric.

Another advantage is that the many overlapping centers of governance can induce interjurisdictional competition, which constrains the power of policymakers and gives them a stronger incentive to respond to constituents' desires. The Ostroms, as leading scholars in public choice economics, used the real-world assumption that government officials are rationally self-interested. Sometimes their self-interest aligns with the welfare of the broader public, but often it does not.[35] Thus, outcomes of public policies are rarely socially optimal and may involve wasted resources. In the presence of the real-world challenges of public administration, polycentric systems allow citizens to pressure government actors in various jurisdictions to change their behavior. Much as competition in markets leads to lower prices and higher-quality goods, competition between governments can lead to better public policies.[36]

Since the citizens have many choices and can "vote with their feet" by moving to the jurisdiction that fits their preferences most closely, government officials must make desirable policies so that citizens choose to remain.[37] As citizens have more freedom to enter and exit various jurisdictions, more competition is introduced into the governance system. The Ostroms repeatedly noted that competition between jurisdictions in the public sector can produce better governance because it can reduce opportunistic behavior on the part of politicians and bureaucrats.[38] Additionally, overlapping jurisdictions often help avoid tyranny because competition effectively limits the power that any policymakers may have.[39] Economists Spencer Banzhaf and Randall Walsh find empirical evidence that people do, in fact, "vote with their feet" for environmental quality.[40] Their tests suggest a link exists between changes in environmental quality and changes in local community demographics.

Competition among jurisdictions in a polycentric system can also help lead to the internalization of externalities. An externality is a side effect or spillover effect of an activity that affects people who are unrelated to that activity. For example, a refinery that emits pollution has little incentive to install costly equipment that will limit its emissions. The pollution is a negative externality because no one owns property rights to the air—the air suffers from a tragedy of the commons. To eliminate the externality, or (in other words) to internalize it, governments can enact regulations.[41] A question still remains: How should an externality like air pollution be regulated? Different people in different places have different preferences. Various jurisdictions can compete to provide the types of public policies that people want. People who do not like the public policies where they live have the option to move to another jurisdiction that suites their preferences better. Of course, there are real-world limitations to this effect since it is costly for many people to move, but interjurisdictional competition still gives policymakers a stronger incentive to be responsive to their constituents' desires than does no competition at all.

Polycentric systems also provide protection against institutional failures and allow governance to be more resilient. When spheres of decision-making are dispersed, errors only affect a small part of the system, not the entire system. If a governance structure is monocentric, any institutional failure will affect all the people under that governance structure. Monocentric systems can only try one version of a policy at a time, and if the policy fails to solve a collective action problem, the failure could mean disaster for the whole system. However, polycentric governance structures mitigate the chance that an institutional failure in one sphere will spill over onto other people in other spheres.[42]

Another benefit of polycentric systems is that small-scale administrative units can, when necessary, band together and create policies that span several jurisdictions. Because decision-making power is dispersed, smaller political units, like counties or states, can come together to solve environmental problems that cross their borders. When larger-scale problems arise, polycentric structures allow smaller-scale units to aggregate themselves and devise institutional solutions that match the scale of the problems.[43] The Colorado River Compact is one example of how several states came together in an attempt to govern water in the arid Southwest. The Colorado River Basin extends across seven states, making the jurisdictions of single states too small to implement effective water-use policies. Direct federal control would have been too large-scale because the scope of the externalities did not extend to the whole country. Although scholars and policymakers have called for an update to the compact's allocations, the polycentric approach to water governance in the Southwest has worked remarkably well for more than fifty years.[44]

It is important to distinguish the concept of polycentricity from simple decentralization or the idea that "local is always better." Vincent Ostrom, and his coauthors Charles Tiebout, and Robert Warren were concerned with devolving governance to the lowest point at which an externality can be internalized.[45] Sometimes this can be done at the lowest local level, but sometimes it is more optimally done at the regional, state, or federal level. The nature and scale of the issue matters when considering the most appropriate governance scheme. For example, local municipalities oversee garbage collection, while the federal government oversees national defense. National defense and local garbage collection both serve the "public," but they are issues with different scales and qualities. Thus, depending on the nature and scale of the issue, the optimal governance structure will be different. A polycentric arrangement provides institutional flexibility so that policymakers can tackle a diverse range of social problems. Several cities in the same county can band together; groups of counties in the same state can cooperate; states can solve problems using interstate compacts; and countries can make multilateral agreements. The key is fitting the scale of governance to the scale of the problem.

Lastly, devolving power in polycentric arrangements can allow large-scale desired outcomes to emerge from the actions at lower levels. Similar to the outcomes of markets, the outcomes of polycentric systems are often emergent orders that have unplanned, but usually desirable, features.[46] The Ostroms' work on polycentricity was influenced by F. A. Hayek, who emphasized the dispersed, local, and tacit nature of knowledge.[47] Polycentric systems allow the many forms of knowledge in a social system to be aggregated and shared, but Hayek and the Ostroms were careful to acknowledge the limits of planning. At first, it seems as if there is a tension between the concept of "designing" a polycentric order and allowing "spontaneous" outcomes to result. The seeming tension, however, is not necessarily a tension at all. For example, markets operate within formal rules and informal norms, and the formal rules are often designed consciously. Even though general rules may be created by design, the outcomes of market interactions are not centrally planned but are generally socially desirable. In terms of environmental problems, the policies that solve problems do not have to be designed by a centralized government. If lower levels of governance are allowed to create policies that incorporate local and tacit knowledge, the desired outcomes are likely to emerge from the actions at lower levels. As actors in the various decision-making spheres respond to dynamic changes in the world, they can adapt and change the rules to fit new and changing circumstances. As in markets, the resulting outcomes are broader system effects that people desired, but that no centralized entity designed.[48]

Although there are benefits to polycentric governance systems, these systems are not a cure-all and will still encounter problems. Polycentric systems have weaknesses, and scholars and policymakers should be aware of both the benefits and the potential problems.[49] Since polycentric systems involve some degree of decentralization, lower levels of government and private associations may fail to achieve their goals, or politicians and bureaucrats may find creative ways to practice opportunism and cronyism. Multiple centers of decision-making authority may facilitate "buck-passing," making it difficult for citizens to know whom they should hold accountable for what outcomes. Because polycentric systems have complex spheres of overlapping decision-making, it is not immediately clear how a problem will be solved or who will solve it. Relatedly, understanding how the polycentric system works may place cognitive burdens on citizens. In the real world, many polycentric systems have difficulty addressing the constant, dynamic change of social and environmental systems.[50] Thus, the question is not whether polycentric systems are perfectly capable of addressing problems, but whether they produce better results than alternative systems. Polycentric governance, although fallible, may be the best option that societies have to overcome complex environmental problems. As Elinor Ostrom said, "No governance system is perfect, but polycentric systems have considerable advantages given their mechanisms for mutual monitoring, learning, and adaptation of better strategies over time."[51]

3. Sage-Grouse Conservation through Polycentric Governance

From 2010 to 2015, federal, state, and local policymakers, as well as private associations, cooperated to conserve the greater sage-grouse populations in the western United States. This success story is just one example of a polycentric approach that solved an environmental collective action problem, and it is instructive because it shows how various governments, businesses, and nonprofit organizations can facilitate self-governance in a polycentric system. Policymakers can use the sage-grouse example as a learning opportunity to understand what aspects of the conservation effort worked well and what aspects could be improved on.

The greater sage-grouse is a species of bird that lives on the sagebrush steppes of western North America. Although the historical range of the species was much larger, the species is currently present in eleven states and one Canadian province. The birds are ground-dwelling and can grow up to two feet tall. Greater sage-grouse are a favorite among bird-watchers because of the intricate courtship displays that males perform to attract females.[52] Sage-grouse are also a favorite among hunters as a game bird.

One of the most important institutions for species conservation in the United States is the Endangered Species Act (ESA) of 1973, which gives the US Fish and Wildlife Service (USFWS) the authority to list species as "endangered" or "threatened." It is illegal for a person to "take" an individual of a listed species, with *take* defined as to "harass, harm, pursue, hunt, shoot, wound, kill, trap, capture, or collect, or to attempt to engage in any such conduct."[53] There are civil and criminal penalties for unlawfully taking an individual of a listed species, on either private or public land. Additionally, the USFWS can designate critical habitat areas, but these designations affect only federal agency actions or federally funded or permitted activities. Once the USFWS designates a critical habitat, other federal agencies are required to consult the USFWS if their actions may "destroy or adversely modify" this habitat.[54]

When the ESA was first passed, it was a relatively inflexible piece of legislation that imposed severe sanctions on people. Over time, however, amendments to the law and changes in how it is implemented have made it more flexible and adaptive. For example, the 1982 amendments to the ESA created "incidental take" permits, which allows people with the permits to "take" a listed species in a way that would otherwise be unlawful. Individuals can receive an incidental take permit if they submit a habitat conservation plan that is approved by the USFWS. These plans demonstrate how negative effects to a listed species will be minimized or mitigated, among other details.[55]

From 2002 to 2004, several individuals and organizations, including ecologist Craig C. Dremann, Institute for Wildlife Protection, and American Lands Alliance, submitted petitions to have the greater sage-grouse listed under the ESA. The USFWS conducted a review, and in 2005, it found that the greater sage-grouse did not warrant listing under the ESA.[56] Western Watersheds Project was not satisfied with the 2005 finding and sued the USFWS. On December 4, 2007, the US District Court of Idaho ruled that the USFWS's 2005 finding was arbitrary and capricious under the Administrative Procedure Act. The court reversed the USFWS's decision and remanded the finding back to the USFWS.[57]

In 2010, after two years of reviews, the USFWS announced that a listing of the greater sage-grouse was "warranted but precluded," which means that the USFWS should take action but would not immediately because of other higher priorities.[58] A "warranted but precluded" determination is essentially a temporary deferral of action. Thus, the greater sage-grouse was identified as a "candidate species" for full listing under the ESA. A candidate species designation does not give statutory protection under the ESA, but the USFWS encourages federal agencies, state governments, and private associations to work on conservation efforts to avoid a full listing in the future. Those working toward conservation have a wider range of options to experiment with under a candidate species designation because the full statutory requirements of the ESA are not in effect.[59]

One of the most contentious issues associated with a full listing under the ESA is the disproportionate distribution of costs and benefits—the people who bear the largest burden of the costs are not usually the people who receive the largest benefits. Groups that do not want to bear the costs of a full listing find it in their interest to negate the need for a full listing by engaging in conservation efforts. Federal, state, and local policymakers wanted to avoid a full listing of the sage-grouse because a large portion of sage-grouse habitat exists on public lands where ranching and resource extraction are common.[60] Landowners and people in resource extraction industries wanted to avoid a full listing because of the stringent and restrictive land-use policies that the USFWS can impose.[61] Additionally, private associations of hunters, bird-watchers, and conservationists had a strong incentive to maintain the sage-grouse populations to protect their preferred means of recreation.[62]

The candidate species designation sparked a polycentric effort to boost the sage-grouse population in order to avoid a formal listing as endangered or threatened. The success of these various overlapping policies from policymakers and private associations ultimately removed the need for a listing. The polycentric efforts included federal management plans, candidate conservation agreements, the Sage Grouse Initiative, the Greater Sage-Grouse Comprehensive Conservation Strategy, state management plans, and local working groups. The rest of this section describes how the polycentric system generally succeeded and what its shortcomings were.

The Role of Federal Agencies in Sage-Grouse Conservation

Federal agencies play an important role in sage-grouse management because sage-grouse are often found on federal lands. Officials in both the Bureau of Land Management (BLM) and US Forest Service (USFS) wanted to ensure that the sage-grouse would not be listed as endangered. Since sage-grouse live on hundreds of millions of acres of federal land, a full listing would have significantly raised the costs of using federal land for any type of development or resource extraction. To avoid such costs, the agencies began drafting new management plans after the candidate species designation, and they adopted finalized plans in 2015. The new plans amended the previous plans for 98 BLM and USFS units to increase the protection for sage-grouse on nearly 70 million acres of federal land across much of the western United States.[63] The BLM and USFS plans led the way for community management. The BLM's and USFS's 2015 plans took a polycentric approach because they focused on the development of state sage-grouse management plans that also facilitated "voluntary, multi-partner private lands effort to protect millions of acres of habitat on ranches and rangelands across the West." Additionally, the BLM and USFS plans facilitated collaboration among federal, state, and private-sector scientists to research the most effective and efficient means of conservation.[64]

Another polycentric approach that federal officials used was candidate conservation agreements (CCAs). CCAs are voluntary agreements between the USFWS and another party, such as a state government, a private landowner, another federal agency, a local government, or a tribal government. Parties that opt into CCAs commit to reduce threats to candidate species.[65] Several state governments, including those of Idaho, Wyoming, and Oregon, all entered into sage-grouse CCAs.[66] From 2013 to 2015, CCAs were implemented on 5.5 million acres, including both private and federal lands.[67]

One CCA in eastern Oregon provides a clear example of how CCAs function. Many cattle ranchers in eastern Oregon lease BLM land for grazing, but this grazing land is also habitat for the greater sage-grouse. In 2013, the USFWS, the BLM, and the Oregon Cattlemen's Association entered into a "programmatic CCA," which is a broad umbrella agreement among those three entities. The programmatic CCA allows the Oregon Cattlemen's Association to identify conservation measures that benefit sage-grouse and to assist individual ranchers using BLM land to development "allotment CCAs." Allotment CCAs are tailored for each rancher's unique circumstances in order to ameliorate threats to sage-grouse and to encourage grazing practices that benefit sage-grouse on BLM land in Oregon. The BLM and USFWS work with participating permittees to select conservation measures that address threats and provide benefit to greater sage-grouse on the leased BLM land. The conservation measures are voluntary actions performed by private ranchers that supplement mandatory actions under the BLM's resource management plan or other regulations.[68] In eastern Oregon, the sage-grouse CCAs allowed private ranchers greater flexibility to figure out the measures that work best for their unique circumstances, and that also help conserve sage-grouse.

In addition to new management plans and CCAs, one of the most effective and polycentric approaches to sage-grouse conservation from the BLM and USFS was the partnerships formed through the Sage Grouse Initiative (SGI). More than 1,100 private individuals across the West participated in the SGI, which had the dual goal of restoring about 4.4 million acres of sage-grouse habitat while also allowing economic development on federal lands.[69] The SGI works through voluntary cooperation, incentives, and community support to protect sage-grouse habitat and increase sage-grouse populations. The initiative accomplishes these objectives by aiding ranchers with conservation measures on private rangeland, such as by preventing the spread of noxious weeds, removing conifers that threaten sage-grouse habitat, securing conservation easements in residential areas, performing wetland restoration projects, and making fences more visible to sage grouse to reduce deadly collisions.[70] The SGI is funded through the Natural Resources Conservation Service, which has spent more than $296.5 million on the SGI between 2010 and 2018. A further $128.0 million has come from other conservation partners and landowners, bringing total SGI investment $424.5 million.[71] It should be noted, however, that the example of the SGI may have limited applicability to the vast majority of imperiled-species problems because game species and other charismatic species often attract more attention and financial resources than non-game or less charismatic species.

The Role of State Governments in Sage-Grouse Conservation

Just as the candidate-species listing prompted federal officials to revise their sage-grouse management policies, it also prompted state officials to create new policies to avoid the need for a full listing under the ESA. In 2011, Secretary of the Interior Ken Salazar invited the eleven states with sage-grouse populations to produce updated sage-grouse management plans. These plans could be individualized to each state, and Secretary Salazar encouraged state policymakers to balance economic development and management of the species.[72] Several western governors, including the governors of Idaho, Wyoming, and Montana, issued executive orders to implement state conservation plans that would eliminate the need for listing the species under the ESA.[73] By 2015, most of these western states had implemented new conservation strategies or strengthened their existing strategies for sage-grouse preservation.[74] Federal plans focus on only federal lands, which makes state plans important because they restrict activities across entire states. In some respects, state management may be more influential than federal management because it covers a broader area of sage-grouse habitat—not just habitat on federal lands.

Before and after the 2010 candidate species designation, western states have engaged in a "laboratory of democracy" in which different states have taken different approaches to sage-grouse conservation. Even though they experimented with different approaches, the states have pursued a common purpose. State leaders learned from the successes and failures of the plans adopted in other states, and they tailored their conservation strategies to comport with the desires and cultures of local people. One of the clearest examples of mutual learning and interjurisdictional cooperation is the Greater Sage-Grouse Comprehensive Conservation Strategy. This strategy was formed by the Western Association of Fish and Wildlife Agencies (WAFWA) in 2006 to facilitate partnerships and mutual learning between state wildlife agencies. (WAFWA is an association of the various wildlife agencies from twenty-four states and Canadian provinces.) The Greater Sage-Grouse Comprehensive Conservation Strategy is an ongoing endeavor in which various state and provincial officials meet with one another in forums and workshops, discuss various approaches to sage-grouse conservation, and engage in mutual learning by reviewing successes and failures.[75] Additionally, many of the conservation actions funded by the SGI are tied to decisions made in the Greater Sage-Grouse Comprehensive Conservation Strategy.[76]

The Role of Local Working Groups in Sage-Grouse Conservation

Some states were able to devolve the implementation of their conservation plans further, facilitating an even more polycentric structure. For example, Utah's policymakers created a new sage-grouse management plan in 2013 and implemented it in 2015.[77] Roughly half of Utah's greater sage-grouse live on private lands, which means that local communities and private landowners are necessary participants for successful conservation. One of Utah's strategies for sage-grouse conservation has been the Community-Based Conservation Program (CBCP) and local working groups. The CBCP is run by a Utah State University extension program and staffed predominantly by university-affiliated researchers. The goal of CBCP was to provide incentives for private landowners and local communities to engage in conservation as an alternative to direct regulations. The CBCP facilitates local working groups for sage-grouse conservation throughout Utah.[78]

Each local working group incorporates representatives of many parties and interests, such as university scientists, federal officials, state officials, county officials, private landowners, livestock operators, private organizations, industry leaders, and grazing associations.[79] Local working groups were first implemented in 1996 to bring together state and federal agents, local landowners, and other interested parties to conserve sage-grouse.[80] Each group has its own conservation plan and works to reverse the decline of sage-grouse in its area. Utah currently has eleven local working groups, and several other states have formed similar groups. Now there are more than sixty across the western United States and Canada.[81] Utah's local working groups are financially supported by the Utah Division of Wildlife Resources, Utah State University Extension, the Berryman Institute, private landowners, public and private natural resources management organizations, and wildlife conservation organizations.[82]

The Parker Mountain Local Working Group in central Utah brought together Utah land managers, USFS officials, USFWS officials, Utah State University Extension county agricultural agents, county commissioners, local agricultural producers, and members of a relatively large private grazing association. The group decided to first gather information on local sage-grouse populations before making any management changes. After each phase of the various research projects, the group convened to discuss the findings and propose management plans. The group determined that mechanical and chemical treatments were effective at making the habitat more conducive to sage-grouse reproduction.[83] Mechanical treatments, such as mowing, and chemical treatments, such as the herbicide tebuthiuron, are meant to improve the growth and dietary quality of sagebrush for sage-grouse.[84] Plots that were treated with tebuthiuron had the highest sage-grouse habitat selection, so the USFS, the BLM, and the Utah Division of Wildlife Resources decided to treat larger brooding areas with tebuthiuron, which increases the herbaceous understory that is necessary for sage-grouse.[85]

The West Desert Local Working Group in Utah also succeeded in boosting local sage-grouse populations. Participants included officials from a variety of federal, state, county, and tribal agencies, as well as from grazing associations, recreation agencies, and conservation districts. In spring 2015, the group held several brainstorming sessions about ways to understand and manage the continuing decline of the area's sage-grouse population. Adopting a unique approach to the situation, the group discussed bringing sage-grouse from other places to augment the local sage-grouse population. In 2016, the group began a translocation project to bring in sage-grouse from two areas in Utah with stable populations. This project provided data on how the newly translocated sage-grouse survived, reproduced, and moved. [86]

The efforts and results of these working groups illustrate how conducting management and research at the local level has allowed local knowledge to be used in conservation. The several local working groups in Utah have "capitalized upon one another's research results."[87] Because Utah State University Extension serves as a hub, local working groups throughout the state can see how other groups have engaged in research and management. For example, the West Desert group was able to learn from other local working groups about the value of conifer removal for sage-grouse habitat improvement.[88] In addition to facilitating knowledge-sharing, the polycentric model of local working groups built a sense of legitimacy and ownership over the sage-grouse conservation project that may not have existed if research plans and management strategies had been forced upon local actors by far-removed federal officials.[89]

The case study of the greater sage-grouse shows how federalism can enable "laboratories of democracy." Using multiple jurisdictions as laboratories of democracy is closely related to the popular concept in conservation biology of adaptive management. Adaptive management refers to the integration of design, management, and monitoring to systematically test assumptions in order to adapt and learn. Adaptive management includes the modification of management decisions when better information is available.[90] Elinor Ostrom argued that polycentric systems have "mechanisms for mutual monitoring, learning, and adaptation of better strategies over time."[91] Scholars and policymakers who are concerned with using adaptive management strategies in conservation should focus more on the advantages of polycentric solutions that allow for learning and adaptation to take place. The connection between the Ostroms' body of research and the adaptive management literature is an area ripe for future study.

Although Utah has experienced conservation successes through its highly polycentric approach, wildland resource scholars Lorien Belton, Nicole Frey, and David Dahlgren warn that such an approach may not work everywhere. They argue, "The scale of engagement in sage-grouse issues across the western United States, as reflected in Utah, is unprecedented and therefore may be difficult to use as a model."[92] The exact framework of Utah's system may not be applicable everywhere, but polycentric approaches can take many different forms. The exact configuration of the system and the specific authorities in any given level can be tailored for different circumstances.

Learning from the Polycentric Approach to Sage-Grouse Conservation

From 2010 to 2015, federal, state, and local officials were able to prove that they could engage in effective conservation efforts. The USFWS decided in September 2015 to withdraw the greater sage-grouse from the candidate species list and not to list it as threatened or endangered. The justification for the decision stated,

> Based on the best available scientific and commercial information, the Service has determined that the primary threats to sage-grouse have been ameliorated by conservation efforts implemented by federal, state, and private landowners. . . . Therefore, the Service has determined that listing the sage-grouse in all or a significant portion of its range is not warranted at this time.[93]

Policymakers and scholars must be careful not to oversimplify the successes of the sage-grouse case study. From 2010 to 2015, the polycentric governance structure appears to have "solved" the collective action problem related to sage-grouse conservation, but the sage-grouse has several characteristics that make it unique. Game species and other charismatic species like the sage-grouse can often serve as "flagships" that stimulate public support for conservation in a particular area.[94] Not only is the sage-grouse a flagship species, it also has a widespread range across several states, popularity with recreationalists, and relatively abundant conservation funding from both private and public sources. Much of the grouse habitat restoration money, especially money used by the Sage Grouse Initiative, came from oil and gas operations, farming and ranching associations, mining corporations, and private land trusts.[95] The combination of interests that contributed to the sage-grouse conservation efforts had more financial resources than the interests that work to conserve many other species of concern. Without such a widespread, well-funded conservation effort, the sage-grouse conservation effort may not have been as successful.

Events since 2015 show that the situation is complex, and conservation of the greater sage-grouse is not guaranteed into the future. The legal protections for sage-grouse under federal law are politically tenuous. For example, the Trump administration has changed the BLM and USFS land management plans for sage-grouse conservation.[96] The Trump administration has also changed several regulations under the ESA, which largely motivated state and private actions for sage-grouse conservation.[97] Congress is also considering bills that would change the ESA, and several changes made in 2019 have directly affected the greater sage-grouse. The Consolidated Appropriations Act of 2019 stipulates that no appropriated funds "by this or any other act" may be used to list the greater sage-grouse under the ESA. It is uncertain how long that stipulation will exist or how it will affect sage-grouse conservation in the future.

Owing to various institutional changes at the federal level, sage-grouse populations may fall in the future. However, even though federal policies may change, the polycentric setup of the American system can still help conserve sage-grouse. States and counties can make their own policies. States can make compacts with one another, like the Greater Sage-Grouse Comprehensive Conservation Strategy, to preserve the sage-grouse even without federal oversight. Private organizations and individuals can attempt to persuade their neighbors to engage in conservation. The polycentric character of sage-grouse conservation may still aid conservation efforts if states create new policies or maintain the restrictions that federal land management agencies under the Trump administration have now relaxed. For instance, state oil and gas commissions may continue to regulate under the older, more stringent restrictions even after the BLM has weakened its protective mitigation standards. Likewise, some state agencies may choose to keep stricter regulations on the books or experiment with more effective policies. Thus, the polycentric arrangement for sage-grouse conservation provides protection against institutional failure because policy changes at the federal level do not necessarily determine the entire outcome. Interstate associations, states, counties, and private associations have the ability to continue engaging in conservation, even if the federal government has rolled back some protections.

From 2010 to 2015, there were undeniably top-down policies affecting sage-grouse conservation, especially the threat of the full listing under the ESA. In the case of the sage-grouse, the trigger for the highly polycentric approach to conservation was the threat of a top-down imposition of public policies through the ESA. However, since federal officials allowed lower levels of government to engage in their own conservation policies, sage-grouse populations were able to increase, removing the need for a full listing. Power may be highly decentralized in a polycentric system, but there is still a role for higher levels of government. In this case, the pressure of federal agencies served as a catalyst for a polycentric conservation effort. In other instances, such federal pressure may be unnecessary or unwarranted. As Elinor Ostrom argued, "Patterns of relationships among individuals and groups tend to be relatively complex and rarely lend themselves to simple explanations. Reforms based on overly simplified views of the world have led to counterintuitive and counterintentional results in both urban and CPR environments."[98] Although public administration is a complex phenomenon, polycentric systems "are more likely than monocentric systems to provide incentives to self-organized, self-corrective institutional change."[99]

4. Conclusion

Each society faces its own unique environmental challenges, and there are countless ways to tackle those challenges. Solutions can come from formal policymakers, private associations, communities, markets, or any combination of these entities. Balancing effective environmental policy with democratic self-governance can be a challenge. The Ostroms' research, however, has shown how polycentric systems can effectively solve environmental problems while also promoting a form of citizen-centered governance.

Sage-grouse management in the western United States provides a clear example of a polycentric approach to self-governance because the people who live near and interact with the environmental problems at hand are intimately involved in the formation, monitoring, and enforcement of social rules. Sage-grouse management was democratic because people directly affected by environmental problems were given the freedom to create institutions that resolved those problems. Each institution was tailored to the specific contexts and cultures of the local people. As Vincent Ostrom explained, "What it means to live in a democratic society is much more demanding than electing representatives who form governments. Not only are democratic societies constructed around the essential place of citizens in those societies, but they cannot be maintained without the knowledge, moral integrity, skill, and intelligibility of citizens in the cultivation of those societies."[100]

The Ostroms' normative and analytical approach is much more widely applicable across environmental policies in the United States and throughout the world. Policymakers should look for ways to facilitate polycentric structures or community governance in these arenas. With more self-governance, local people will be able to use their dispersed and tacit knowledge to devise new ways of tackling problems. When local people are involved in the rulemaking process, they see rules as legitimate and help monitor and enforce these rules. Systems with these characteristics become self-enforcing, decreasing the need for centralized oversight. As new environmental problems arise in the world, polycentric systems offer one of the most robust and innovative ways to find solutions in a world of dynamism and diversity.

Pacific Salmon Fisheries Management: An (Unusual) Example of Polycentric Governance Involving Indigenous Participation at Multiple Scales

Shane Day

BOTH VINCENT AND ELINOR OSTROM are well known for their foundational work in public choice theory and the formulation of the Institutional Analysis and Development (IAD) and Social-Ecological Systems (SES) frameworks. Their work has garnered much attention across various policy domains, but it is perhaps in the areas of environmental policy and natural resource management where their insights have had the most influence. An enduring insight of their work is that natural resource issues are complex, and that analysts should eschew "panacea," or one-size-fits-all, solutions to such complex problems.

A common inference drawn from their research is that highly centralized regulation—Garrett Hardin's classic solution to the tragedy of the commons—is not *always* the best approach, and that small-scale, informal associations of user groups *may* effectively self-manage public and common-pool resource goods. However, the Ostroms cautioned that there are plenty of cases of failure across both of these broad types, and that successful management of collective action dilemmas and successful adaptive responses to ecological disturbances are multifaceted, contextual, and dependent on developing complex institutions that are well-matched to the wide array of ecological and social conditions that surround a particular issue. Their work surrounding the concept of polycentricity is particularly salient, and suggests that multiple independent authorities working in a particular issue domain at multiple scales can effectively coordinate and manage resources, if institutions are designed to facilitate trust, coordinate action, and effectively manage conflict and disagreement.

It is relatively less well known that both Vincent and Elinor had an abiding interest in the politics, rights, and arts of indigenous peoples. Such was the level of their interest that there is a significant permanent collection of indigenous arts in their name at the Mathers Museum of World Cultures at Indiana University. Indigenous groups, as sovereign entities, were interesting subjects to the Ostroms because they represented a particular type of user group whose members often successfully self-manage their own resources. Thus these groups were commonly subjects for their extensive fieldwork that delved into the questions of how smaller-scale user groups effectively manage common-pool resources. However, it turns out that indigenous groups can also be important *governmental* actors in their own right, serving as influential institutional partners in regimes that manage complex and large-scale resource systems. The regime governing the management of salmon in the eastern North Pacific is an interesting and unusual example of such participation by indigenous groups at all scales—international, regional, and local—in which the tribes serve as central and important coordinating actors. This chapter examines how combinations of institutional rules shape the participatory authority of indigenous groups at different levels of the regime.

Employing an analysis rooted in both IAD and SES frameworks, I demonstrate how Pacific salmon management is an example of complex polycentric governance that involves an unusual tribal role entailing significant coordination and decision-making responsibilities at a level coequal to that of state and national actors. I argue that *position rules, boundary rules, choice rules*, and *aggregation rules*, as conceived of in the IAD framework, configure in various ways that determine the level of what I term *participatory authority* of a particular group within an institutional setting.

There is a stark contrast between Canadian and American indigenous groups' roles at multiple levels within the regime. What explains this difference in the power and influence of various indigenous peoples in this regime, particularly at the international scale? And how do institutional rules shape the bargaining relationships between indigenous groups and other institutional actors? Most scholarship on Native American policy tends to characterize indigenous governments either as being akin to other "nonstate actors" or as quasi-government actors subordinate to federal and state governments. At an international scale, indigenous groups are overwhelmingly construed as operating within the system of international governance as nonstate actors agitating for internationally recognized human rights to serve as a check on their own national governments. Relatively less attention is given to examining the ways in which tribes exercise high degrees of de facto sovereignty and significant policymaking authority alongside international organizations, national governments, and other subnational governments.

1. The Polycentric Governance System of the Pacific Salmon Regime

As Elinor Ostrom and her coauthors illustrated, common-pool resource management faces at least two broad types of collective action problems: "appropriation" problems and "provision" problems.[1] One of the things that makes the salmon SES so complex is that the various governance functions addressing these types of problems are disaggregated across a wide range of institutions at multiple levels. Many actors within the salmon SES "wear multiple hats" insofar as they are formal members of more than one of the constituent institutions in the overall SES, and thereby constitute policy actors who connect the various other actors within the SES and may thus bring a greater degree of coherence to the overall system. Therefore it is necessary to map the institutional relationships that exist and to locate where various governance functions reside within those relationships. Mapping those relationships requires distinguishing among at least four levels of institutional rulemaking government organizations: international, transnational, regional, and local.

1.1 International and Transnational Governance

At the international level, the North Pacific Anadromous Fish Commission is an organization created to implement the various provisions of the Convention for the Conservation of Anadromous Stocks in the North Pacific Ocean, which was negotiated by the United States, Canada, Japan, and Russia, and which came into force in 1993 (South Korea also joined the convention in 2003).[2] Essentially, the focus of this convention is to prohibit the targeted fishing of salmon on the high seas (i.e., in the areas beyond each nation's exclusive economic zone, or EEZ, which extends out to 200 nautical miles from shore) in order to maximize the numbers of fish returning to each country's waters, and to collaborate in minimizing the bycatch of salmon in all other fisheries within each nation's EEZ.[3] Each party to the convention can nominate up to three representatives to the commission. Commission decisions must be made by consensus, with each party receiving one vote.[4]

A more significant management role is played at the transnational level in the Eastern Pacific by the Pacific Salmon Commission (PSC). The PSC is a bilateral organization created by the United States and Canada to address the issue of interceptions and overharvesting of fisheries that range across the borders of these two countries. The PSC was created to address the macroscale (transnational) appropriation problems relating to salmon, although the institution has evolved beyond its original exclusive focus on appropriation issues to include a variety of provision activities. The commission itself does not have regulatory authority over the salmon fisheries but provides regulatory advice and recommendations to the two countries. A key exception to this is that the PSC does exercise regulatory authority over Fraser River sockeye and pink salmon stocks through the Fraser River Panel, a regulatory authority that is a vestige of bilateral salmon management agreements that were administered through the International Pacific Salmon Fisheries Commission, the organizational precursor to the PSC.[5] PSC staff promulgate and enforce fishing regulations in both American and Canadian territorial waters known as the Fraser River Panel Area, which encompasses the areas around southern Vancouver Island, the Washington coast, the Strait of Juan de Fuca, Puget Sound, and the Strait of Georgia. Instream enforcement of fishing regulations on the Fraser is the responsibility of the Department of Fisheries and Oceans (DFO), also known as Fisheries and Oceans Canada, and must comply with the overall target harvest allocations set by the PSC.[6]

Beyond this, the PSC has responsibility for "all salmon originating in the waters of one country which are subject to interception by the other, affect the management of the other country's salmon or affect biologically the stocks of the other country."[7] Under the terms of the Pacific Salmon Treaty (PST) and subsequent agreements the PSC consists of a sixteen-member body, with four commissioners and four alternates from each side. The commission's primary role is to hash out agreements regarding the targeted escapement goals for each species of fish that is known to migrate across national boundaries and thus become susceptible to interception, and then to set specific American and Canadian harvest allocations for particular stocks. Each country is responsible for making regulatory decisions to implement the suggestions of the PSC; thus in effect the PSC gives both countries a forum through which to resolve their differences and collaboratively determine acceptable harvest levels and decisions regarding targeted habitat improvements. According to the PST, "Each section shall have one vote in the Commission. A decision or recommendation of the Commission shall be made only with the approval of both sections."[8] This effectively gives each country veto power over any activity of the commission.

An institutional analysis of the PSC reveals a much more nuanced picture than the simple one-country, one-vote dynamic, however. The IAD framework identifies seven broad types of rules, four of which I argue particularly shape the level of participatory authority of each of the interests that fill positions of power within any institution. *Position rules* specify the specific positions of authority in any decision process, connecting particular actors to authorized actions.[9] *Boundary rules* specify the process of choosing who fills particular positions, by defining "1) who is eligible to enter a position, 2) the process that determines which eligible participants may enter (or must enter) positions, and 3) how an individual may leave (or must leave) a position."[10] *Choice rules*, meanwhile, specify the range of actions that a "participant occupying a position must, must not, or may do at a particular point in a decision process."[11] Thus, choice rules fundamentally outline the conditions under which authoritative decisions may be made by particular actors in a decision-making process. Finally, *aggregation rules* specify whether an authoritative decision may be made by a single participant, or whether multiple participants are required to collaboratively make a decision.[12] In other words, aggregation rules capture the voting rules and processes behind the making of authoritative institutional decisions.

Position rules are important in the sense that having multiple representatives for a particular national delegation increases the likelihood that indigenous groups (and other groups that are usually characterized as *nonstate actors*) obtain some measure of formal representation, in contrast with the one-member, one-vote form of representation that characterizes many international organizations. Boundary rules specifying the processes by which indigenous representatives are selected are more important for indigenous participatory authority to the extent that they allow relatively unchecked authority of indigenous groups to select whomever they want to fill these positions. Choice rules meanwhile are important in that they fundamentally outline the conditions under which authoritative decisions may be made by particular actors filling particular positions in a decision-making process. In a general sense, choice rules impacting participatory authority in international institutions would entail the degree to which such groups have a formal vote on all, some, few, or none of the decisions taken by the organization. Aggregation rules are very important in that they are related to conditions under which an authoritative decision can be made. Whether the aggregation rules in effect are nonsymmetric or symmetric will significantly influence the level of authority of any actor in an institutional setting.[13] For instance, if an authoritative decision can be made unilaterally by a specific actor within an institutional setting (a nonsymmetric rule), then aggregation rules favor the decision-making power of that particular actor. However, if all actors must agree on any decision taken by the group—a symmetric aggregation rule that effectively grants each actor veto power—then all actors could be termed relative coequals in terms of power within the institution, a situation that would likely be significant in determining bargaining relationships and coalition-forming within groups.

Position rules pertaining to commissioners for both delegations are spelled out at the constitutional level in article 2 of the PST: "The Commission shall consist of not more than eight Commissioners, of whom not more than four shall be appointed by each Party. Each Party may also appoint not more than four alternate

Commissioners, to serve in the absence of any Commissioner appointed by that Party."[14] In addition, each delegation must choose an individual to serve as the delegation's primary representative, with these two individuals serving as commission chairman and commission vice-chairman (these positions alternate between the two countries on an annual basis).[15] It is worthwhile to note here that informal norms at the operational level have evolved such that there is virtually no differentiation between the "formal" and "alternate" commissioner positions, such that all eight members are essentially coequal.[16] Because each delegation has established its own aggregation rules for determining what the position of the national delegation will be in any particular instance, as will be demonstrated shortly, the active differentiation between commissioners and alternates essentially becomes moot. Boundary rules specify that both commissioners and alternates "shall hold office at the pleasure of the Party by which they were appointed,"[17] essentially deferring decisions on who is eligible to serve at the Commissioner level, the process by which potential individuals may enter these positions, and processes by which individuals may leave these positions to a collective-choice process governed independently by each delegation.

The commission represents the most authoritative level of decision making within the PSC, given the broad authority granted to it by choice rules articulated at the constitutional level in the PST: "Subject to the approval of the Parties, the Commission shall make such by-laws and procedural rules for itself, for the Panels . . . , and for the committees . . . as may be necessary for the exercise of their functions and the conduct of their meetings."[18] Thus, all determination of constitutional-level rules governing collective-choice processes at the panel and committee levels rests with the commissioners. Furthermore, "The Commission may make recommendations to or advise the Parties on any matter relating to the Treaty."[19] Other choice rules granting sole authority over budgeting,[20] disbursement of funds,[21] appointment and oversight of the Secretariat staff,[22] and creation and elimination of panels and committees[23] grant the commission broad latitude to determine the entire range of decision functions undertaken by the organization.

Because of the broad deference granted to each delegation to determine additional rules at the collective-choice level for its own delegation, divergent patterns of decision making exist that impact the relative participatory authority of American versus Canadian indigenous groups in the PSC, with the treaty tribes of the United States holding relatively greater participatory authority than their Canadian counterparts. Two distinct groupings of participating treaty tribes from the United States can be identified based on the specific areas in which they are located and the different collective fishing regimes that each group employs. The first group consists of twenty treaty tribes from Washington State that hold special treaty rights "to fish in usual and accustomed places" and "in common with the citizens of the territory."[24] These treaty rights have been interpreted by the courts in *United States v. Washington* and various ancillary cases to allocate roughly 50 percent of the annual salmon harvest to the tribes, to allow tribal fishing beyond reservation borders, and to grant the tribes "co-management authority" with the state. These tribes fish independently of one another but are collectively assisted by the Northwest Indian Fisheries Commission (NWIFC), which acts as a support agency that attempts to resolve intertribal collective action problems and to provide political and technical assistance to each of the member tribes[25]. The second group consists of four tribes in the Columbia River basin of Washington, Oregon, and Idaho—the Umatilla, Nez Perce, Yakama, and Warm Springs—that have similar treaty provisions to fish. These tribes collectively regulate, through the Columbia River Inter-Tribal Fish Commission (CRITFC), a commercial fishery over a group of shared common fishing areas on the Columbia River[26]. Owing to dam construction on the Columbia, which flooded multiple traditional platform fishing areas, in 1988 Congress established several "treaty fishing access sites" in several locations along the reshaped river basin as a remediation effort to replace these usual and accustomed fishing areas.[27]

Boundary rules regarding who may serve as PSC commissioners actively distinguish between the NWIFC and CRITFC tribes. In the case of the American delegation to the PSC, the Pacific Salmon Treaty Act of 1985 serves as the implementing legislation of the PST, and outlines most of the rules at the collective-choice level that impact the commissioner roles. Section 3(a) of this act mandates that

> one shall be an official of the United States Government who shall be a nonvoting member of the United States Section; one shall be a resident of the State of Alaska and shall be appointed from a list of at least six qualified individuals nominated by the Governor of that State; one shall be a resident of the States of Oregon or Washington and shall be appointed from a list of at least six qualified individuals nominated by the Governors of those States; and one shall be appointed from a list of at least six qualified individuals nominated by the treaty Indian tribes of the States of Idaho, Oregon, or Washington.[28]

Although these positions are subject to Senate confirmation, owing to significant backlogs in the confirmation processes for presidential appointees across all departments and agencies of the federal government, each federal, state, and tribal party essentially has de facto authority over choosing the particular individual who fills these positions, and individuals often serve without formal confirmation.[29] Because of the evolution in norms in the PSC's rules of procedure, which effectively no longer distinguish between the roles of commissioners and alternates, the structure of the American delegation now consists of two federal representatives, two Alaska representatives, one representative from Washington State, one from Oregon, and two from the treaty Indian tribes.

In terms of the tribal representatives, a significant operational-level norm has been to have both the NWIFC and the CRITFC submit a list of three nominees, and to select one individual from each list.[30] Historically, additional boundary rules determined at the operational level and negotiated between representatives of the NWIFC and the CRITFC rotated the positions of full and alternate tribal commissioners between the NWIFC representative and the CRITFC representative on an annual basis. In light of the fact that full and alternate commissioners are no longer effectively distinguished from one another, which of the two groups has full or alternate representation is now merely a nominal matter.[31] Combined with the fact that none of the PSC commissioners in recent years has been selected according to the confirmation process outlined in section 3(a) of the Pacific Salmon Treaty Act the treaty tribes hold de facto authority to fill their allocated commissioner positions with virtually anybody they wish.[32] Thus the nomination and selection processes for filling the commissioner positions are essentially internal processes of the NWIFC and the CRITFC, despite the boundary rules set forth in the act.

In terms of choice rules directly pertaining to the tribes, any tribal representative can initiate any item both within the American delegation and at all joint international sessions at the commission, panel, and technical committee levels.[33] This gives tribal representatives an enhanced agenda-setting role that the tribes have often used to push particular issues. Because all decisions made by the PSC must be approved at the commissioner level, the tribes through their commissioner positions have a formal vote on all items of business.[34]

Aggregation rules pertaining to decision making of the commissioners from the American delegation are somewhat complex. The Pacific Salmon Treaty Act specifies that "the United States Section shall operate with the objective of attaining consensus decisions in the development and exercise of its single vote within the Commission. A decision of the United States Section shall be taken when there is no dissenting vote."[35] Unwritten operational-level rules in recent years have required that all eight full and alternate commissioners collectively determine the position of the American delegation.[36]

The Pacific Salmon Treaty Act declares the federal representatives of the PSC to be nonvoting members,[37] which would appear to effectively grant individual veto power to each of the two commissioners representing Alaska, to the commissioner from Oregon, to the commissioner from Washington State, to the commissioner representing the NWIFC tribes, and to the commissioner representing the CRITFC tribes. Veto authority is limited, however, by a preemption clause contained in the act which states that the federal government may preempt inaction owing to gridlock between the various commissioners, in order to avoid the violation of international treaty obligations. This preemption clause has served to temper enthusiasm for the veto authority held by the tribes in particular, who believe that preemption effectively gives the federal government veto authority over their veto in any case where there has been an inability to reach consensus.[38] The general perspective held by all participants—federal, state, and tribal—however, is that the mere threat of veto authority by the states and tribes, and the power of preemption by the federal government, effectively force negotiation among the parties, as evidenced by the fact that neither an official veto nor an act of preemption has taken place.[39] Not all participants in the PSC hold this rather positive perspective of the American voting structure. Fears of gridlock, concerns that several veto points complicate intra-delegation and bilateral negotiation patterns, and unease that the level of authority held by the American tribes could set a precedent for increased demands a higher level of participation by First Nations representatives are widespread in the literature and were mentioned several times during my fieldwork.[40]

The relative participatory authority of the Canadian delegation's First Nations groups offers a stark contrast to that of the US delegation's tribal representatives. A very broad distinction between Canada and the United States is the nature of each country's federal system. Canada represents a sort of "double federation" that is based on both territory and special recognition of the rights and political status of particular peoples, rather than a federalism based primarily on territory, as in the United States.[41] A consequence of this federal structure is that the national government is pulled in different directions by various stakeholders and by the provinces themselves, with the federal and provincial governments asserting authority over their own spheres of influence and sometimes fighting for ascendancy vis-à-vis one another in particular policy domains, especially in situations where the special status of a particular protected class of people serves to pit the provincial and federal governments against each other.

Environmental policy in Canada is quite complex and creates a major fault line between the provinces and the federal government. In contrast to "cooperative federalism," which characterizes the modern application of federalism in the United States, environmental policy in Canada conforms more to a "dual federalism" model of shared authority in which the different orders of government have sole spheres of influence. This frequently results in coordination problems and "jurisdictional confusion about which problems can or should be attacked by which level of government."[42] The general federal relationship is that the provinces retain control over natural resource development and exploration while the federal government has sole jurisdiction over designated federal lands, international trade, shipping and navigation, and fisheries.[43] Therefore, primary authority over fisheries policy, other than that in some limited inland jurisdictions that have been granted to the provinces, is vested in the federal government through the Fisheries Act, which designates DFO as the sole regulatory agency.

The broad discretion of the Minister of Fisheries, Oceans, and the Canadian Coast Guard and his or her delegates (such as the Regional Directors General), provides a stark contrast to the pattern of fisheries comanagement in the United States. The Fisheries Act has historically contained a multitude of provisions that grant the Minister broad discretion in setting a wide range of regulatory policies pertaining to fisheries. Formerly, the Minister had full discretion to allow fishing without limitations, broad latitude to allocate fish among different stakeholders, and generally broad bureaucratic discretion in promulgating rules, without any formal provisions to prohibit overfishing or mandate action on particular depleted fish stocks, a level of authority that was a "unique power in fisheries management and conservation" compared to other nations.[44] Recent Changes to the Fisheries Act made in 2019 maintain significant levels of authority on the part of the Minister, but now require a balancing approach from among multiple criteria, including the application of precautionary and ecosystem approaches; consideration of scientific evidence; incorporation of indigenous and community knowledge; and various social, economic, and cultural factors in fisheries management.[45]

An additional notable example of a constraint on ministry authority is the international treaty agreement for joint US-Canadian regulatory power over Fraser River salmon stocks under the auspices of the PSC. As a consequence of DFO having broad authority, the boundary, choice, and aggregation rules employed by the Canadian delegation are often developed and exercised at the operational level, and specific rules are often not formally articulated or written down as official policy. The general implication of the Fisheries Act is that DFO calls all the shots when it comes to passing and enforcing regulations pertaining to fisheries. In the context of the PSC, this is most notably manifested by the informal aggregation rule that the official stance of the Canadian delegation is solely determined by the Regional Director General for the Pacific region, who always sits as the commission chairman of the Canadian delegation.[46] An outgrowth of this unilateral decision-making authority on the part of DFO within the PSC is that there is a strong informal rule mandating a unified Canadian position in the context of bilateral negotiations within the PSC.[47] Disagreements between commissioners are expected to be articulated only within the confines of the domestic caucus that precedes bilateral negotiation,[48] and there is an informal norm that generally the majority opinion will prevail and DFO will vote accordingly. The DFO vote, however, fundamentally determines the Canadian position and could feasibly contradict a majority opinion within the commission.[49] The implication is that the asymmetric aggregation rule implies a general informal choice rule that gives the Regional Director General the sole discretion to make decisions for the entire Canadian delegation. The other commissioners' ability to initiate action items is thus restricted to within the confines of the domestic caucus, before PSC meetings.

Boundary rules specifying who fills the Canadian delegation's commissioner positions are highly informal and fluid. A general pattern throughout most of the history of the PSC has been to have two commissioners who are DFO personnel, two commissioners who represent commercial fishery interests, two commissioners who represent recreational fisheries, and two commissioners who represent First Nations groups—although there is no official written policy that specifies this composition.[50] In recent years, there has been a slight shift such that the delegation now consists of two DFO officials, two First Nations representatives, and one representative each for the commercial fisheries sector, recreational fisheries, the province of British Columbia, and environmental groups.[51] The ability to shuffle the specific sectors represented in the commission stems from DFO's status as sole authority over fisheries policy and is due to the fact that there is no official policy delegating seats on the commission to particular interests.[52]

The process for appointing commissioners to the Canadian delegation is similarly informal. The regional director general solicits nominations for each position and then narrows each of these lists down to three finalists. These are reviewed by the Minister of Fisheries, Oceans, and the Canadian Coast Guard in Ottawa, who ultimately appoints the individual commissioners.[53] Thus the Regional Director General has significant input and serves as a sort of gatekeeper, in that he or she controls the recruitment process for candidates for commissioner positions and has the opportunity to identify his or her three preferred candidates. Various stakeholders have criticized the solicitation process, arguing that it is not comprehensive and targets individuals or groups sympathetic to the general DFO position on salmon fisheries.[54] Another criticism points to the fact that the relatively few positions available at the commission, panel, and committee levels mean that DFO cannot possibly accommodate within the PSC structure representatives from all interested indigenous groups, because there are more than 250 such bands in British Columbia.[55] A related problem is that there is no effective pan–First Nations representative body in Canada akin to that of the NWIFC and the CRITFC.[56]

Why then does DFO accommodate the particular interests that it does in the commission? The entrée of Canadian stakeholders into the PSC stems from a general culture of public-private consultation, which is fundamentally different from the American delegation's recognition of state and tribal governments as comanagers of fishery resources. *Consultation policy* refers to a complex array of rules and norms derived from court mandates, general policy directed from the Privy Council of Canada, and, in the case of DFO, a general bureaucratic culture dating back to the 1970s.[57] DFO had been at the forefront of formalizing consultative policy before it was mandated to do so under the directive of the national government, using the PSC in particular as an experiment in involving multiple stakeholders in consultative processes in order to defuse conflict between the various Canadian stakeholders. This precedent has created an expectation on the part of various groups that they will be actively consulted by DFO during the regulatory process.[58]

The participatory authority of First Nations groups in Canada relative to that of the treaty tribes of the United States is clearly much more constrained. Lacking any real decision-making authority (given the monopoly over decision making that the Regional Director General has in the Canadian delegation), the First Nations groups are essentially restricted to bringing agenda items to the attention of DFO within the confines of the domestic caucus, and mechanisms are in place allowing for the removal of individuals who do not toe the party line. Also, First Nations groups in Canada have much less power to choose their own representatives to the PSC than do the American treaty tribes. Owing to the recognized "duty to consult," however, it may be infeasible for the government of Canada to totally do away with First Nations representation in the PSC, even if it wanted to do so. By virtue then of the relative entrenchment of these positions, the PSC at least represents a formal forum through which First Nations interests can bring to the attention of DFO issues of concern to them, and a number of individuals from each of the sectors represented in the Canadian delegation indicated that this has resulted in a marked increase in the "face time" experienced between First Nations representatives and DFO officials. Therefore it might be said that the relative influence of First Nations groups within the PSC is much more subtle than that of American treaty tribes, and that the PSC offers these groups an advantaged, behind-closed-doors lobbying position to advance their particular interests.

1.2 Regional Governance

Once allocations are agreed upon and set by the PSC, harvest management activities proceed to the regional level. Each country is distinct in the processes it uses to handle its own regional appropriation and provision policies. On the American side, the Magnuson-Stevens Act institutions, created by the Magnuson-Stevens Fishery Conservation and Management Act and its amending reauthorization act,[59] exercise regulatory authority over fisheries within both EEZ and territorial waters. However, there are two different patterns concerning which specific actors have regulatory authority over salmon: one for Alaska and one for the contiguous forty-eight states. In the contiguous forty-eight states, regulatory authority is exercised through the Pacific Fishery Management Council (PFMC), which covers the area extending from three nautical miles to the two hundred nautical-mile limit. The council consists of fourteen voting members, "including 8 appointed by the Secretary . . . at least one of whom shall be appointed from [California, Idaho, Oregon, and Washington], and including one appointed from an Indian tribe with Federally recognized fishing rights from California, Oregon, Washington, or Idaho."[60]

The predominant work of the PFMC, as with the other Magnuson-Stevens Act institutions, is to set appropriation and harvest regulations; however, the council also engages in some provision-type activities through its Habitat Committee, which

> . . .evaluates essential fish habitat . . . including adverse impacts on such habitat and the

consideration of actions to ensure conservation and enhancement of such habitat [and] provides expert advice on the effects of proposed management measures on fish habitat and other habitat related matters brought before the Council for action. The Habitat Committee also reviews activities, or proposed activities, to be authorized, funded, or undertaken by any federal or state agency that may affect habitat of a fishery resource under the jurisdiction of the Council.[61]

In Alaska, the North Pacific Fishery Management Council (NP-FMC) exercises authority similar to that of the PFMC, except that it delegates its regulatory authority over salmon, crab, and herring fisheries to the state of Alaska, primarily because the vast majority of these fisheries lie within the three nautical mile zone.[62] This represents a significant devolution of regulatory control from the federal government to the state of Alaska, a situation which is unique among the eight regional Magnuson-Stevens Act institutions. According to the act, "The North Pacific Council shall have 11 voting members, including 7 appointed by the Secretary . . . (5 of whom shall be appointed from the State of Alaska and 2 of whom shall be appointed from the State of Washington)."[63] Washington State is granted formal membership primarily in order to provide a forum for addressing Washington's concerns over Alaskan interceptions of migratory groundfish that range into Washington waters.

In the contiguous forty-eight states, once allocations and other regulatory issues are determined by the PFMC for the ocean fisheries within the three- to two-hundred-nautical-mile range, regional regulatory oversight shifts to the states. For the states of Oregon and Washington, the "North of Falcon" planning process coincides with the March and April meetings of the PFMC.[64] (The term "North of Falcon" refers to Cape Falcon in northern Oregon, which marks the southern border of active management for Washington salmon stocks.) During this process, near-shore commercial troll and recreational fishing seasons and catch limits off the coasts of Washington, Oregon, and California are decided.[65] Representatives from the state governments of Oregon and Washington and representatives from the treaty tribes within each of these states engage in a comanagement process, with input from federal representatives from the National Marine Fisheries Service. This planning process is an integral step in the hierarchical process of setting specific appropriation regulations. According to the Washington Department of Fish and Wildlife,

> The North of Falcon process starts in late February when the run-size forecasts are first available. Wild and hatchery run sizes for all salmon species from various areas of the state are considered in planning fisheries for the upcoming season. Expected Alaskan and Canadian harvest levels are also considered, as fishery managers and the public consider the seasons that will meet conservation goals for all salmon stocks.[66]

Therefore, two broad regional patterns in the United States can be discerned. In Alaska, all regulation of salmon, from the shoreline to the two-hundred-mile EEZ limit, is exercised by the state of Alaska, although the NPFMC nominally has this authority and delegates it to the state under special agreement. In the contiguous forty-eight states, the PFMC is responsible for the regulatory oversight of fisheries between the three- and two-hundred-nautical-mile range, while the state and tribal governments have collective management authority from the shore to the three-nautical-mile mark.

On the Canadian side, DFO holds sole regulatory authority over both EEZ and internal waters (with the exception of the Fraser River stocks, which are regulated by the PSC, as mentioned previously); thus in Canada, as in Alaska, regional and local appropriation policy is fused and under the domain of a single organization. After negotiating the shared allocation of salmon between the United States and Canada, DFO allocates ocean commercial harvests and then allocates recreational and First Nations instream harvests. First Nations have a wide range of specific allocation rights to salmon that vary considerably from group to group. This situation requires DFO to address individual tribes' allocation to salmon on a case-by-case basis, which complicates planning and decision making. Formal recognition of a First Nations fishing right stems from section 35 of the Constitution Act, although rights specific to fishing were not formally affirmed until the Canadian Supreme Court decision in the case *R. v. Sparrow*, which recognized "food, ceremonial, and social" allocations to a wide number of First Nations bands. While these rights are supposed to take priority over all other considerations, except for conservation, the ill-defined nature of the rights and of how they should be used in setting allocations continues to render them a point of contention between DFO and many First Nations groups, who believe that commercial and recreational fishing interests continue to take priority.[67] Furthermore, some tribes have specific rights that go beyond these basic food, ceremonial, and social rights—one example is the recently court-recognized right of the Nuu-Chah-Nulth to conduct commercial fisheries.[68] There is also a specific allocation to the Nisga'a First Nation of each year's adjusted total allowable catch for Nass River salmon under the Nisga'a Final Agreement, which amounts to 13 percent of the sockeye harvest and 15 percent of the pink harvest.[69]

In Canada, the distribution of indigenous property rights to fish is thus very heterogeneous, but in no case approximates the position enjoyed by the American treaty tribes, as detailed below. DFO is 100 percent responsible for determining not only the total allowable catch, in accordance with guidelines handed down from the PSC, but also the specific numbers of fish allocated to First Nations, commercial, and recreational fisheries, as well as for all determinations regarding the processes by which allocation decisions are made.[70] Furthermore, allocations must be done in accordance with federal "consultation policy" guidelines, which require that regulatory agencies consult with recognized stakeholders regarding any proposed regulatory action.[71] As a consequence, any group identified as a relevant stakeholder must be consulted during policy development decisions. Recognized stakeholders now include certain nongovernmental groups (various First Nations, the Pacific Salmon Foundation, the Sport Fishing Institute of British Columbia, and various interest groups representing commercial fisheries) that participate in formal consultations at multiple levels.[72]

In terms of regional provision activities, under the Oceans Act of 1997, DFO is the lead agency for developing and implementing a national strategy for the management of Canada's estuarine, coastal, and marine ecosystems.[73] DFO's Oceans Action Plan is a set of principles and strategic initiatives, including ecosystem monitoring activities and the development of Marine Protected Areas, meant to coordinate the activities of twenty federal government organizations over a wide variety of habitat-improvement and other programs in saltwater environments.[74] Provisioning activities related to freshwater habitat are overwhelmingly addressed by the provincial government of British Columbia, owing to its central role in natural resource management related to issues such as mining and forestry, and to their potential impacts on salmon.

1.3 Local Governance

On the US side, there is again a distinction between the local management regimes of Alaska and the states in the contiguous forty-eight, owing to the fact that the state of Alaska has integrated regulatory authority over the entire fishery, from stream to the two hundred mile limit of the EEZ. In the states of the Pacific Northwest, regulatory authority over internal waters falls under the jurisdiction of state-tribal comanagement, which is performed on a watershed-by-watershed basis. There are two distinct governance systems at this local level. In Washington State, the Washington Department of Fish and Wildlife coordinates with the twenty treaty tribes, each of which holds special treaty rights "to fish in usual and accustomed places" and "in common with the citizens of the territory", which as a result of *United States v. Washington* and various ancillary cases, have been interpreted to guarantee to the tribes roughly 50 percent of the annual salmon harvest, allow for tribal fishing rights that extend beyond reservation borders, and grant "co-management authority" with the state.[75] The tribes are collectively assisted by the NWIFC, which acts as a support agency that attempts to resolve intertribal collective action problems and to provide political and technical assistance. Along the Columbia River, *United States v. Oregon* similarly established fishing rights and a comanagement regime involving four tribes—the Umatilla, Nez Perce, Yakama, and Warm Springs—that collectively regulate a commercial fishery over shared common fishing areas, with the CRITFC serving as the sole regulatory authority within these treaty fishing access sites, as mentioned previously.

It is useful to differentiate between these two tribal comanagement roles. In the case of the Washington coastal and Puget Sound tribes, each individual tribe coordinates technical and regulatory activity with the Washington Department of Fish and Wildlife, assisted by the NWIFC. In Oregon's comanagement regime, the

Umatilla, Nez Perce, Yakama, and Warm Springs tribes, working collectively through the CRITFC, predominately deal with the federal government in the establishment of sites to mitigate loss of usual and accustomed fishing grounds. They then negotiate with the states of Oregon (primarily, because most treaty fishing access sites are located on the Oregon side of the Columbia River) and Washington to ensure target escapement totals of returning salmon, after which tribal, commercial, and recreational inland allocations are negotiated according to the fifty-fifty share provisions outlined in *United States v. Washington* and its sister case, *United States v. Oregon.*

Owing to the vast array of land-use practices that have potential impacts on salmon productivity, a wide range of provisioning-type activities are conducted by a host of state and local governments in conjunction with particular private organizations. Various rules pertaining to logging practices on private lands, for instance, have been promulgated in Washington State under the Forests and Fish Plan, with the treaty tribes playing significant monitoring and enforcement roles.[76] Because there are such a wide variety of these types of provision arrangements, entailing everything from agricultural practices to mining practices and beyond, no effort will be spent here to catalog them all. A host of provision-related activities are carried out in a very disaggregated and rather ad-hoc manner when it comes to activities that impact salmon's freshwater habitats, and typically entail a high degree of collaboration involving multiple stakeholders, with the state and treaty tribes consistently present as comanagers.

2. Contrast between American and Canadian Indigenous Participatory Authority

Several contrasts between Canadian First Nations and American treaty tribes are worthy of note. On the American side, comanagement between federal, state, and tribal interests is conducted at virtually all levels of the salmon regime, for both appropriation and provision functions. (Notable exceptions to this rule are the North Pacific Anadromous Fish Commission at the international level and the NPFMC governing Alaskan waters, in which tribes do not have any formal representation.) Because of this situation, each actor—federal, state, and tribal—can be characterized as having a high level of network centrality within this multiscale regime. Owing to their complex matrix of interactions, all three actors have direct contact with one another, resulting in little network segmentation. On the Canadian side, one actor, DFO, has a high degree of centrality and serves to coordinate the exchanges between actors across all action situations within all scales of the overall regime, while other actors have a more constrained set of decision responsibilities than their American counterparts.

Because of the conventional wisdom that indigenous peoples and nonstate actors do not commonly hold significant authority within international institutions, perhaps the most interesting aspect of the overall regime is indigenous activity within the PSC. Because of the specific constellation of choice and aggregation rules, all the actors on the American side maintain direct connections to the federal representative on the Canadian side, and in some instances maintain direct links with the other commissioners of the Canadian delegation, despite DFO's desire to control decision making within the auspices of the domestic caucus.

The available access points of American indigenous participation in salmon management at all scales are considerable. The PSC has multiple natural resource management responsibilities and has disaggregated specific functions to several panels and committees that have primary responsibility in certain areas. Beyond the commissioner level, the organization consists of four panels—the Fraser River, Southern River, Northern River, and Transboundary River panels—which serve as the venues for setting targeted escapement levels and harvesting levels for stocks subject to international interceptions. There are also nine "technical committees" (the Chinook, Coho, Chum, Data Sharing, Fraser River, Northern Boundary, Selective Fishery Evaluation, Transboundary, and Habitat and Restoration Technical Committees), which serve as the primary monitoring and information-sharing venues of the institution and address a variety of technical issues relevant to management of salmon in general. Two additional special Restoration and Enhancement Fund Committees, one for the north and one for the south, exist to provide funding for a variety of habitat restoration efforts and improvements in technical data gathering and sharing. These were created by the 1999 renegotiation of the PST and can best be construed as bodies involved in "investment activities" related to "provision problems" rather than the typical "appropriation problems" that have traditionally been the focus of the PSC's work. Therefore, these committees represent significant institutional drift in the responsibilities of the PSC, into non-harvest-related activities.

A few instances of "self-organizing activities" are of particular interest to this study. Starting around 2003, several Canadian First Nations representatives, including the two First Nations commissioners in the PSC, pushed for the creation of a First Nations Caucus to serve as a direct consultative body between Canadian First Nations representatives and DFO within the PSC.[77] The caucus was seen as a necessary tool for promoting First Nations interests in light of the fact that no organization collectively speaks for Canadian First Nations interests in the way that the NWIFC and the CRITFC speak for the American treaty tribes.[78] First Nations representatives in the PSC successfully obtained limited funding to support an intertribal caucus process, through the Aboriginal Aquatic Resource and Oceans Management program, which was designed to improve the consultative capacity of DFO vis-à-vis indigenous groups. The caucus seems to have been fairly successful at mitigating the intertribal disputes that have frequently come up during PSC negotiations. However, there have been concerns voiced from the Canadian PSC commissioners representing the commercial and recreational fishery sectors that the closed-door nature of the First Nations caucus potentially complicates the ability to present a unified front in opposition to the US delegation, which they believe should be the primary goal of the Canadian delegation.[79]

Building on the precedent set by the First Nations Caucus, since 2008 there has been a "joint tribal caucus" within the PSC, where all tribal and First Nations representatives at the commissioner, panel, and technical committee levels meet to try to work out differences between American and Canadian indigenous groups *before* official negotiations take place at the annual meetings.[80] The ability to work out differences before negotiations begin is particularly relevant for the deliberations of the Fraser River Panel, because almost all of the American allocation of Fraser River sockeye accrue to particular American treaty tribes in Northern Puget Sound, and this pits these groups against the various Fraser River First Nations groups that themselves face major intertribal conflicts based on their respective geographic locations on the river.[81] Transnational intertribal negotiation prior to the meetings is a new development and it is unclear how effective it will be in facilitating compromise between the American tribes and the Canadian First Nations groups, but it does represent an interesting new dimension of cross-border interaction that the indigenous group representatives themselves believe to be useful and of high value.[82] It is not without controversy, however, because DFO and other Canadian stakeholders have expressed reservations about the legal authority of First Nations groups to engage in "foreign" negotiations. In order to alleviate these concerns, indigenous actors have been careful to characterize the forum as merely another example of the many "hallway conversations" that occur during PSC meetings.[83]

3. Conclusion

Indigenous peoples hold unique and significant levels of authority at multiple scales of the regime governing Pacific salmon. This regime is necessarily complex owing to the sheer ecological complexity of salmon as a resource and the range of societal interests with a stake in salmon use and preservation. The regime is interesting in that indigenous groups, particularly on the American side, hold significant positions of authority and serve as coordinating actors across the multiple centers of power that operate at the international, national, regional, and local levels. An examination of the ways in which position, boundary, choice, and aggregation rules combine better illustrates the channels through which indigenous groups employ influence within institutions than do other policy frameworks, that might characterize indigenous group activity as merely reflecting the roles usually attributed to outside interest groups or coalition partners.

During field research for this project, key informants frequently asserted that the American tribes in particular, which occupy significant and protected positions of authority in virtually every institution in the polycentric structure of salmon governance, serve as a necessary coordinating mechanism both horizontally and vertically within the regime. Furthermore, the salmon-allocation regime represents an interesting test bed in evaluating the ways in which institutional rules configure in such a way as to grant relative power and authority to indigenous peoples within international institutions, groups which might otherwise erroneously be considered "non-governmental", falling outside the scope of authoritative decision-making or otherwise merely behaving as special-interest lobbying groups.

Applying the logic of institutional analysis to other international institutions that have mechanisms for indigenous inclusion or that make room for the accommodation of indigenous rights and interests, such as the Arctic Council and the International Whaling Commission, would help elucidate models and processes for greater inclusion of indigenous peoples as truly sovereign actors, particularly within international institutions. Analyses regarding whether such participation promotes the stability of such regimes and enhances the sustainable management of the resources in question should also be improved by the more nuanced picture of the power and influence of indigenous groups that comes from such an approach to institutional analysis.

Population Growth and the Governance of Complex Institutions: People Are More Than Mouths to Feed

Pierre Desrochers and Joanna Szurmak

D ISCUSSIONS OF ELINOR OSTROM'S KEY contributions to the study
of polycentric governance of complex institutions are often
framed as a challenge[1] to biologist Garrett Hardin's classic essay "The Tragedy of the Commons" (TC).[2] Ostrom herself used
the word "challenging"[3] to describe TC, a contribution that both
encapsulates and expands on Hardin's then long-standing concern with the preservation of finite resources through human
population control.[4] By now, the consensus on this relationship
between Ostrom's and Hardin's work—Ostrom as the challeng-
er of Hardin's "freedom in a commons brings ruin to all" dic-
tum[5]—is nearly universal.[6] Brad Wible, senior commentary editor in *Science*, in a preface to a symposium assessing the impact
of TC on the fiftieth anniversary of its publication, wrote, "Hardin questioned society's ability to manage shared resources and
avoid an environmentally and socially calamitous free-for-all. . . .
Considerable work, notably by Nobelist Elinor Ostrom, has challenged Hardin, particularly his emphasis on property rights and
government regulatory leviathans as solutions."[7] A recent work
refines this established perspective: "Elinor Ostrom dedicated
much of her career to demonstrating how commons in the real

world had not and do not inevitably lead to tragic ruin, as Hardin had insisted."[8]

These analyses are, by preponderance of evidence and repeated agreement of peers, overwhelmingly correct. As perceptive and essential as these observations are, they take two analytical shortcuts that are, to our knowledge, almost universal in the literature of the Ostrom-Hardin challenge. First, these scholars focus their critiques, and their comparisons between Ostrom's and Hardin's work, on one aspect of Hardin's TC, the economic implications of his interpretation of the term "commons."[9] Eminent economics professors Brett Frischmann, Alain Marciano, and Giovanni Battista Ramello, in what is arguably the most accomplished and up-to-date analysis of the economic legacy of TC with respect to Ostrom's work, identify and discuss the conceptual failures of Hardin's understanding of the commons.[10] Second in our list of shortcuts, analysts typically assume that Hardin, like Ostrom, was primarily concerned with the management of scarce resources in a commons, such as pastures, forests, and fisheries. This is a misconception. In fact, Hardin's primary conundrum was the proposition, encapsulated in TC's tagline, that "the population problem has no technical solution; it requires a fundamental extension in morality."[11] Indeed, Hardin revived the overexploited commons metaphor from political economist William Forster Lloyd (1794–1852) to illustrate, as Lloyd had done, the necessity of controlling human population numbers.

Many economists and resource analysts have continued to focus on Hardin's metaphorical hook while avoiding his main argument and concern, particularly when contrasting Hardin's and Ostrom's work, but a few researchers have commented on the key issue in TC. As the prominent Marxist geographer David Harvey observed, Hardin's key message was that the "personal decision to have children would, he feared, lead eventually to the destruction of the global commons (a point that Thomas Malthus also argued). The private, familial nature of the decision was the crucial problem. The only solution, in his view, was authoritarian regulatory population control."[12] Another geographer, David Correia, similarly wrote that the main message of TC is often misunderstood, for "unlike Ostrom, Hardin wasn't writing about forests or oceans or pastures when he used the word 'commons,' he was talking about population."[13] Ostrom was well aware of Hardin's emphasis on population control[14] and realized that the commonly accepted understanding, even among scientists, of the term "tragedy of the commons" might lead to overgeneralizations in what she called "metaphorical use of models"[15] in the study of resource management, and, more importantly, to policy prescriptions concerning both the environment and population control.

This is, in fact, the key idea on which we have built this chapter: The typical interpretation of the phrase "tragedy of the commons" does not align with the key message of Garrett Hardin's work "The Tragedy of the Commons," which is the need for authoritarian, top-down population control in the name of preserving limited resources.[16] The key contributions of Elinor Ostrom's work do, in fact, address the management of the commons explicitly, but have deep implications for the nature of decision-making in complex, polycentric settings. We aim to show in this chapter that, even though the key issue in TC is population control, not resource management, the implications of Ostrom's work are still significant philosophically in reinforcing the importance of governance models, and decision-making processes, that are nonauthoritarian. Rather than offering an economic analysis of Ostrom's and Hardin's views on the question of the management of the commons, as has been done by others, most recently by Frischmann, Marciano, and Ramello,[17] we provide a historical perspective of the population-control issue at the heart of TC, bringing together Hardin's and Ostrom's perspectives on the issue.

Our goal in this chapter is to provide a broader context for the debates launched by Hardin's classic essay. First, we introduce his work and summarize his stance about the absolute necessity of population control, articulated in TC and throughout his career. In the second and third sections, we revisit long-standing arguments for and against population control that deal specifically with Hardin's main concerns—environmental impact, resource depletion, and economic growth—by using sources that (often long) predate the case he made in TC and elsewhere, typically stopping our analysis with sources available in 1968, the year of TC's publication. As will be demonstrated, Hardin's thoughts were hardly original and he, like virtually all neo-Malthusians[18] in the past two generations, failed to engage with contrary facts and arguments. Where he arguably stood out, however, was in his willingness to articulate and debate publicly some unpalatable logical implications of his Malthusian worldview. In the final three sections, our chapter will draw connections between Hardin's ideas and Ostrom's challenges to his "systems" model of human behavior and resource governance.[19] We trace Ostrom's insights into polycentric governance and the properties of the Institutional Analysis and Development framework in the area of population growth, particularly as a counterpoint to Hardin's viewpoints. We conclude that the implications of Ostrom's research are consistent with a cautious brand of population optimism centered on individual agency.

1. Garrett Hardin's Legacy of the "Tragedy of the Commons": Population Growth, Environmental Degradation, and Resource Stewardship

As the web page of his personal archive acknowledges, Garrett Hardin "wrote on and publicly supported birth control and eugenics (including abortion and sterilization), conservation, ending of foreign aid, and restriction of immigration as solutions to overpopulation."[20] Apart from TC, Hardin is best known for promoting the concept of carrying capacity[21] and for developing the lifeboat ethics as an alternative to the Spaceship Earth metaphor,[22] topics we discuss later in this chapter.

Like the views of other prominent American environmental writers of his day, Hardin's core values regarding natural resource management and population-control policy were shaped by prior eugenicist and Malthusian thinking.[23] In fact, Hardin's intellectual roots were "equal parts Malthusian political economy and Cold War systems science,"[24] nourished and given prominence by the "'Malthusian moment' [that] swept population biology, policy discussions, and the political imaginaries of diverse publics."[25] Hardin's views also derived from his formal training in microbial ecology and population biology, first at the University of Chicago and then at Stanford University. His 1941 PhD dissertation examined *Oikomonas*, uniflagellate protozoans common in stagnant water, soil, and sewage, reacted to changes in their environment and food availability.[26] Hardin's research on algal ecology had as its goal increasing the human food supply.[27] Instead of embracing that motivation, Hardin confronted, for the first time, what he saw as a failure of science to deal with the root cause of the food supply problem: the increasing rate of human population growth.

Hardin's main concern in his postgraduate work and throughout his life remained human population growth as the ultimate cause of resource waste and environmental degradation. He wrote about the preservation of natural resources and population control in the first edition of his textbook *Biology: Its Human Implications*.[28] In his view, any well-meaning policy—whether it involved research on alternative foodstuffs or poverty relief—that resulted in increased human numbers was ultimately self-defeating. Politically, Hardin was hostile to both laissez-faire free market policies and communism if the outcome was greater human encroachment on the natural ecosystems. Writing for an American audience in TC, he insisted that little progress would be made toward reaching "optimum population size" until the "spirit of Adam Smith in the field of practical demography" (i.e., the notion that an individual who "intends only his own gain" is "led by an invisible hand to promote . . . the public interest") had been properly exorcized.[29]

The main problem with Smith's philosophy, Hardin argued in TC, was that it contributed to "the dominant tendency of thought that has ever since interfered with positive action based on rational analysis, namely the tendency to assume that decisions reached individually will, in fact, be the best decisions for an entire society. If this assumption is correct it justifies the continuance of our present policy of laissez faire in reproduction."[30] In a short reflection piece published three decades after TC, Hardin summarized the evolution of his thought on the subject:

> With Adam Smith's work as a model, I had assumed that the sum of separate ego-serving decisions would be the best possible one for the population as a whole. But presently I discovered that I agreed much more with William Forster Lloyd's conclusions, as given in his Oxford lectures of 1833. Citing what happened to pasturelands left open to many herds of cattle, Lloyd pointed out that, with a resource available to all, the greediest herdsmen would gain—for a while. But mutual ruin was just around the comer. As demand grew in step with population (while supply remained fixed), a time would come when the herds-men, acting as Smithian individuals, would be trapped by their own competitive impulses. The unmanaged commons would be ruined by overgrazing; competitive

individualism would be helpless to prevent the social disaster.[31]

Hardin clearly stated his anti-individualist stance contra Smith on this issue, pointing out what even Malthus missed in his analysis:

> As I see it, Malthus walked right past the heart of the population problem. . . . The problem is simply this: can the necessity of population control be reconciled with the apparent demands of *individualism* . . . ? I conclude that there is a fatal contradiction between these two necessities; and that the survival of civilization will require us to modify significantly the powers we now grant to individual "rights."[32]

Lloyd's *Two Lectures on the Checks to Population* (1833) were largely forgotten until Hardin resurrected interest in the – still rarely read – work of this Malthusian British political economist." They dealt in part with a comparison of societies: societies where the "burden of a family [was thrown] entirely on the parents" and others where "the children maintain themselves at a very early age" were compared to the "parallel cases of inclosed grounds and [open] commons" in which cattle is stocked. Lloyd asked, Why "are the cattle on a common so puny and stunted? Why is the common itself so bare-worn, and cropped so differently from the adjoining [better-maintained] inclosures?" The key explanation, he argued, was how "an increase of stock in the two cases affects the circumstances of the author of the increase," especially in the case of a "number of adjoining pastures, already fully stocked . . . at once thrown open, and converted into one vast common." The key problems were that if "individuals are prudent [they do not] alone reap the benefit" and, "if they [are] imprudent [they do not] alone feel the evil consequences."[33]

Hardin later acknowledged that he and Lloyd were really addressing a subset of traditional commons-management issues for an unmanaged resource, although, on the basis of how he phrased the issue, it is probably fair to say that Lloyd was more aware of the problem. Ostrom called these unmanaged commons such as pastures common-pool resources.[34] Summing up his thought on the issue in 1998, Hardin observed, "A 'managed commons' describes either socialism or the privatism of free enterprise. Either one may work; either one may fail: 'The devil is in the details.' But with an unmanaged commons, you can forget about the devil: As overuse of resources reduces carrying capacity, ruin is inevitable.'"[35] He further clarified,

> Both privatism and socialism can either succeed or fail. But, except in the smallest of communities, *communism* cannot succeed.[36] An unmanaged common fails because it rewards individual exploiters for making the wrong decisions— wrong for the group as a whole, and wrong for themselves, in the long run. Freedom in the commons does *not* produce a stable prosperity. This is Lloyd's revolutionary point. Popular prophets, intoxicated by laissez-faire, simply could not hear Lloyd.[37]

Whatever shortcomings TC—"a qualitative modeling exercise wrapped in a parable about a hypothetical public pasture"[38]— might have exhibited in explaining the problem of unmanaged commons, however, ultimately Hardin always remained adamant that the commons degradation or "pollution problem is a consequence of population [growth]."[39] In fact, Hardin saw overpopulation as an ecological problem of the human species with a "narrow statist" solution,[40] summarized in his lifeboat ethics metaphor. This trope partitioned a global problem into discrete national subproblems instead of leaving it as a question for a Spaceship Earth to resolve. As Hardin saw things, the Earth was not a spaceship, since a ship has a captain with real power while the Earth (in the absence of global governance) does not.

In Hardin's lifeboat ethics metaphor, "each rich nation is in effect a lifeboat full of comparatively rich people."[41] By contrast, since the lifeboats representing poor nations are uncomfortably overcrowded, "the poor fall out of their lifeboats and swim for a while in the water outside, hoping to be admitted to a rich lifeboat, or in some other way to benefit from the 'goodies' on board." Hardin then asked, "What should the passengers on a rich lifeboat do? This is the central problem of 'the ethics of a life boat.'" Hardin's argument was that the unavoidable and ethically correct thing to do was to let the poor swimmers drown, however morally repugnant that might seem to us, in order to prevent an even worse outcome through a "suicidal . . . generous immigration policy."[42]

Scholars of philosophy and history of science Sebastian Normandin and Sean Valles saw Hardin's lifeboat ethics and the concomitant immigration and reproduction control philosophies as representing an "almost anti-ecological" stance, "insofar as it runs counter to any holistic perspective on the worldwide environmental problems related to population growth."[43] The environmental policy analyst John S. Dryzek commented on Hardin's narrow and authoritarian stance along the same lines: "Hardin made a connection to childbearing decisions: if the world is a commons, each additional child adds stress to the commons, even though calculations of private interest determine that the child should be conceived, born, and raised."[44] Since each individual child is akin to a free rider on the commons and an interloper against the carrying capacity, those private interests bringing a child into being cannot be allowed to prevail when considering both the carrying capacity and the lifeboat ethics metaphors.

Hardin's metaphors display not just an overreliance on static physical capacity concepts, but a scientistic attitude: He placed too high a value on a narrow analysis of a complex topic, assuming that this analysis was the sole correct method for dealing with the problem.[45] His scientism implies that a "fully rational and dispassionate analysis of complex human circumstances is possible"[46]—and that it is, indeed, sufficient—and that both the natural resources needed and the actual number of human beings the earth can support can be mathematically calculated solely as "a function of per capita demands of those individuals."[47] Thus, in Hardin's world, the scientific and political elite of each sovereign country would calculate the state's population carrying capacity and enforce the correct sustainable population numbers. Individuals should not have the agency to decide whether, and when, to reproduce, because the Smithian decisions optimizing individuals' own outcomes would be sure to impinge on the scientifically determined carrying capacity calculated for the collective.

Hardin famously concluded TC by stating that the "only way we can preserve and nurture other and more precious freedoms is by relinquishing the freedom to breed, and that very soon." He further explained that "freedom is the recognition of necessity," and "it is the role of education to reveal to all the necessity of abandoning the freedom to breed. Only so, can we put an end to this aspect of the tragedy of the commons."[48] As Hardin would again write toward the end of his life, "The reality that underlies all the necessary curtailments [to individual freedom] is always the same—population growth."[49]

Although in time his rhetoric would shift somewhat in terms of the dire consequences he feared,[50] Hardin always maintained that population growth in the context of finite resources could only result in disastrous outcomes and, because of this, mandated a severe curbing of individual freedom. As he argued in TC and in many other places, "The more the population exceeds the carrying capacity of the environment, the more freedoms must be given up."[51] In his 1997 open letter to the American Civil Liberties Union, recounted in his obituary by energy analyst Vaclav Smil, Hardin argued that "when a woman elects to have a child, she is committing the community to something like $100,000 for bearing and rearing of that child. Is it wise to extend individual rights that far?"[52] Hardin's solution was a policy of "mutual coercion, mutually agreed upon."[53] Political scientist and Ostrom's collaborator Amy Poteete summarizes his stance in terms of the outcome of the tragedy of the commons as a model: it "predicts that a set of individuals will be unable to engage in collective action without outside intervention."[54] According to Hardin, efficiencies must be externally imposed by a governing elite in an attempt to "achieve 'normalization' . . . based on a single perspective."[55] In other words, the lifeboat needs a captain.

Hardin's desirable institutional framework, therefore, always relied on elite guidance in accordance with a single perspective through—if practical—coercion. Indeed, a fair reading of Hardin's other writings on the issue leaves little doubt that he supported "mutually agreed upon" measures only to the extent he deemed them sufficiently drastic in terms of reducing population growth. In this sense, Hardin's stance epitomized the single-solution consensus common to many pessimistic environmentalist thinkers of the post–World War II era who opined on these issues before TC's publication. Like these thinkers, Hardin failed to discuss in any meaningful way the contrary arguments and the empirical evidence put forward by the optimist analysts whose case is presented in section 3. Hardin's stance against unchecked human population growth—always the main driver in his attempts at interdisciplinary synthesis—would remain unchanged for the rest of his life.

Hardin was arguably more willing that contemporary neo-Malthusians to think, write, and say what many others deemed unacceptable in the policy arena,[56] and he was a radical (if not always a consistent one) in both life and death. He and his ill wife committed suicide together shortly after their sixty-second wedding anniversary—but together they had raised four children,[57] more than the one child per every man or woman he had reportedly advocated.[58]

2. The Neo-Malthusian Case in Brief

We now turn to a more detailed discussion of the key insights of the conflicting discourses: that is, the neo-Malthusian pessimist perspective and the optimist one. It is essential that we become acquainted with the historical precursors of Hardin's ideas so that we can assess, first, where Hardin's ideas were rooted intellectually and, second, what was truly novel about his additions to the pessimist side of the population debate. We will find congruence between Hardin's views and those of the pessimists, whereas the optimist perspective will give us some additional insights into Ostrom's critique of Hardin in our concluding section. In addition, becoming familiar with the optimist side of the population debate will foreground arguments, for the most part as old as those of the pessimists, that were available to Hardin had he wished to disprove them specifically, or to address any of the associated empirical findings. We will see that, like most neo-Malthusian thinkers, Hardin chose not to address optimist arguments in detail or in a serious manner, preferring instead to launch largely ad hominem attacks against economists as poorly trained nonscientists.[59]

As stated earlier, our choice was to use material that predates the publication of TC, material that would therefore have been accessible to Hardin and other post–World War II neo-Malthusian writers.[60] For the most part we will discuss both Hardin and Ostrom within the range of the literature available to them when they wrote the key works in question, such as TC and, in Ostrom's case, works published before her Nobel prize in 2009. There will be exceptions to this material selection constraint in the final section and in the conclusion, but the majority of such exceptions will illustrate points about Hardin's or Ostrom's views, not new empirical or theoretical insights on the topic of population growth and resource management. To provide an example of this exclusion, this chapter does not engage with the population implications of China's one-child policy or of its repeal at the end of 2015, because neither Ostrom nor Hardin addressed the former in great detail,[61] and they had no opportunity to learn of the latter.

Pessimists have long argued that, if not checked by voluntary or coercive means, a population tends to outgrow its limited supply of food and natural resources or else inflicts irredeemable environmental damage on its surroundings, resulting in famine and societal collapse. Writers in this tradition, with whom Hardin was arguably more familiar than with most other post-World War II neo-Malthusians,[62] typically invoked the arguments we summarize below using sources that predate the publication of TC. While pessimist thought reaches back further in time than the fifteenth century (where we start this section), the following survey of key Malthusian and neo-Malthusian arguments situates us at the ground zero of Hardin's ideas on population.

Pessimist Argument 1: Continued
Growth in a Finite System Is Unsustainable

In the early sixteenth century, Niccolò Machiavelli observed that "when every province of the world so teems with inhabitants that they can neither subsist where they are nor remove elsewhere, every region being equally crowded and over-peopled," the world will purge itself through floods, plagues, or famines.[63] In the mid-1700s, the Danish cleric Otto Diederich Lütken anticipated Malthus by forty years, at the same time neatly encapsulating the ideas of limits to growth and the carrying capacity of the earth:

> Since the circumference of the globe is given and does not expand with the increased number of its inhabitants, and as travel to other planets thought to be inhabitable has not yet been invented; . . . it follows that the proposition "that the world's inhabitants will be happier, the greater their number" cannot be maintained, for as soon as the number exceeds that which our planet with all its wealth of land and water can support, they must needs starve one another out.[64]

In 1886, the former Methodist minister and birth control activist Joseph Symes wrote that "no matter how large the country," in the absence of deliberate efforts to the contrary, "the land will be over-stocked with people," the food supply will be "too scanty," and "even standing room will soon be wanting." What was true of any country was, prefiguring Hardin's lifeboat metaphors, "equally true of the world at large, the raft to which we cling in the boundless ocean of space."[65]

A generation later, the eugenicist Edward Isaacson argued that "the time must come when the countries which now export food will be filled up to the point where they will need all they produce for themselves, and can no longer supply the over-populated countries at any price."[66] Although emigration had acted as a safety valve in the past, this could only continue "so long as there is a place for it; but what then?" Isaacson's solution, echoing John Stuart Mill, was a steady state of economic development in which "population must be kept down to the numbers which [over-populated countries'] land with the best management can support."[67]

While we do know that Hardin's main inspiration for TC was the output of William Forster Lloyd, particularly *Two Lectures on the Checks to Population*, we can see from this section's selections that both the idea of limits dictating a carrying capacity and the image of humanity clinging precariously to boats or rafts, in fear of extinction, are mainstays of the pessimist discourse.

Pessimist Argument 2: Everything Else Being Equal, a Reduced Population Will Enjoy a Higher Standard of Living

As evinced in the previously quoted passages by Machiavelli and Lütken, population control by catastrophic crashes due to famine, war, or epidemic illness was a common motif in the pessimist literature. Short of such disasters, pessimists argued that coercive population control was a necessity for attaining human prosperity. While Malthus admitted that the inhabitants of a country "depopulated by violent causes" such as wars would "probably live in severe want," he suggested that population reduction without destruction of the capital stock (say, the aftermath of an epidemic disease) would benefit the remaining inhabitants, as they could "cultivate principally the more fertile parts of their territory" and not have to cultivate more marginal lands.[68] Writing in 1879, Edward Henry Stanley, the fifteenth Earl of Derby and a prominent British public officer and politician, opined that "it is better to have thirty-five millions of human beings leading useful and intelligent lives, rather than forty millions struggling painfully for a bare subsistence."[69]

In 1948, ornithologist and population control activist William Vogt observed in his *Road to Survival*—the biggest environmental best seller of all time until the publication of Rachel Carson's *Silent Spring* in 1962—that "drastic measures are inescapable" in light of worldwide environmental destruction by the pressures of overpopulation.[70] Vogt's harsh rhetoric is a direct precursor of Hardin's: "Irresponsible breeding . . . imposes a drain on the world's wealth . . . when this wealth might be used to improve living standards and survival chances for less people."[71]

Pessimist Argument 3: Decreasing Returns to Investment in Natural Resources Result in Lower Standards of Living

Because valuable natural resources such as land suitable for agriculture and mineral resources come in different grades and are found in more- and less-convenient locations, pessimist writers have long made the case for unavoidable decreasing or diminishing returns to economic effort over time, the result of which will be retardation and the eventual termination of economic growth.

The decreasing-returns perspective in the population-resource debate is usually traced back to the second edition of Malthus's *An Essay on the Principle of Population*, where he argued that making less-productive parts of the landscape fit for agricultural production would require more time and labor than was previously necessary. As a result, the "additions that could yearly be made to the former average produce must be gradually and regularly diminishing."[72] This argument was endorsed by John Stuart Mill in his *Principles of Political Economy*, where he even disputed the utility of the additional labor new individuals could contribute in a zero-sum world.[73]

The distinguished American scientist and eugenicist Edward Murray East worried about decreasing returns in agricultural production. In particular, "Food exportation from the younger countries will sink rapidly, as it did in the United States during the decades before the [First World] war, so rapidly that overpopulated countries will have the greatest difficulty in adjusting themselves to the change."[74]

In 1951 Robert Carter Cook, a prominent American geneticist, demographer, and eugenicist, commented that the world's growing population will force the use of marginal lands, which in general are extremely expensive to exploit. More and more human energy will have to be devoted to the basic problem of producing food, and the standard of living, instead of going up, will remain at subsistence level in the areas where it now stands at that, while the wealthier areas will find their standards of living declining.[75]

This argument has long been applied to carbon fuels. For instance, in 1865 the economist William Stanley Jevons suggested in his classic *The Coal Question* that, over time, the price of this resource would become "much higher than the highest price now paid for the finest kinds of coal" because the most "cheaply and easily" accessible fields and seams would always be developed first.[76]

Most pessimist writers were content to apply the decreasing returns argument to agriculture and other instances of natural resource exploitation, but they rarely extended it to manufacturing activities. Hardin did, in order to condemn economic growth in toto as an irresponsible and unscientific idea,[77] thus anticipating later degrowth literature. In a relatively rare foray into an economic argument, Hardin contrasted economies of scale with what he called "diseconomies of scale" that crop up "at some level of production";[78] Hardin proceeded without giving illustrations or explanations of this phenomenon, but it is an analogue to the idea of diminishing returns. The critique of Hardin's argument, although beyond the scope of our chapter, would focus on Hardin's assumption of a static nature of "diseconomies" in an innovation-poor setting.

Pessimist Argument 4: Technological Innovation and Synthetic Products Cannot Be Substituted for Natural Capital

As we observed in the previous subsection, technological innovation and change were not highly regarded by pessimist thinkers. Writing in 1948, Henry Fairfield Osborn Jr., a conservationist and longtime president of the New York Zoological Society, insisted that the "grand and ultimate illusion would be that man could provide a substitute for the elemental workings of nature."[79] His examples of endeavors in which technology must fail humanity in the long run included chemical fertilizers,[80] now known to be one of the great successes of early agrochemical engineering.

William Vogt similarly considered agricultural innovation and mechanization "of dubious value to the land, as it is more purely extractive than older methods,"[81] bringing poorer land under cultivation, being too dependent on rapidly dwindling petroleum reserves, and triggering a migration from rural to urban areas, thereby reducing agricultural populations that should be kept on farms as human buffers in case of future recessions. Moreover, Vogt observed, agricultural machinery had little to contribute to the land: one does "not find a manure pile outside the tractor shed."[82]

Pessimist Argument 5: The Prosperous Should Not Help the Poor

Like Hardin, several Malthusian thinkers opposed famine relief and other measures to help the poor, arguing that they would only make a bad situation worse. Writing in the middle of the nineteenth century, the French mutualist theorist Pierre-Joseph Proudhon thus condemned Malthusianism as having been from its beginning "the theory of political murder; of murder from motives of philanthropy and for love of God . . . [Malthusians] cannot conceive how, without some sort of an organization of homicide, a balance between population and production can exist."[83] Half a century later, the Catholic economist Charles Stanton Devas observed that the practical results of Malthusian thinking had "been a grave discouragement to all works of social reform and humane legislation, which appeared as foolish sentiment defeating its kind aims by encouraging population."[84]

The case against helping the poor was restated forcefully at the end of World War II by prominent writers, who urged policymakers to let nature run its course rather than ship vast quantities of new synthetic pesticides and medicine to poor economies. William Vogt, for one, considered such measures inadvisable. He even argued that the "flank attack on the tsetse fly with DDT or some other insecticide," then being carried out by "ecologically ignorant sanitarians, entomologists, and medical men," was going to make things worse because there was no "kindness in keeping people from dying of malaria so that they could die more slowly of starvation."[85]

In a 1952 presidential address to the British Association for the Advancement of Science that would later be denounced by both the Kremlin and the Vatican,[86] distinguished British scientist Archibald Vivian Hill—who also happened to be brother-in-law to famous economist, eugenicist, and neo-Malthusian John Maynard Keynes[87]—asked, "If men were certain that the present overpopulation trends would eventually engulf them, would they be right in withholding such things as insecticides, fertilizers, and anti-malarial and anti-tuberculosis drugs?" and if "men bred like rabbits should they be allowed to die like rabbits?"[88] Novelist and philosopher Aldous Huxley laid out the same logic in his 1958 essay *Brave New World Revisited*:

> We go to a tropical island and with the aid of DDT we stamp out malaria and, in two or three years, save hundreds of thousands of lives. . . .

Quick death by malaria has been abolished; but life made miserable by undernourishment and over-crowding is now the rule, and slow death by outright starvation threatens ever greater numbers.[89]

Pessimist Argument 6: Past Successes in Overcoming Natural Limits Are Irrelevant to Present Conditions

To Hardin, as to most pessimist thinkers, humanity was living in a most perilous time, facing uniquely difficult problems. In 1923, Edward Murray East opined in his influential book *Mankind at the Crossroads* that the

> facts of population growth and the facts of agricultural economics point . . . severally to the definite conclusion that the world confronts the fulfillment of the Malthusian prediction here and now. Man stands to-day at the parting of the ways, with the choice of controlling his own destiny or of being tossed about until the end of time by the blind forces of the environment in which he finds himself.[90]

There was no comfort in looking at past developments, he argued, as the "present age is totally unlike any previous age."[91]

A few years earlier the prominent British economist Alfred Marshall had also turned to Malthus, but in order to absolve him for not foreseeing the technological revolution in transportation and power generation brought about by the steam engine, which had delayed the Malthusian population catastrophe. Marshall noted that that grim future was getting nearer by the day, however, "unless the checks on the growth of population in force at the end of the nineteenth century are on the whole increased."[92]

Two prominent American pessimists, Robert Carter Cook and the geochemist and eugenicist Harrison Brown, wrote similar reflections on Malthus's work half a century later. As Cook put it, Malthus "lived at the threshold of an age in which a profound revolution in the physical circumstances of Western life was to occur" in terms of new modes of transportation, the opening of new territories, and scientific advances.[93] Unfortunately, "the nineteenth-century refutation of the population crisis is still a part of most contemporary belief" and the "man in the street sees no compelling reason to be apprehensive that the science which has served him so handsomely thus far will fail him in the future."

For his part, Brown similarly excused the deficiencies of Malthus's extrapolation into the future, as they "suffered not from lack of proper reasoning, but from lack of sufficient knowledge of the potentialities of technological development." Brown was a better observer of the nature of technological and population changes through the nineteenth and early twentieth centuries, as he wrote of Malthus,

> Further, he could not have foreseen the extent to which the changed way of life in an industrial age would result in drastically declining birth rates coupled with decreasing mortality. In short, the scientific knowledge of his time was too meager to permit his drawing valid quantitative conclusions, no matter how sound his reasoning was.[94]

Brown was referring to the demographic transition brought about by increasing prosperity and galloping technological innovation, the shift from a high-fertility society of large families to a society with increasingly fewer children. The implications of the demographic transition are important to us, and we will return to the economic relationship between population growth, technological progress, and the rise in individual prosperity as denoted by rising per capita incomes in industrializing countries of the nineteenth and twentieth centuries.

Hardin's views, as expressed over nearly five decades of his life, did indeed resonate with those of earlier neo-Malthusian writers and pessimist eugenicists, as we have indicated throughout this section. Although Hardin was more familiar with the history of thought than most of these writers, like other pessimist writers of his time he nevertheless failed to engage with the opposing view and he did not entertain the idea that past historical outcomes might be problematic for his outlook.

3. The Optimist Case in Brief

We now turn to a more detailed examination of the insights of the optimist writers. Since the early decades of the nineteenth century, optimist analysts have drawn their readers' attention to key empirical facts such as the increasing longevity, better health, higher incomes, and burgeoning technological innovation accompanying an increasing population as proof of the validity of their perspective. To the extent that pessimists acknowledged such facts,[95] they saw them as fleeting aberrations, intellectual shiny objects that have the power to distract those who do not understand the science of limits. The unspoken critique of optimists' reliance on such facts was their lack of a theoretically satisfactory explanation, expressed in a way that met the conventions of modern science, of the mechanisms behind the simultaneous increases in population and prosperity that could overcome natural limits. Hardin's sarcastic "Grow! Grow! Grow!"[96] was just such an indictment of the seemingly limitless economic and population growth endorsed by optimists.

There is, however, at least one elegant theoretical model that reconciles the empirical observations of the simultaneous population and prosperity growth of the Industrial Revolution while predicting the current postindustrial demographic transition. We will present this model before fleshing out the optimist case, because the model gives a context for the predominantly empirical arguments that follow.

In 2000, Israeli economist and influential theorist Oded Galor, and David N. Weil, American economist and Galor's Brown University colleague, proposed a relationship between population growth, technological progress, and the increase in individual prosperity. For Galor, this work culminated a decade later in the introduction of unified growth theory, a holistic approach to the complex problem of development grounded in the entire span of human history. Galor and Weil modeled the behavior of population growth, technological progress and individual prosperity over long periods of time, identifying three distinct regimes. The first regime is known as Malthusian and it is characterized by what economists call stagnation: a near-zero population growth, no long-term increase in individual incomes, and very little technological change.[97]

While Malthus turned out to be right about the properties of this regime, we also know that Malthus's description did not apply to the population-wealth-technology relationship during the Industrial Revolution in the eighteenth and nineteenth centuries. The regime witnessed, but not characterized, by Malthus during early rapid industrialization, according to Galor and Weil, was the Post-Malthusian Regime.[98] In this regime population was increasing and technological development was accelerating, yet individual incomes were also rising. Thus, unprecedented population levels coexisted with unprecedented prosperity while appearing to ratchet up the pace of technological progress. Galor and Weil did, in fact, show there is a feedback mechanism between these variables,[99] but what put the loop in motion?

Before we analyze this further, we must return to today's Modern Growth Regime, characterized by "steady growth in both income per capita and the level of technology . . . [with] a negative relationship between the level of output and the growth rate of population,"[100] so that the richest countries have population growth rates near zero.

What connects these three regimes is, in fact, population growth, at least according to the Galor and Weil model[101] (to which we will add a proviso shortly). In the Malthusian Regime, each increase in wealth also increased the population. Initially, as income per capita rose, population grew more quickly. In places like industrializing Europe, however, economic output increased fast enough to allow income per capita to continue rising even as population was rising. Galor and Weil explained this as follows: "During this Post-Malthusian Regime, the Malthusian mechanism linking higher income to higher population growth continued to function, but the effect of higher population on diluting resources per capita, and thus lowering income per capita, was counteracted by technological progress, which allowed income to keep rising."[102] Thus, "a feedback loop between technology and population generates a transition from the proximity of a Malthusian equilibrium to the Post-Malthusian Regime."[103] The key mechanism of this shift was the accelerating technological progress, facilitated by the growing, denser, and more efficiently interconnected population.

The shift from the Post-Malthusian to the Modern Growth Regime was marked by the demographic transition. This momentous societal shift in reproductive strategies was noticeable even to the pessimist writer Harrison Brown.[104] The demographic transition happens when parents stop having numerous children, presumably of lower societal fitness, "human capital," or "child quality,"[105] and start raising fewer children with substantially increased human capital—represented in the Galor and Weil model, as most often in life, by education. Significantly, Galor and Weil pointed out that the disequilibrium caused by the rapid and unabated technological change was what changed the value of, or the rate of return on, human capital.[106] Parents reacted to the higher valuation of human capital by having fewer children but educating each child as much as they could afford.

The conclusion of Galor and Weil's research was even more shocking: The very stable and seemingly inevitable Malthusian steady state can vanish, and will vanish

> in the long run because of the impact of population size on the rate of technological progress. At a sufficiently high level of population, the rate of population-induced technological progress is high enough that parents find it optimal to provide their children with some human capital. At this point, a virtuous circle develops: higher human capital raises technological progress, which in turn raises the value of human capital.[107]

Thus, the transition from the Malthusian steady state into the Post-Malthusian dynamic regime of rapid increase is triggered by population growth and sustained by technological change that can be generated only through—yes—higher and more efficiently interconnected populations. The threshold of technological innovation at which progress really does take off is a function of population size: the greater the population, the faster the rate of innovation. The transition into the next steady state of Modern Growth is triggered by the parental shift of child-rearing strategies toward producing very few, but very highly educated, children that best succeed in the high-tech, high-prosperity, high-population (but low-population-*growth*) society of today.

The elegance of the Galor and Weil model[108] is not only in how it shows the key significance of the population variable in setting economic development in motion, but also in how it demonstrates that the Modern Growth Regime is a near-steady state of near-zero population growth and a steady (not exponential) rise in incomes and innovations. There does not need to be an infinite exponential growth of incomes and population because, for the foreseeable future, humanity can maintain a constant rate of income and technological growth at this higher population plateau. Applying Hardin's prescription of population control would needlessly thwart the stability of Modern Growth by trying to force humanity right back to the Malthusian steady state, with much individual and societal suffering, particularly in the economies that need the human capital the most to get to the new stable state.

It is time for our proviso. The Galor and Weil positive feedback loop between population growth and technological innovation can only function where the social and political climate is sufficiently hospitable to change. Many writers have pointed out the foundational value of openness to social and economic change in political institutions and cultures.[109] In Ostrom's work, not only do we find further support for the importance of institutions to the flourishing of cooperation and prosperity, we also find practical support for the key fact that such institutions can develop between willing individuals in a matrix of acceptance and awareness from above, not rigid top-down control. The right institutions matter, and they are not a function of authoritarian power.

Although Ostrom wrote little about population, she by and large adopted a perspective according to which humans are not only mouths to feed, but also hands to work and brains to think up solutions to pressing problems. Consequently, a brief discussion of the key points made by more optimistic writers is useful in providing additional historical context for her work. Let us now examine the historical insights of the optimist thinkers in light of the theoretical and empirical support for their observations.

Optimist Argument 1: A Larger Population That Engages in Trade and the Division of Labor Will Deliver Greater Material Abundance per Capita

In 1821 the French economist Jean-Baptiste Say criticized the belief that a reduction in population would "enable those which are left to enjoy a greater quantity of those commodities of which they are in want" as nonsensical because it ignored the fact that a reduction in manpower simultaneously destroyed the means of production.[110] After all, one did not see in thinly populated countries that "the wants of the inhabitants are more easily satisfied." On the contrary, it was "abundance of productions, and not the scarcity of consumers, which procures a plentiful supply of whatever our necessities require."[111] This is why the most populous countries were generally better supplied.

In 1879, anticipating the insights of Galor and Weil with observations,[112] Henry George, the American political economist who might arguably be called the most widely read economist of the nineteenth century, similarly noted that while one could see "many communities still increasing in population," they were also "increasing their wealth still faster."[113] Indeed, "among communities of similar people in a similar stage of civilization," the "most densely populated community is also the richest" and the evidence was overwhelming that "wealth is greatest where population is densest; that the production of wealth to a given amount of labor increases as population increases. These things are apparent wherever we turn our eyes." In the end, the "richest countries are not those where nature is most prolific; but those where labor is most efficient—not Mexico, but Massachusetts; not Brazil, but England." Where nature provides modest resources, George commented, "twenty men working together will . . . produce more than twenty times the wealth that one man can produce where nature is most bountiful."[114] This was because the

> denser the population the more minute becomes the subdivision of labor, the greater the economies of production and distribution, and, hence, the very reverse of the Malthusian doctrine is true; and, within the limits in which we have reason to suppose increase would still go on, in any given state of civilization a greater number of people can produce a larger proportionate amount of wealth, and more fully supply their wants, than can a smaller number.[115]

One of the best short overviews of the anti-Malthusian stance can be found in an anonymous essay published in 1889 in the *Westminster Review*:

> The Malthusian theory does not accord with facts. As population grows, instead of production being less per head, statistics clearly prove it to be greater. The intelligence which is fostered in large communities; the advantages of the division of labour; the improved transit, which increases in efficiency with an enterprising people in proportion as numbers become large, and is impracticable until population has developed— are more than a match in the competition of production for any advantage a thinly scattered community may in some respects gain on a virgin soil. Malthus and his followers, while bringing prominently forward the needs of an increasing population, keep out of view the increasing means

of supply which the additional labour of greater numbers will produce. . . . And so long as there are a pair of hands to provide for every mouth, with intelligence and energy ample production is assured, unless society erects artificial barriers by means of its laws regarding the distribution of wealth.[116]

Of key importance to us in considering Ostrom's position is the optimist writers' repeated emphasis on human cooperation and emergent organization, whether they make transportation or manufacturing more efficient or provide more diverse markets for goods. Ostromian insights align with the importance of individual choice as well as of group coordination in achieving complex social goals.[117]

Optimist Argument 2: Human Creativity Can Deliver Increasing Returns

A long-standing tenet of population optimism is that knowledge, or creative application of the human intellect, is the key factor in overcoming scarcity and diminishing returns. As American resource economists Harold Barnett and Chandler Morse observed two generations ago, "Recognition of the possibility of technological progress clearly cuts the ground from under the concept of Malthusian scarcity," and the historical evidence "mainly show[s] increasing, not diminishing, returns."[118]

What optimist writers have also long understood is that a greater division of labor also favors the development of new ways of doing things. Writing in 1857, the social theorist Herbert Spencer observed,

By increasing the pressure on the means of subsistence, a larger population again augments these results; seeing that each person is forced more and more to confine himself to that which he can do best, and by which he can gain most. Presently, under these same stimuli, new occupations arise. Competing workers, ever aiming to produce improved articles, occasionally discover better processes or raw materials.[119]

Spencer believed this made possible not only the development of better alternatives to what had existed before, but also the development of things not possible before. For instance, the replacement of stone tools by similar bronze tools paved the way for the development of new things that could not have been made out of stone. These advances, in turn, would increase the manipulative skill, comfort, and intelligence of the population, refining "their habits and tastes," transforming "a homogeneous society into a heterogeneous one"[120] and ultimately resulting in social and political change.

A generation later Henry George, criticized by Hardin as unscientific for documenting the rapid growth of the Post-Malthusian Regime,[121] commented that "even if the increase of population does reduce the power of the natural factor of wealth, by compelling a resort to poorer soils, etc., it yet so vastly increases the power of the human factor as more than to compensate."[122] The American entrepreneur, inventor, and economic writer Edward Atkinson observed at about the same time that the "mind of man when applied to the direction of natural forces is the principal agent in material production, in fact, the controlling element. Those who claim that labor is the source of all production are utterly misled because they do not admit this fundamental principle."[123] The basic Malthusian hypothesis was thus "utterly without warrant either in fact or in experience," because "Malthus appears to have had no imaginative faculty, a very essential quality in dealing with economic questions." As Atkinson saw it, Malthus "could not forecast the future nor foretell the wonderful results that would be attained through the new scientific discoveries and the better understanding of the art of production and distribution which had begun even in his own day to work a profound change in the relations of men to each other."[124] Atkinson further discussed the case of land that "itself may be exhausted when treated as a mine," but "may be maintained when worked as a laboratory" and might one day be potentially enriched by diverting "nitrogen and carbon from the atmosphere and converting these elements into food for man and beast,"[125] a prediction that, in the case of nitrogen, would become a large-scale reality a few decades later.

A few years before he coauthored the *Communist Manifesto*, a young Friedrich Engels argued that the "productive power at mankind's disposal is immeasurable: and the 'productivity of the soil can be increased ad infinitum by the application of capital, labour and science'"[126] In later decades, several German and Russian writers expanded on this point.[127] Vladimir Lenin thus argued that the law of diminishing returns "does not at all apply to cases in which technology is progressing and methods of production are changing" and "has only an extremely relative and restricted application to conditions in which technology remains unchanged."[128] Writing nearly five decades later, Mao Zedong celebrated China's big population and argued that even "if China's population multiplies many times, she is fully capable of finding a solution; the solution is production." He dismissed the "absurd argument of Western bourgeois economists like Malthus that increases in food cannot keep pace with increases in population" as both having been "thoroughly refuted in theory by Marxists" and exploded in practice in the Soviet Union and in other Marxist regimes. He added that "of all things in the world, people are the most precious. Under the leadership of the Communist Party, as long as there are people, every kind of miracle can be performed."[129] Although most scholars working within the Marxist tradition today have converted to the pessimist ideology, mainline Marxists dismissed neo-Malthusian thought for most the twentieth century.[130]

British economist and historian of economic thought Edwin Cannan opined that while one might occasionally observe "diminution of returns," these have typically been only temporary until the development of "inventions and the introduction of better methods." Indeed, the belief that "diminishing returns was the general rule throughout history" was "so contrary to the results of direct observation that it seems difficult to believe that it could ever have been accepted."[131] As a matter of fact, "no reasonable person can have any doubt that the productiveness of agricultural industry has enormously increased" and that "the population of the civilized world is much better fed, and yet has to spend far less a proportion of the whole of its labor on the acquisition of food." If agricultural returns had actually diminished in agriculture, a "larger and ever larger proportion of the world's labor would clearly have to be expended in producing food,"[132] something that obviously did not happen in the early years of the twentieth century.

Writing at the end of World War II, the agricultural economist Karl Brandt observed,

> During World War I and immediately after, the belief was common among scholars and statesmen that Malthus' doctrine was still valid and that, owing to the progressive propagation of man, scarcity of food was not only inevitable in the long run but characteristic also for the second quarter of the twentieth century. A few years after the war the situation in the world market contradicted

those assumptions. The war had fostered rapid progress in farm technology. It brought the internal combustion engine into general use for agriculture, first in America and later elsewhere. The truck, tractor, and combine were some of the machines in which it was applied. Millions of horses were replaced, and millions of feed acres were released for food production. Enormous savings in manpower and in production costs became possible. New varieties of plants made available for crop production many areas that previously could be used only for scanty grazing. Research in animal nutrition and genetics also led to much greater efficiency in converting feed into animal products. The really revolutionary progress in food production technology revealed the economic fallacy of the more than century-old secular "law of diminishing returns," as commonly applied to food production. It became apparent that technological progress made increasing economic returns and a lowering of the costs of food production possible within sufficiently wide boundaries.[133]

In a personal reply to and further face-to-face conversation with Malthus, the American diplomat Alexander Everett suggested that an expanded division of labor not only made people more productive, but further laid the foundation for "the invention of new machines, an improvement of methods in all the departments of industry, and a rapid progress in the various branches of art and science" that resulted in a level of labor productivity that far exceeded the proportional increase in population numbers.[134] A belief in decreasing returns, he argued, ultimately assumed that "labor becomes less efficient and productive in proportion to the degree of skill with which it is applied; that a man can raise more weight by hand, than by the help of a lever, and see further with the naked eye than with the best telescope."[135]

Friedrich Engels also stood Malthus on his head by observing that "science increases at least as much as population. The latter increases in proportion to the size of the previous generation, science advances in proportion to the knowledge bequeathed to it by the previous generation, and thus under the most ordinary conditions also in a geometrical progression."[136] More than a century later, Barnett and Morse similarly commented that "a strong case can be made for the view that the cumulation of knowledge and technological progress is automatic and self-reproductive in modern economies, and obeys a law of increasing returns" as "every cost-reducing innovation opens up possibilities of application in so many new directions that the stock of knowledge, far from being depleted by new developments, may even expand geometrically."[137] Interestingly, the economic insights of Galor and Weil do bear out these observations via the positive feedback loop between population growth and the accompanying growth of innovation.[138]

One can thus identify at least two key arguments on the benefits of growing population numbers in terms of delivering increasing returns. The first is that the more human brainpower becomes available, given some means of creating communities of interest, the greater the likelihood of new beneficial inventions. As the British political economist William Petty observed more than a century before Malthus, it was "more likely that one ingenious curious man may rather be found out amongst 4,000,000 than 400 persons."[139] Cannan similarly disagreed with the notion that agricultural productivity would have been greater in his time if population numbers had remained small, because fewer active individuals would have meant that fewer advances would "have been discovered and introduced."[140]

The second key argument points to the cumulative nature of technological development: the fact that present and future advances build on past ones. In his 1944 book *The Theory of Economic Progress*, institutionalist economist Clarence Ayres emphasized the importance of "the principle of combination" to human creativity and applied it in a variety of ways. The exponential growth or proliferation of technical devices could be explained, for instance, because "the more devices there are, the greater is the number of potential combinations" and because the cross-fertilization of ideas was a key component of the discovery process.[141] Ayres added that natural resources, which he termed "materials," were therefore not static:

> The history of every material is the same. It is one of novel combination of existing devices and materials in such fashion as to constitute a new device or a new material or both. This is what it means to say that natural resources are defined by the prevailing technology, a practice which is now becoming quite general among economists to the further confusion of old ways of thinking (since it involves a complete revision of the concept of "scarcity" which must now be regarded as also defined by technology and not by "nature").[142]

The economist Fritz Machlup perhaps put it best more than half a century ago when he distinguished between the "retardation school" of technological change, whose proponents believed that "the more that has been invented the less there is left to be invented," and the "acceleration school," according to which "the more that is invented the easier it becomes to invent still more" because "every new invention furnishes a new idea for potential combination with vast numbers of existing ideas" and the "number of possible combinations increases geometrically with the number of elements at hand."[143] The roles of individuals as well as of their communities in developing governance solutions is, indeed, a key point of Ostrom's work, as we will see in the next section.

Optimist Argument 3: Human Standards of Living Are Not Constrained by Local Resources

Henry George famously observed that of "all living things, man is the only one who can give play to the reproductive forces, more powerful than his own, which supply him with food."[144] Other animals survive on what they find and can only grow as numerous as their food sources allow, but increases in human numbers are possible because of their ability to produce more food:

> If bears instead of men had been shipped from Europe to the North American continent, there would now be no more bears than in the time of Columbus, and possibly fewer, for bear food would not have been increased nor the conditions of bear life extended, by the bear immigration, but probably the reverse. But within the limits of the United States alone, there are now forty-five millions of men where then there were only a few hundred thousand,[145] and yet there is now within that territory much more food per capita for the forty-five millions than there was then for the few hundred thousand. It is not the increase of food that has caused this increase of men; but the increase of men that has brought about the increase of food. There is more food, simply because there are more men.[146]

George added that a key difference between animal and human was that both "the jay-hawk and the man eat chickens, but the more jay-hawks the fewer chickens, while the more men the more chickens." Similarly, "both the seal and the man eat salmon, but when a seal takes a salmon there is a salmon the less, and were seals to increase past a certain point salmon must diminish." Humans, however, "by placing the spawn of the salmon under favorable conditions" can increase the numbers of salmon to such an extent as to more than make up for their catches.[147]

George was thus making an argument about the management of common-pool resources without recourse to the tragedy of the commons. In the end, George argued, "while all through the vegetable and animal kingdoms the limit of subsistence is independent of the thing subsisted, with man the limit of subsistence is, within the final limits of earth, air, water, and sunshine, dependent upon man himself."[148] The ultimate limit to human population was therefore physical space, not raw resources.

Historically one of the main ways to break local limits was to increase agricultural outputs on the same piece of land, by introducing new crops, developing new crop rotations, improving the productivity of existing crops, or enriching the soil through various means. Commenting on the last case, the anarchist theorist and physical geographer Pyotr Kropotkin observed that the high agricultural productivity of Belgian farmland had nothing to do with some inherent superior fertility of the local soil—because,

> to use the words of [Émile Louis Victor de] Laveleye, "only one half, or less, of the territory offers natural conditions which are favourable for agriculture;" the other half consists of a gravelly soil, or sands, "the natural sterility of which could be overpowered only by heavy manuring." Man, not nature, has given to the Belgium soil its

present productivity. With this soil and labor, Belgium succeeds in supplying nearly all the food of a population which is denser than that of England and Wales.[149]

Commenting on the market gardens that surrounded Paris, Kropotkin wrote that in "market-gardening the soil is always made, whatever it originally may have been." It was therefore a "usual stipulation of the renting contracts of the Paris *maraîchers* [market-gardeners] that the gardener may carry away his soil, down to a certain depth, when he quits his tenancy," because he had created it.[150]

More generally, optimist writers belonging to otherwise antagonistic schools of thought have long dismissed the notion of limited natural resources. To give but one illustration, the institutionalist economist Erich Zimmermann observed more than eight decades ago that, before the emergence of humans, "the earth was replete with fertile soil, with trees and edible fruits, with rivers and waterfalls, with coal beds, oil pools, and mineral deposits; the forces of gravitation, of electro-magnetism, of radio-activity were there; the sun sent forth his life-bringing rays, gathered the clouds, raised the winds; but there were no resources."[151] Resources, he argued, are in reality "highly dynamic functional concepts; they are not, they become, they evolve out of the triune interaction of nature, man, and culture, in which nature sets outer limits, but man and culture are largely responsible for the portion of physical totality that is made available for human use."[152] Like Ostrom, Zimmerman thus recognized the importance of human institutions in creating and maintaining viable resources.

Optimist Argument 4: Past
Successes Are Grounds for Optimism

More than a century ago, Edward Cannan took issue with John Stuart Mill's ambivalence about whether future improvements could overcome decreasing returns. The problem with Mill, Cannan argued, was that he limited his discussion to "fairly recent times" in which "it does not appear to be possible either to prove or disprove [the argument]."[153] Fortunately, Cannan observed, a longer-term perspective yields a more promising outlook. While commodity prices go through cycles, in the long run valuable resources typically become less scarce and less expensive. Because of historical precedents, he added, pessimistic future projections based on very recent trends should not be taken seriously.

In his 1964 prognosis of the needs for and the availability of natural and industrial materials, the economist Hans Hermann Landsberg commented that "the indications are that the American people can obtain the natural resources and resource products that they will need between now and the year 2000" because "neither a long view of the past, nor current trends, nor our most careful estimates of future possibilities suggest any general running out of resources in this country during the remainder of the century."[154]

4. Elinor Ostrom's Environmental
Perspective: From Polycentricity to Game Theory

Before we examine the conflict of views between Garrett Hardin and Elinor Ostrom, we will briefly sketch the key ideas in Ostrom's background, and eventual research output, that may help in evaluating her stance as a cautious population optimist.

The concept of polycentricity, vital to Ostrom's study of the dynamics of common-pool resource governance, may be traced to Michael Polanyi's 1951 philosophical analysis of the relationships between freedom, authority, control, and coordination in such diverse human pursuits as scientific research and economic activity. Polanyi posited that overarching, centralized authority or a strict hierarchical organization in domains such as science or art would paralyze their progress.[155] Such human endeavors benefit from an informal social organization and do best when not forced toward a rigid methodology, relying instead on the concept of freedom that "consists in the right to choose one's own problem for investigation, to conduct research free from any outside control, and to teach one's subject in the light of one's own opinions."[156] Polanyi further noted how freedom enhances coordination:

> The existing practice of scientific life embodies the claim that freedom is an efficient form of organization. . . . if the scientists of the world are viewed as a team setting out to explore the existing openings for discovery, it is assumed that their efforts will be efficiently co-ordinated if only each is left to follow his own inclinations.[157]

Thus, Polanyi's "optimum coordination [would be] achieved here by releasing individual impulses." How does this individual freedom of mature scientists in the social matrix of science enhance coordination? "The co-ordinative principle of science thus . . . consists in the adjustment of each scientist's activities to the results hitherto achieved by others."[158] This adjustment is a spontaneous phenomenon emergent from individual communication efforts.

Polanyi applied this insight of polycentric social organization toward showing the impossibility of the socialist calculation problem.[159] The market, as a polycentric system similar to the self-coordinating network of scientific research, is a "web of many agents that constantly adjust their behavior to the decisions made by others."[160] The proponents of socialist central planning, or any other command system, expected to do much better than the market at reaching equilibrium provisioning through the elimination of overlap and "pointless" competition. On the surface, this made sense, but as Polanyi pointed out, the self-coordinating, nonhierarchical mechanism of emergent order was still, and will always be, more efficient than central planning:

> I affirm that the central planning of production— in the rigorous and historically not unwarranted sense of the term—is strictly impossible. . . . My point is that it can be demonstrated that an overwhelming reduction, amounting to a standstill in the possible rate of production, must arise from the administrative limitations of a system of central direction. . . . The operations of a system of spontaneous order in society, such as the competitive order of a market, cannot be replaced by the establishment of a deliberate ordering agency.[161]

Thus, polycentricity, as presented by Polanyi, offered two key principles that differentiated it from a hierarchical and centrally imposed authority: (1) It emphasized the importance of individual agency and motivation to work toward an abstract goal in the choice of activities, and (2) it reinforced the observation that those individual decisions take place within a self-organizing social matrix where choices of any given agents are constantly influenced by, and adjusting to, the actions of others. Polanyi's polycentric social matrix is thus one of constant internal calibration and exquisite sensitivity to many feedback channels.

American political economist and Elinor's husband Vincent Ostrom, working with his colleagues Charles Tiebout and Robert Warren, adopted Polanyi's polycentricity construct as a general organizing principle applied to the problem of municipal government.[162] Their summary of the then de rigueur understanding of metropolitan governance as inefficient and chaotic highlights the parallels between Polanyi's theoretical work and their emergent application of polycentricity:

> This [standard pre-polycentric] view assumes that the multiplicity of political units in a metropolitan area is essentially a pathological phenomenon. The diagnosis asserts that there are too many governments and not enough government. The symptoms are described as "duplication of functions" and "overlapping jurisdictions." Autonomous units of government, acting in their own behalf, are considered incapable of resolving the diverse problems of the wider metropolitan community. The political topography of the metropolis is called a "crazy-quilt pattern" and its organization is said to be an "organized chaos." . . . A political system with a single dominant center for making decisions is viewed as the ideal model for the organization of metropolitan government.[163]

Vincent Ostrom and his coauthors contrasted this orthodox view with the "polycentric political system" where "'polycentric' connotes many centers of decision-making which are formally independent of each other."[164] Nonhierarchical organization and coordination happens when polycentric organizations evolve the right rules via social choice mechanisms. Polycentricity allows for a characterization of the concept of emergent order even—in the case of social governance systems—without a price mechanism.[165] While polycentricity is evident in markets, the scientific community, and municipal or federal governance, Elinor Ostrom proposed to apply and adapt the concept to the study of arrangements for the governance of common-pool resources (CPRs)—resources that, like deep-sea fishing stocks, bridges, and irrigation water, will be depleted through use but from which users or "extractors" are very difficult to exclude.[166]

In the opening lines of her Nobel lecture, Elinor Ostrom noted that her research on the institutional arrangements for public goods and CPR governance "builds on classical economic theory while developing new theory to explain phenomena that do not fit in a dichotomous world of 'the market' and 'the state.'"[167] One of the reasons, she suggested, that the dichotomy of the market and the state did not adequately represent the governance issues emerging with CPRs and public goods was that it did not allow researchers to model human behavior as involving agency and nonrational, or noneconomic, motivations. Ostrom recognized that people evolve economic structures and systems for a variety of reasons that are themselves multilayered, changeable, and subject to feedback loops: "The humans we study have complex motivational structures and establish diverse private-for-profit, governmental, and community institutional arrangements that operate at multiple scales to generate productive and innovative as well as destructive and perverse outcomes."[168] Ostrom's Institutional Analysis and Development (IAD) framework was flexible enough to model different social variables and complex behaviors but also rigorous enough to support quantitative and qualitative investigations.[169]

Elinor Ostrom's outside-the-box insight and analytical finesse may indeed be the key factors contributing to her ability to counter the "tragedy of the commons" perspective on development and population growth championed by Hardin. Ostrom's first powerful insight was understanding the philosophy behind the scientific tools she and her colleagues were using. Ostrom, a political scientist among economists, appears to have appreciated how scientific theories, falsifiable hypotheses[170] derived from theories deductively, and models focusing on particular outcomes predicted by theories differ from one another . In addition, she added to this fundamental philosophical understanding a recognition of the difference between such models, the theories they relate back to, and the metaphors that may be used to highlight model outcomes. In the first chapter of her magisterial analysis of institutions, *Understanding Institutional Diversity*, Ostrom stated, "While the usefulness of a universal *model* of rational behavior is challenged in chapter 4, the assumption of a universal *framework* composed of nested sets of components within components for explaining human behavior is retained throughout the book."[171] Insightfully, Ostrom thus dispensed with a "systems" school (Hardinian) approach of hierarchical modeling in favor of a looser framework of nested components, each steeped in its context.

Elinor Ostrom retained the desire to craft elegantly simple theories: "As a scholar committed to understanding underlying universal components of all social systems, I do not introduce complexity lightly. I view scientific explanation as requiring just enough variables to enable one to explain, understand, and predict outcomes in relevant settings."[172] Yet Ostrom's genius was to be acutely aware of the level of abstraction at which she was working, given a metaphor, model, theory, or framework, and what kinds of generalizations, if any, could be made from it to other situations. She noted that "explanations occur at multiple levels and different spatial and temporal scales."[173]

That exquisite sensitivity to the extent and nature of what she called the action arena—composed of participants and the action situation[174]—allowed Ostrom to find and utilize the optimal analytical tool: game-theoretical analysis.[175] With the power of game theory, a tool that incidentally allowed for quantitative descriptions of the dynamics of action arenas, Ostrom was poised to explore human institutions at many levels, and to do justice to the complex interactions, choices, and kinds of communication that were affecting behaviors leading to observed outcomes: "Whenever interdependent individuals are thought to be acting in an organized fashion, several layers of universal components create the structure that affects their behavior and outcomes they achieve."[176] Within the IAD framework, any action arena is composed of a set of dependent variables that may also be complexly interconnected: the various rules participants use within their relationships, the properties of the world—Ostrom called them "biophysical and material conditions"[177]—that affect the action arena, and the community structure.

Ostrom not only understood the difference between these tools, but she also understood their unique domains, their overlaps, and the conditions under which each could become invalid. Indeed, much of the IAD framework may be used to refute formulations such as the "tragedy of the commons" as applied to CPRs, not because the outcome described by the metaphorical story is always invalid, but because Ostrom's analysis can show rigorously that it may be invalid under many different circumstances, and to a differing degree, just as it may occasionally be valid under other circumstances and with another set of actors. In other words, Ostrom brought to the analysis of human governance of CPRs an understanding of scale and degree, a granularity that placed everything from the nature of goods to the behaviors of people on a continuum, finally freeing economic analysis of social behavior from navigating between extremes. Ostrom wrote,

> The diversity of regularized social behavior that we observe at multiple scales is constructed, I will argue, from universal components organized in many layers. In other words, whenever independent individuals are thought to be

acting in an organized fashion, several layers of
universal components create the structure that
affects their behavior and the outcomes they
achieve.[178]

An excellent example of Ostrom's analytical finesse is her input into the redefinition of Paul Samuelson's theory of public
goods.[179] The classical understanding of the differences between
private goods and public goods focused on whether individuals
must compete for depletable or finite units of a good—so whether
the goods necessitate rivalry among users—and on whether one
may exclude others from partaking in such a good. Pure public
goods cannot be exhausted through use, so they are, in the classical sense, nonrivalrous. They are also nonexcludable. For example, a transmitter-to-air broadcast signal from a radio station is a
public good: One cannot prevent others from taking advantage of
the signal if they have the receiver (local signal jamming aside),
and additional listeners do not deplete the signal for others. Peace
is Ostrom's example of a public good.[180] Private goods are the exact opposite of pure public goods, in that they are both rivalrous
and excludable: A loaf of freshly baked olive bread may be desired by many customers of a small bakery, but only the few lucky
individuals who shop when the batch becomes available will be
able to obtain a unit of that good. In addition, it is easy to exclude
others from access to such a good. This classical picture lacked
detail when it came to goods that may be depleted by use but
are essentially nonexcludable—CPRs such as deep-sea fisheries or
irrigation systems—and when it came to excludable but nonrivalrous goods such as private parks or satellite TV, which Samuelson
called "club" goods.[181]

Ostrom's analysis brought a nuanced understanding of human actions to the latter two classes of goods, revolutionizing
their definitions. Ostrom refocused the discussion of the non-

excludable, rivalrous goods on the subtractability of use by resource appropriators: "the extent to which one individual's use subtracts from the availability of a good or service for consumption by others."[182] Her definition of CPRs touched on both properties of those goods: "Common-pool resources yield benefits where beneficiaries are hard to exclude but each person's use of a resource system subtracts units of that resource from a finite total amount available for harvesting."[183] The problem at the core of CPR use is the free-rider problem: "A strong incentive exists to be a free-rider in all situations where potential beneficiaries cannot easily be excluded for failing to contribute to the provision of a good or service."[184]

In addition to the nuanced substitution of the concept of rivalry (a human behavior) for subtractability of a resource (a property of the system), Ostrom introduced the concept of a continuum of gradations to evaluate the extent of subtractability or the difficulty of exclusion. Ostrom's picture of every instance of a "tragedy of the commons" moved the analysis beyond a dualistic system and into the realm of the IAD framework, a "multitier conceptual map."[185] Instead of envisioning participants driven to act blindly on one kind of incentive, Ostrom developed the concept of the action arena in which "participants and an action situation . . . interact as they are affected by exogenous variables . . . and produce outcomes that in turn affect the participants and the action situation."[186] The strength of this approach is the built-in understanding that participants are indeed that—individuals who make choices, not pawns driven blindly by instinct or by force—and that they actively respond to feedback.

5. Ostrom versus Hardin: A Philosophical Conflict

A discussion of Ostrom's framing of the CPR problem brings our analysis back to Garrett Hardin, authoritarian control methods in the socioeconomic arena, TC, and the tragedy of the commons, the issue most often associated with the governance of CPRs.

Hardin's legacy has taught analysts to see the tragedy of the commons as a conflict between two behaviors: (1) the individualistic response exemplifying the liberty of rational self-interest of the laissez-faire approach (with the assumption that an individual will always elect to subtract from the CPR without contributing to its maintenance); and (2) top-down authoritarian governance that would rein in the self-interest of the individual in a prescribed and coercive manner." It is worth mentioning that despite significant interactions with economists and free market environmentalists,[187] Hardin ultimately saw no real value in economic analysis and the optimist case built on human creativity.[188] Hardin dismissed both Marx's and George's arguments, according to which a larger population would be better provided for than a smaller one, by denigrating them as "pre-Darwinian" because the authors "baldly assume[d] that the laws of nature which govern all other species of plants and animals were negated for man by the God of *Genesis.*"[189] Apart from the optimist economist's refusal to admit that humans live "in a limited physical world subject to limitless demands," such an economist's main mistake, Hardin wrote, was the belief in economies of scale.[190] Fortunately, Hardin wrote, "Scientists know better. At some level of production, the balance shifts to diseconomies of scale" and "in reality, there is no anti-Darwinian world: wherever there is growth, diseconomies of scale ultimately rule."[191]

Ostrom appears to have been well aware of the philosophical and theoretical undercurrents of Hardin's work, even if we have no evidence that she conceptualized them as part of the larger pessimist discourse. We do know that Ostrom attended a lecture by Hardin after the publication of TC in 1968.[192] She described her immediate reaction to Hardin's ideas during her conversation with Margaret Levi:

Hardin gave a speech on the [Indiana University Bloomington] campus, and I went to it, and he indicated the more general—but then it was that he really was worried about population. . . . He was very serious about it. . . . I was somewhat taken aback: 'My theory proves that we should do this,' and people said, 'Well don't you think that that's a little severe?' 'No! That's what we should do, or we're sunk.' Well, he, in my mind, became a totalitarian. I, thus, had seen a real instance where his theory didn't work.[193]

Ostrom had both a visceral reaction to Hardin's dogmatic authoritarianism and a methodological issue with his refusal to admit that his hypothesis was falsifiable or questionable.

While Ostrom did not contribute to the debates on human population and fertility choices, she noted that "Hardin himself used the grazing commons as a metaphor for the general problem of overpopulation."[194] Consequently, she understood the significance of the metaphor and its ubiquitous use in the literature and in popular culture.[195] Ostrom's own dissection of Hardin's tragedy-of-the-commons metaphor used the tools of game-theoretical analysis to mobilize both the quantitative aspect and its modularity: She formalized Hardin's parable as a prisoner's dilemma game, a "noncooperative game in which all players possess complete information . . . , communication among the players is forbidden or impossible or simply irrelevant."[196] Each player has a dominant strategy: to defect, thus exploiting the commons and the other players. When there are no other considerations in the game (such as interplayer communication), all players choose the dominant strategy of abusing the commons and all obtain a suboptimal outcome. The prisoner's dilemma game demonstrates "the paradox that individually rational strategies lead to collectively irrational outcomes."[197] On the strength of metaphors such as the tragedy of the commons and their game theory representations such as the prisoner's dilemma game, it would appear that the optimistic expectations of individual choices benefiting the group are unrealistic. It would appear that perhaps Hardin and the pessimists are right: people will not voluntarily pass up fleeting individual gain for the good of the community.

Ostrom, however, was able to expose the weaknesses of such pessimist conclusions. Ostrom was scrupulous in documenting instances when tragedy-of-the-commons models do indeed obtain realistic outcomes, but she followed this with a warning about the generalizability of these approaches: "What makes these models so dangerous—when they are used metaphorically as the foundation for policy—is that the constraints that are assumed to be fixed for the purpose of analysis are taken on faith as being fixed in empirical settings."[198] Hardin's tragedy of the commons is thus a tragedy of researcher assumptions, participant isolation, lack of communication, and lack of agency. His pawn-like humans exhibit a single-minded and unwavering commitment to one of the worst long-term outcomes possible, a feature that hardly reflects the reality of human choice in social settings. Individual participants in CPR problems seek to understand the rules of engagement and to change the constraints imposed on them through communication and other mechanisms. Hardin's humans, on the other hand, appear to be captives, or—worse yet—zombies. Ostrom noticed this feature of the prisoner's dilemma: "As long as individuals are viewed as prisoners, policy prescriptions will address this metaphor. I would rather address the question of how to enhance the capabilities of those involved to change the constraining rules of the game to lead to outcomes other than remorseless tragedies."[199]

Thus, in Ostrom's view, Hardin's model fails to account for variables affecting the action arena of CPR governance from the participant's point of view. There is, however, a more fundamental failure at the heart of how the tragedy of the commons is used in both theoretical and policy discussions. As Ostrom pointed out, Hardin's original article used the commons pasture as a metaphor.[200] Hardin and others then started doing more than using the metaphor to rapidly convey information about the superficial features of a situation: they started modeling solutions on the assumption that the metaphor was harboring deeper truths about human action at many levels.[201] In effect, they exceeded the carrying capacity of the metaphor.

Ostrom analyzed this problem:

> The similarity between the many individuals jointly using a resource in a natural setting and the many individuals jointly producing a suboptimal result in the model has been used to convey a sense that further similarities are present. By referring to natural settings as "tragedies of the commons," "collective-action problems," "prisoner's dilemmas," "open-access resources," or even "common-property resources," the observer frequently wishes to invoke an image of helpless individuals caught in an inexorable process of destroying their own resources. . . . Public officials sometimes do no more than evoke grim images by briefly alluding to the popularized versions of the models, presuming, as self-evident, that the same processes occur in all natural settings. [This is] an empirically incorrect inference. . . . As such, it has been assumed that the individuals have been caught in a grim trap. The resulting policy recommendations have had an equally grim character.[202]

Most researchers commenting on the tragedy of the commons are unaware of the methodological and philosophical shortcomings of the metaphor. A few may be less worried about its adherence to the truth than they are about the "wrong" policies being enacted. Indeed, Hardin's tragedy-of-the-commons model envisioned the biosphere and the habitable world as the limited commons, albeit broken up into statist jurisdictions. Hardin's users had so little agency that they are hardly worth describing as participants. Consequently, the metaphor strains the model by negating any human agency, choice, or reflection, and any social capacity for communication or feedback. As in all pessimist formulations of the natural resources problem, people are only users, never creators.

The distortions created by Hardin's constantly reused yet "empirically incorrect inference"[203] led him and others to advocate policy solutions with equally biased governance implications. When arguing that political systems everywhere were failing to protect the environment in an adequate manner, Hardin claimed that human inability to do better had much to do with a "cloud of ignorance" that allowed people to be complacent.[204] Hardin lamented that humanity, through such ignorance and lack of leadership, has failed to realize that there is only one real solution, a coercive and authoritarian one brought about from above through "whatever force may be required to make the change stick."[205] Indeed, Hardin continued: "If ruin is to be avoided in a crowded world, people must be responsive to a coercive force outside their individual psyches, a 'Leviathan.'"[206] This distortion was an abuse of the metaphor leading to both biased science and lopsided policy: "The presumption that an external Leviathan is necessary to avoid tragedies of the commons leads to recommendations that central governments control most natural resource systems."[207]

As Ostrom and her numerous colleagues have shown over the decades, reality is much more complex than the simple prisoner's dilemma. Empirical situations deny researchers the comfort of an obvious outcome:

> Instead of there being a single solution to a single problem, I argue that many solutions exist to cope with many different problems. Instead of presuming that optimal institutional solutions can be designed easily and imposed at low cost by external authorities, I argue that "getting the institutions right" is a difficult, time-consuming, conflict-invoking process.[208]

According to Ostrom, instead of relying on one overly general metaphor to fit every issue, a scientist wanting to understand the issues of CPR governance should do empirical work without presumptions that may dictate a biased outcome. "Large studies of irrigation systems in Nepal and forests around the world challenge the presumption that governments always do a better job than users in organizing and protecting important resources."[209] Thus careful fieldwork and theory building, such as Ostrom carried out, must precede heavy-handed policy prescriptions.

6. Conclusion: Was Ostrom a Population Optimist?

By the time Hardin published his seminal TC essay, if Galor and Weil are correct, all the developed countries had reached the Modern Growth Regime with respect to the population-prosperity-technology relationship, and most developing countries were in the rapid-growth Post-Malthusian regime[210] The Malthusian regime had been left behind by decades or by centuries, while the Malthusian doctrine itself had been debated for over a century and a half. The opponents of the doctrine had been proved largely correct in the context of market economies. Among the optimists, the author of the anonymous 1889 *Westminster Review* essay thus wrote in unequivocal terms that

> statistical evidence incontrovertibly proves that a large community, other things being equal, is capable of producing more food and more wealth generally, man per man, than is possible in a smaller community. Europe has overgrown the dread of famine, and no doubt in future days will outlive the dread of pestilence. Famines are objects of terror in the early stages of social growth when numbers are numerically weak. Thus the last great famine that visited England was in the fourteenth century. At the present day, with a population in round numbers eleven times greater, a famine is so exceedingly improbable that such a calamity is no longer feared.[211]

By the mid-twentieth century, Harrison Brown had to acknowledge that the "disaster which Malthus foresaw for the Western World did not occur. Instead, Western populations [are] far beyond the levels he would have considered possible, and the poverty and deprivation so widespread in Malthus's time [have] enormously decreased." Brown even added that "so widely divergent were the predictions from the actual course of events that, if we were to look only at the predictions divorced from the reasoning, we would be inclined to say that he was incompetent."[212] Now we know Malthus was correct within a range of population-wealth-technology relationships that were stable over long time periods and low population densities, but not inevitable. Despite much contemporaneous evidence and some familiarity with the opposing perspective, and despite potential access to both empirical and theoretical results challenging his assertions,

Hardin was and remained an avowed neo-Malthusian from the 1940s to his death in 2003.

What about Ostrom? We have seen that she considered Hardin's ideological position repugnant and opposed Hardin's model because of its misrepresentation of the participants and the action arena. The evidence presented here shows that rather than being an outright optimist Ostrom was a cautious one, a researcher more likely to opt for Popper's falsification than for any self-serving, and ultimately impossible, proof.[213] Ostrom would be perhaps better characterized as a cautious optimist about the ability of individuals to arrive at collaborative solutions that best fit the needs and properties of their action arenas. She reacted negatively to the tendency of pessimists, statists, and dichotomous thinkers to strip participants of their ability to choose, cooperate, and reflect. She insisted, "Instead of basing policy on the presumption that the individuals involved are helpless, I wish to learn more from the experience of individuals in field settings."[214]

In that mode of thoughtful individual empowerment, in her IAD framework mindset of seeing individuals as actors in complex feedback loops, Ostrom appeared to express optimism about humanity's ability to resolve its resource issues cooperatively. One of the lessons and potential policy prescriptions we can learn from the Ostrom-versus-Hardin debate over the tragedy-of-the-commons metaphor we have outlined is a distrust of persistent yet poorly articulated metaphors that masquerade as theories or frameworks for systemizing knowledge. The Hardinian tragedy of the commons violates Ostromian principles in a variety of ways, the chief being its propensity to find the authoritarian solution a panacea. As Ostrom wrote, "'One-size-fits-all' policies are not effective."[215]

Mark Pennington summarized three Ostromian arguments against Hardinian central planning and totalitarian solutions.[216] These are fitting recommendations for what to avoid in developing governance solutions or metaphors. First, Pennington noted that central authorities lack situated and tacit knowledge about the action arena and, in particular, about the nature of incentives facing resource users.[217] Some central authorities, nodding along with Hardin, may not care about such knowledge; what they impose on the resource users will be a much poorer fit as a result. Second, the "very act of regulating from the center undermines the incentive for resource users themselves to devise an appropriate set of rules."[218] Third, centrally imposed solutions remove the motivation for users to learn about what would work best for them.[219] For Ostrom, denying participants the opportunity to learn may be one of the most sinister legacies of Hardin's metaphor. With learning, change for the better is possible for participants and for our shared environment—and so is the hope for more improvement.

In the most generous sense, Ostrom's cautious optimism is optimism about the human capacity to learn, and this optimism embraces population growth as well. Even though Ostrom does not address human reproduction as a CPR issue directly, her empirically supported outcomes show that people do evolve methods for dealing productively and positively with scarcity. At the very least, Ostrom's framework is open to many actors and many processes, showing that restricting such inputs is not at all necessary to the success of cooperative ventures revolving around both resource provision and depletion. Ostrom's outlook champions individuals' ability to find the best solutions for their resource issues through a collaborative process emphasizing choice, trust, and feedback mechanisms, not a reliance on solutions imposed coercively from above. To be fair, Ostrom's eight rules for successful CPR governance emphasize the importance of institutions that are conducive to the support for, and the nurturing of, cooperative learning and decision-making.[220] As with the population-technology feedback loop in the Post-Malthusian Regime, without institutional support for nascent polycentric governance, or for new technology, change is impossible. But given institutional openness, Ostrom's research echoes the insights of Julian Simon, a prominent environmental and population optimist, who found that humanity's endless creativity and resourcefulness were the "ultimate resource."[221]

Contracting and the Commons: Linking the Insights of Gary Libecap and Elinor Ostrom

Eric C. Edwards and Bryan Leonard

In 2009, Elinor Ostrom won the Noble memorial prize in economics sciences for, in the words of the prize committee, "demonstrating how local property can be successfully managed by local commons without any regulation by central authorities or privatization."[1] This account of Ostrom's contribution focuses on how her work presented a "third way" of governing the commons in direct contrast to the two solutions suggested by Garrett Hardin.[2] In critiquing Hardin's view, Ostrom studied many cases in which resource users, in the presence of weak, dysfunctional, or nonexistent governments, created resilient institutions to manage resource use. In these settings, she demonstrated that self-regulating common-pool resource (CPR) governance can take the place of other institutional arrangements more familiar to economists and political scientists.

Because many of Ostrom's groundbreaking findings emerged from studies of local, self-sustaining governance built on informal norms, economists have tended to view her work as less relevant to governance questions related to industrial resource use in developed countries where formal property rights, regulation, and contracts also play a role.[3] One clear exception is found in the work of economist Gary Libecap, who examines settings where the ultimate governance structure is either a contract between resource users or the creation of new formal property rights. Libecap's approach treats the outcome of property right negotiations as a collective action problem, and in this chapter, we explore how his approach complements and extends Ostrom's work. We also explore key areas of divergence between Libecap, and property rights scholars generally, and the work of Ostrom and other commons scholars—unsurprising given Ostrom's skepticism of property right solutions as a panacea.[4]

Starting with Arthur Cecil Pigou, economists have analyzed natural and environmental resource problems against the benchmark of a social planner making optimal decisions.[5] In this view, idealized solutions are clear, and the realities of if, or how, they are implemented are a secondary concern. Ostrom and Libecap turn this on its head, studying as their primary research objective how users deal with factors that cause coordination and collective action problems, rather than treating these problems as obstacles to achieving some desired optimal outcome. Both Libecap and Ostrom see the world through the lens of collective action and individual incentives. While Ostrom and her colleagues looked broadly at collective governance, Libecap found parallels between CPR governance and collective action through formal contractual agreements: group characteristics, information problems, and the proportionality of resource distributions being key determinants of success. These results build on Ostrom's work and provide important insight into contemporary environmental and natural resource challenges, where the same factors that cause difficulties in collective action and coordination prevent the adoption of optimal regulatory solutions.[6]

In comparing Libecap and Ostrom, we acknowledge that both authors have large bodies of work grounded in the empirical realities of numerous cases. It is difficult to fully generalize each author's work, and that is not our goal. Instead, we use an illustrative selection of their writings and those of related scholars to make two key arguments: (1) Ostrom's work is applicable to the study of property rights and regulation, as well as self-governing regimes; and (2) the type of property rights and contracting results Libecap discussed, under some circumstances, move resource users toward effective CPR governance. We first provide examples of how the study of collective action in the work of both authors yields important insights for both property rights and contracting. We then focus on one apparent area of divergence: Libecap's emphasis of the effectiveness of property rights in contrast to Ostrom's emphasis on trust. We argue that trust and clearly defined property rights serve similar functions in some cases, and that because of this they can be viewed as partial substitutes.

The chapter is organized as follows: Section 1 provides a framework for understanding collective action and the management of natural resources. In the subsequent sections 2–4, we examine similar empirical findings from both Libecap and Ostrom centered on group characteristics, information, and proportionality. In section 5 we discuss how contracting solutions might overcome some of the difficulties encountered in the self-organizing collective management Ostrom observed. Section 6 concludes with a discussion of the ongoing importance of Ostrom's work beyond the settings she studied.

1. Collective Action to Manage Common-Pool Resources

The common-pool resource problem, as traditionally viewed by economists, is a market failure. Specifically, there is an externality in consumption or production of the resource whereby one user's use imposes a cost on other users. The solution suggested by Pigou was to make each resource user liable for the damage caused to other users.[7] While taxes or other regulatory remedies could be potential solutions, the level of resource use that maximizes value could also be achieved by consolidating ownership under one individual or entity that could then optimize resource use. One obvious choice for such an entity is a central government, which could plan for optimal extraction and impose restrictions on users in order to achieve it.

This top-down prescription for resource management fails for several reasons, however, two of which appear to have motivated the work of Libecap and Ostrom. First, Ostrom takes exception to the idea that an existing overarching authority is necessary or sufficient for managing CPRs, suggesting that the users could themselves form the authority and might be able to do so more effectively.[8] Ostrom asks under what circumstances collective action will lead to successful, self-regulating CPRs.[9] Second, Libecap takes exception to the idea that a central government is interested in choosing resource use that maximizes aggregate value. Instead, he suggests that a government is made up of politicians who care about resource user constituencies as well as about the public's preferences.[10] Libecap asks under what circumstances resource users will act collectively to improve the management of their CPR.[11]

Both authors, upon questioning the standard economic conception of CPRs, arrive at a similar starting point for their analysis: users must find some way to coordinate when their individual interests are not aligned. To understand this problem, both authors pay particular attention to the work of Mancur Olson on collective action. In particular, they ask why users might successfully act collectively when Olson suggests there are significant barriers to action: "Unless the number of individuals is quite small, or unless there is coercion or some other special device to make individuals act in their common interest, *rational, self-interested individuals will not act to achieve their common or group interests.*"[12]

In Libecap's framework, users attempt to change contracts or property rights to capture more value from the resource. The question is whether individuals' expected rents are greater under open (or limited) access or under a contracting regime. Individuals will only agree to an assignment of formal property rights via a contractual arrangement if the expected value of their formal right is at least as great as their expected rents under the status quo, absent contracting.[13] When these conditions are not easily met, collective action is needed to develop an initial allocation of individual property rights or to reconfigure contracts such that each user is made as well off. If agreement is reached, contracts are enforced by an external authority. However, the initial collective action problem is still not easily solved.[14]

Ostrom and her colleagues often viewed CPR governance through the framework of social-dilemma games. If the games are one-shot or are repeated for a preset, finite number of rounds, agreements must be enforced by an outside authority.[15] Infinitely repeated social-dilemma games can support a variety of equilibria. However, the extent to which coordination allows resource users to solve the collective action problem articulated by Olson had not been addressed with systematic and rigorous analysis.[16] The problem articulated by Ostrom and her colleagues is determining what factors allow users to forgo selfish behavior in the present, instead taking actions that, although not immediately self-interested, would in the long run yield greater benefits.[17] When individuals exhibit reciprocity, forgoing gains in the short run to demonstrate cooperative intentions, they build trust and over time groups are able to establish long-term commitments to act in the group interest.[18] Often, a group establishes norms or rules, formal or informal, to govern the CPR, and this builds reciprocity into behavior to the point that selfish acts may be viewed distastefully or not considered.[19]

Acting consistently with their broader bottom-up approach to resource governance, both Libecap and Ostrom focused on how the characteristics of resources and of the groups themselves, as well as external pressures, affect individual incentives by shaping benefits and costs. In many of the cases Ostrom studied, the group must find a way to enforce its choices for resource use, while Libecap's resource users rely on the state's contract enforcement capability once an agreement is reached. Although the institutions differ, the factors that lead to success or failure of the entire enterprise are similar. Ostrom's and Libecap's focus on individual incentives stands in contrast to models of optimal resource governance that measure efficiency in the aggregate without comparing the distribution of individual payoffs under alternative institutional arrangements.[20] Focusing on the users themselves yields generalizable results, because the same factors that cause the problem with managing the resource in the first place, such as resource complexity, lack of information, high costs, and divergences in user expectations and outcomes, prompt users to resist or otherwise foil top-down solutions.

Both Libecap and Ostrom embraced complexity and empirical observation, studying a wide variety of natural resources, cultures, and institutional settings. Yet taken in the aggregate, these many disparate settings yield common themes, both within and between their works. First, understanding how and why people in groups behave in particular ways is paramount to understanding whether they can solve a CPR problem. Success requires buy-in on a solution from many parties and identifying the problem or externality facing the group is a necessary, but not a sufficient, condition. Second, individual user costs and benefits matter, not just the aggregate outcome. User perceptions of these costs and benefits also matter, and information asymmetry and uncertainty can decrease the likelihood of success. Third, the relationship between costs and benefits matters. In Ostrom's work, this gets at the idea of fairness: unequal proportions of costs and benefits are likely to discourage collective action because individuals are not willing to contribute to the maintenance of a system that they feel does not fairly distribute the gains of cooperation.[21] Libecap perceives proportionality as affecting bargaining, because users seeing similar proportions of costs to benefits are more likely to have their interests aligned.[22]

2. Group Characteristics

Both Libecap and Ostrom identify group characteristics as crucial to successful CPR management because users together must agree on a mutually beneficial set of rules and expectations for behavior. Based on earlier work on collective action, group size and heterogeneity are a focus for both authors.[23] With large groups, coordinating the bargaining process becomes more burdensome; large groups may increase the level of conflict and costs of arriving at acceptable allocation formulas.[24] Group heterogeneity can affect both the ability to make proportionate allocations and the information available to different users, as discussed above.

In the literature on collective action, no clear consensus has emerged on the effect of group size and heterogeneity. While increases in the number and heterogeneity of bargaining parties tend to increase the transaction costs of negotiation and make agreement less likely,[25] this is definitely not always the case.[26] Because both group size and heterogeneity may be endogenous to the collective action process, success may lead to larger and more heterogeneous groups, while less successful outcomes lead to fragmentation—smaller but more homogeneous groups.[27] Both authors acknowledge this issue and emphasize that the existence of large group sizes or high degrees of heterogeneity are not themselves the cause of the breakdown of collective action. Instead, it is the impact of these factors on variables that actually affect the expectation of the costs and benefits perceived by users. Both authors' work in this area is linked by a rigorous assessment of the key variables that explain perceived costs and benefits over a series of empirical cases.

2.1 Size

Libecap is explicit in his assessment of the issue of group size: "The greater the number of competing interest groups with a stake in the new definition of property rights, the more claims that must be addressed by politicians in building a consensus on institutional change."[28] It is more difficult to bring larger number of users to the bargaining table, have them all agree on the state of the resource and the nature of the problem, and create and enforce a solution. Large resource users internalize more of the rent dissipation, and if a large number of smaller users can free ride on any curtailment, large users are likely to impede agreements.[29] The necessity of including a large number of parties in a contracting situation is often indicative of a more complex and interconnected resource.

Ostrom argues that the key to understanding the role of aspects like group size lies in embracing the complexity of social-ecological systems;[30] in her social-ecological systems (SES) framework the number of users is one of nine traits of resource users that affect collective action, and all nine traits are interrelated. For this reason, Ostrom is more muted than Libecap in her assessment of group size: "The effect of the number of participants facing problems of creating and sustaining a self-governing enterprise is unclear." She continues, "Analyzing the conflict levels over a subtractable good and the transaction costs of arriving at acceptable allocation formulas, group size may well exacerbate the problems of self-governing systems."[31] Correlated factors make it difficult to directly assess the impact of group size. Small groups allow for more interactions and the ability to build trust, but may also decrease the resources available to mobilize and run the group.[32]

Political scientist Amy Poteete and Ostrom suggest that the relationships between group size and heterogeneity and collective action are not likely to be linear, although their examples suggest that these nonlinearities may stem from correlated factors.[33] For instance, the size of a group might interact with other factors, such as the distribution of wealth: "Appropriators who possess more substantial economic and political assets may have similar interests to those with fewer assets or they may differ substantially on multiple attributes."[34] A large group's size might facilitate allowing enough wealthy individuals to lead the collective action endeavor to make it successful in situations where interests are aligned. Alternatively, where the interests of the wealthy diverge, the lack of repeated interactions and trust in large groups might lead to a breakdown in collective action.

This argument appears to be at odds with Libecap's assessment that large groups tend to increase both complexity and heterogeneity. One explanation for the divergence in views is that the groups studied by Ostrom may have been quite small or homogeneous (or both) relative to those studied by Libecap.[35] Alternatively, the correlation of size with other factors predicting success, including the overall gains from coordination, might limit consensus. Still, Libecap and co-author Steven Wiggins's argument that having few, large firms on an oil or gas field can allow for a rapid agreement is analogous to Ostrom's view that appropriators with substantial assets may facilitate agreement, if the total number of users is held small and constant.[36] Increasing the number of firms, Libecap argues, decreases the willingness of large firms to participate in an agreement that will allow small appropriators to continue to dissipate resource rents.[37]

2.2 Heterogeneity

It is clear in the work of both Libecap and Ostrom that group size and heterogeneity are linked, although the two authors conceive of group heterogeneity in slightly different ways, each aligning their approach to their conception of the collective action problem faced by resource users. Libecap views heterogeneity through the lens of transaction costs.[38] A group whose members face significantly different potential benefits and costs from a proposed solution has higher costs of reaching agreement: "Even when there are aggregate net benefits from implementing management regimes . . . , not all parties perceive individual gains. Therefore, some may resist collective action."[39] A diverse set of economic interests, or more users generally, make finding a mutually acceptable agreement more difficult.

Production cost heterogeneity also affects collective action. During the New Deal, differences in cost structure limited the ability of industrial firms to lobby to enforce collusive policies, while agricultural producers represented by the American Farm Bureau Federation had uniform production costs and successfully retained collusive pricing policies.[40] However, even in agriculture, producer heterogeneity limited the scope for successful collective action, as exemplified by Florida and California citrus producers' inability to agree on effective prorationing rules.[41] Heterogeneity in user incentives, as a result of unequal revenue and cost share distributions, hinders oil and gas unitization agreements when revenue shares are not the same as cost shares, creating differential incentives to exploit the resources.[42]

Alternatively, Ostrom views heterogeneity primarily in terms of its effect on social cohesion and trust: "If groups coming from diverse cultural backgrounds share access to a common resource, the key question affecting the likelihood of self-organized solutions is whether the views of the multiple groups concerning the structure of the resource, authority, interpretation of rules, trust, and reciprocity differ or are similar."[43] In Ostrom's reckoning, trust in a CPR governance regime requires users to have a shared understanding of the world and of the resource system in particular. Heterogeneity can undermine trust when the views and norms held by users are not conducive to building such a shared understanding.

Despite Libecap and Ostrom's different conceptions of heterogeneity, their results are similar: they both find that when interests diverge, it is more difficult to reach a consensus. For example, differential abilities among fishers affect their willingness to organize with others, because those with high skill receive rents even under open access conditions and therefore require larger shares.[44] However, identifying heterogeneity in users is not a sufficient condition for identifying a potential breakdown in collective action. Ostrom discusses this example, but suggests that trust is key, because ongoing, repeated interactions among users help overcome the challenges that heterogeneity creates.[45] Studying forest user groups in Nepal, co-author George Varughese and Ostrom find that heterogeneity does pose a key challenge that can be overcome with innovative institutional arrangements.[46]

3. Information Problems

Although Ostrom's original design principles focused on institutional characteristics rather than resource characteristics, her later development of the social-ecological systems framework also incorporated resource characteristics.[47] Within the context of the framework, Ostrom continuously emphasized users' ability to observe and understand the resource as critical to successful CPR management:

> Characteristics of CPRs affect the problems of devising governance regimes. These attributes include the size and carrying capacity of the resource system, the measurability of the resource, the temporal and spatial availability of resource flows, the amount of storage in the system, whether resources move (like water, wildlife, and most fish) or are stationary (like trees and medicinal plants), how fast resources regenerate, and how various harvesting technologies affect patterns of regeneration. . . . It is relatively easy to

estimate the number and size of trees in a forest and allocate their use accordingly, but it is much more difficult to assess migratory fish stocks and available irrigation water in a system without storage capacity.[48]

Broadly, the challenges that these resource characteristics pose for collective action could be summarized as "information problems" that limit users' ability to understand and predict resource characteristics with sufficient certainty to develop institutions for governance.

Economists have long appreciated the role of information in affecting coordination,[49] and Ostrom explicitly incorporated economic reasoning in her explanation of how information problems affect individuals' willingness to cooperatively develop governance regimes. Drawing on economists Harold Demsetz, Douglass North, and others, Ostrom argues,

> Whether the users themselves are able to overcome the higher level dilemmas they face in bearing the cost of designing, testing, and modifying governance systems depends on the benefits they perceive to result from a change as well as the expected costs of negotiating, monitoring, and enforcing these rules. . . . Perceived benefits are greater when the resource reliably generates valuable products for the users. . . . Perceived costs are higher when the resource is large and complex, users lack a common understanding of resource dynamics, and users have substantially diverse interests.[50]

Ostrom also appreciated that information problems and perceptions about benefits and costs could stymie government-based solutions and formal property rights as well as informal systems for CPR management Criticizing economists and other political scientists for their focus on aggregates in the search for global optima, she focused instead on how local knowledge would affect users' incentives to pursue one form of governance or another. This approach emphasizes the importance of local over "highly aggregated" information about resource stocks in shaping incentives for individuals to solve collective action problems either informally or through the political process, which Ostrom treated as endogenous.[51]

Like Ostrom, Libecap studied the effects of information about resource stocks on individuals' perceived benefits and costs from contracting to solve common-pool problems. Rights-based policy reforms that appear to be Pareto-improving may nevertheless be unacceptable to a majority of resource users, preventing reform.[52] Hence, economists' focus on statistical aggregates (macro-level Pareto improvements) causes them to overlook the important local information that determines whether individual users will actually support a particular institution.

A particularly salient example of the similarities between Ostrom's discussion of information and Libecap's findings is the study of common-pool problems in oil production. In many areas of the United States, rights to subsurface resources were conveyed to landowners when land was first privatized. Conventional oil reservoirs can span thousands of acres, whereas most land parcels were 160 to 320 acres initially. This gave rise to a common-pool problem whereby many landowners could access the same underground oil reservoir but were unable to exclude one another due to the migratory nature of the oil.[53] Libecap's study of this common-pool problem and the associated regulatory and contractual solutions relied heavily on the role of asymmetric and imperfect information about resource stocks—Ostrom's "local knowledge."

Wiggins and Libecap study the effect of imperfect and asymmetric information on contractual solutions to the common-pool problem in seven oil fields.[54] Unitization—the "obvious" contractual solution—involves the formation of a single production unit, which turns over production of the reservoir to a single firm. All the potential users then share the revenues from efficient extraction of oil. The solution is Pareto-improving in the sense that it improves the total rents from oil production relative to competitive extraction. Oil field unitization is conceptually very similar to the CPRs studied by Ostrom in that users must come to a collective agreement about how to manage the resource and distribute the associated benefits. The primary distinction between unitization and an informal CPR regime is that unitization agreements are enforced via formal contracts rather than informal norms and social sanctioning.

Despite the aggregate efficiency gains of joint management, voluntary unitization is somewhat rare, and this is the problem Wiggins and Libecap seek to understand.[55] Contractual solutions that improve aggregate efficiency can nevertheless fail if individuals do not agree to the allocation of shares of net revenue under the unitized contract. Disagreement about these shares—based on parties' limited and differential information about the value of subsurface deposits—is what causes contracts to fail. Though oil can migrate through a reservoir, there is considerable heterogeneity in the productivity of different locations across a given reservoir, but these differential productivities are not observable by all firms. Hence, when firms come to the table, they each have limited information about the productive capacity of all other firms.

Using data from trade journals about the potential unitization of seven oil fields, Wiggins and Libecap study how firms' limited information about subsurface oil reservoirs influences unitization outcomes.[56] Their findings are consistent with their predictions, and with those of Ostrom:[57] they find that unitization is much less likely to occur in oil fields where there is considerable heterogeneity in resource productivity, which makes the information held by individual users more asymmetric. They also find that individual firms that face greater uncertainty about their productivity choose to delay joining units longer because the benefits of unitization relative to open access are less clear when future productivity is hard to forecast.

Libecap's finding that information problems stymie contractual solutions to common-pool problems can be paired with another assertion from Ostrom's work: the same information problems that limit contractual solutions also pose challenges for regulators.[58] Libecap and Wiggins study regulatory responses to common-pool losses in oil reservoirs in Oklahoma, Texas, and Wyoming. The crux of their argument is that the same users that prefer common-pool competition to unitization will also lobby to prevent regulation because they stand to gain from doing so. Libecap and Wiggins find policy on federal lands in Wyoming to be more effective than policy on state lands because federal policy requires unitization before oil field exploration, when all parties are equally uncertain about the resource and there is no local knowledge available.[59] In this setting, firms are less likely to oppose unitization. By contrast, unitization in Oklahoma and Texas can occur only after fields have been developed, at which point certain firms' local information gives them strong incentives to resist unitizing and to resist regulation.

Again, Libecap's approach mirrors Ostrom's emphasis on individual users and their incentives rather than on aggregates. And Libecap and Wiggins explicitly treat regulatory outcomes as endogenous to the information problem, in the same manner called for by Ostrom.[60] Information problems are an especially important arena for treating policymakers as endogenous because policymakers are likely to suffer from the same information problems as resource users. Rather than conclude with pessimism regarding the prospect of effectively governing resources fraught with uncertainty and variability, Libecap and Ostrom both propose that the government should invest in information provision to alleviate the problem. For Libecap, this takes the form of lowering transaction costs,[61] whereas for Ostrom it takes the form of "technological infrastructure" that makes resources less difficult to monitor.[62]

4. Proportionality

Given the challenges of group size, heterogeneity, and imperfect information identified in the previous two sections, how can users design enduring agreements? Both Libecap and Ostrom, examining different resources and institutional settings, find that the proportional allocation of costs and benefit shares is key to ongoing resource management success.

Both authors measure success as the extent to which the value of the resource is maximized. In one example, Ostrom and colleague Roy Gardner examine irrigation ditch management in Nepal, where effective management means a high level of irrigation utilization: more land over more of the year under cultivation.[63] In another example, Libecap and legal scholar Henry Smith look at oil and gas unit management, where effective management means coordinated extraction over time to maximize the amount of the resource extracted.[64] In both settings, costs are incurred separately from benefits and the authors find that when costs are not proportional to benefits, management institutions are less successful.

In Nepal, the key cost is ditch maintenance, which must be performed to ensure that water diversions and deliveries are effective. By allocating these cleanup costs in the form of labor to all users along the ditch, water deliveries are proportionally assigned. Users near the head of the canal are in an advantageous position to extract more water, but agree to a proportional share because they need the labor of others along the canal. When the Nepalese government implemented engineering improvements that made bearing costs to clear the canal unnecessary, the proportional relationship between costs and benefits was disrupted. Users in advantageous positions took advantage by diverting excess water, and overall irrigation utilization decreased dramatically.

In oil and gas extraction, multiple parties may have leasing rights to drill on a particular field, but maximizing extraction requires coordination. The Prudhoe Bay field in Alaska is characterized by a gas cap and an oil rim, which means the natural gas creates pressure in the middle of the formation. As long as the gas is left in the field, oil is driven out of wells at the rim. However, in the creation of the Prudhoe Bay unit agreement, costs and benefits of total field production were not allocated proportionally across all owners because oil and gas revenues and costs were separated. Gas owners then favored increased gas production, increasing the costs of oil extraction and decreasing the ultimate recovery of oil. Conversely, oil owners favored forgoing gas production and using the gas instead as an injectant to further increase oil production. A lack of proportional distribution of benefits and costs led to disagreement among resource users, and ultimately to aggregate losses.[65]

A key empirical finding of both authors is that different settings, even of the same resource, can lead to different rules of proportionality. In examining the Philippine *zanjera* irrigation organizations, Ostrom builds on the work of economist Robert Siy to look at allocation rules for a system requiring considerable manual labor to maintain.[66] Alternative water allocation schemes could increase water use efficiency, as was observed in Nepal,[67] but the use of the water requires large investments of labor by contributing users, and by allocating water in proportion to labor, the system is able to deliver efficiencies in the cost of maintaining infrastructure. Likewise, the allocation of proportional shares of oil and gas production works generally, but breaks down on the subset of formations requiring multiple phases because the proportionality condition is only met within, but not across, phases.[68]

The principle of proportionality laid out by both authors relies on specific knowledge of the characteristics of the resource being managed. In both cases above, understanding the behavior of the resource—the unidirectional flow of water and the forced flow of oil—is critical to understanding why one set of allocation rules is proportional and another is not. Gardner and his colleagues suggest that these lessons can be applied broadly, citing the Montreal Protocol as an example of how a large, global CPR can be managed via proportional cutbacks, and suggesting that failures can be linked to too-large cutbacks or asymmetries in payoffs.[69]

5. Self-Organizing Collective Management and Contracting

Thus far, this chapter has focused on similarities in the conditions for successful resolution of common-pool resource management challenges that Ostrom and Libecap highlighted. Libecap generally focused on formal contracts, contrasting with much of Ostrom's work, which focused on informal governance in settings where such contracts were not available or enforceable owing to absent, weak, or dysfunctional governments. In this section we compare Ostrom's and Libecap's analysis of coordination challenges in the governance of surface water systems, which both authors studied extensively. Their work suggests that, at least in this case, informal institutions and formal property rights serve a similar function, and can be viewed as substitutes.

Irrigation infrastructure—canals, ditches, dams, and reservoirs used to store and convey water to where it is most useful—require large up-front capital costs but entail very low marginal costs once constructed.[70] However, the benefits of infrastructure projects often take time to materialize, particularly in agriculture.

This presents a problem for individual irrigators seeking to develop diversion and storage infrastructure in settings where there is limited access to credit, such as on the nineteenth-century American frontier and in the developing world today.[71]

One way for individuals to overcome high up-front costs is to pool their capital and invest jointly in building larger diversion canals, which can then feed smaller ditches for each individual user. This cost-sharing approach can facilitate the construction of larger, more efficient ditches than would be possible via individual investment.[72] We briefly discussed in the prior section the case of irrigation in Nepal. Once a ditch is constructed, potential users of the ditch face an asymmetric commons dilemma: those closer to the diversion point (head-enders) can access the water before those at the opposite end of the ditch (tail-enders). Because the fixed investment costs are already sunk and the marginal costs of diversion are low, head-enders have an incentive to divert all or most of the water once a ditch has been constructed.[73] Recognizing this potential problem, tail-enders will be unwilling to invest in the first place, creating a classic collective action problem in which all parties would be better off with joint investment, but it is not individually rational for parties to invest.

Ostrom focused on constraints on opportunistic behavior by head-enders that could enable collective action, especially the use of labor and allocation rules. In systems where ex post maintenance labor was critical, rules were more likely to be followed.[74] In the Spanish *huertas*, allocation rules and norms of mutual enforcement made monitoring less costly—the rotational nature of the allocation gave farmers an incentive and ability to monitor others' behavior as they prepared for their own deliveries.[75] In the context of the American frontier, Ostrom emphasized the ability of the Mormon church to serve as a coordinating institution for supporting communal ditch building. The church was able to effectively limit entry by outsiders and link labor and water allocations via construction activities, while also providing strong social sanctions for potential unauthorized diversions after ditch building was complete.[76]

The Nepalese irrigation systems, the *huertas,* and Mormon villages all consisted of homogeneous groups of users with shared cultural backgrounds that facilitated cooperation, either through organizing joint labor or through providing common sanctioning mechanisms.[77] Ostrom emphasized the importance of these shared values by contrasting successes in both the Nepalese and Mormon cases to examples in each setting where the government attempted and failed to solve the same collective action problems in developing irrigation works.[78] In both cases, the government lacked local knowledge and failed to prevent opportunistic behavior by irrigators. Thus, while the government could solve the problem of financing infrastructure, it struggled to resolve collective action problems ex post in the absence of formal property rights.

Libecap's work on the evolution of property rights to resources on the American frontier emphasized a different solution to the same collective action problem. In the context of irrigation development on the frontier, Ostrom's and Libecap's predictions about the role of information problems, the characteristics of the resource, and the scope for formal government management were identical. But where Ostrom emphasized the importance of informal coordinating institutions, economist Bryan Leonard and Libecap, emphasizes the importance of formal property rights to water in solving the collective action problems of infrastructure development.[79] The property right institution in this case is the prior appropriation doctrine, which defined property rights to water on a first-come, first-served basis and allowed water rights to be separated from land ownership. Prior appropriation also entailed priority-based allocation of water during droughts so users with more senior claims had preferential access to water.

Leonard and Libecap characterize the collective action problem of ditch construction exactly as Ostrom did,[80] building their economic framework directly upon Ostrom and Gardner's.[81] However, they focus on the role that priority-based allocation played in enabling users to write contracts to share the costs of ditch construction—a secure property right to water ex post reduced the risk of opportunistic behavior and aligned incentives ex ante. Hence, Ostrom and Leonard and Libecap present two very different solutions to the same collective action problem.[82]

Leonard and Libecap argue that social sanctioning and limits to entry associated with the Mormon church and emphasized by Ostrom were the exception rather than the norm on the western frontier.[83] The successful irrigation systems described by Ostrom may simply not have been feasible for many western communities where a large number of new settlers from diverse cultural and institutional backgrounds were arriving.[84] These settlers lacked a common set of shared social norms to facilitate sanctioning, and there was no way to predict how many irrigators might show up in the future. Under these conditions, a formal property right to water provided the security necessary to facilitate contracting rather than informal coordination. Moreover, the benefits associated with prior appropriation rights (greater ditch investment, higher crop income per acre) were lower in areas of Colorado dominated by Mormon settlement and other preexisting irrigation institutions, suggesting that formal property rights and informal norms were in fact both solving a similar collective action problem based on the broader institutional constraints.[85]

6. Conclusion

The preceding examples and discussion serve to illustrate the congruence between the collective action problems faced by users attempting to define property rights and the collective action problems facing users creating self-enforcing governance institutions. We emphasize three ways in which collective action to contract and collective action to form self-organizing governance institutions are similar: (1) larger and more heterogeneous groups potentially increase the difficulty of collective action, but these challenges can be overcome; (2) information problems associated with the resource and with local knowledge limit collective action; and (3) proportional allocations of benefits and costs aid in successful collective action. Given these similarities, it is natural to ask what differentiates the settings that lead to self-organizing CPR management and those that lead to contracting. To conclude this chapter, we discuss how further research can provide insight into this question. This is especially relevant in applying the lessons of Ostrom, Libecap, and other authors to the improved management of natural and environmental resources.

One question is whether *access* to formal contracts is the only factor that distinguishes the emergence of a formal contract or property right from self-organizing governance. Key cases, and economic intuition, suggest that the relative costs and benefits of different institutions would play an important role. The availability of contracting may lower the cost of collective action but not eliminate the adoption of alternative institutional forms. Where property rights are expensive to enforce, as in the management of groundwater, institutions that look more like self-organizing governance emerge.[86] Groundwater users in Kansas petitioned the state to receive the ability to manage their common-pool groundwater according to local rules and customs.[87] These sorts of hybrid systems where formal and informal institutions exist concurrently are exhibited in Colorado, where users collectively adopted pumping taxes;[88] in Nebraska, where more formal market exchanges were adopted;[89] and in Kansas, where users voluntarily adopted pumping restrictions.[90] In these cases, state laws or state-enforced contracts provide a viable and low-cost end point to collective action to solve CPR problems.

More research is needed to better characterize the conditions under which self-sustaining CPR governance occurs and where contracts and property rights are viable substitutes. For instance, what factors would lead to successful self-organizing CPR governance in countries with strong property rights and a viable court system? This question is key if changes in policy or knowledge can allow for the adoption of alternative, more successful institutional forms. Ostrom suggests one of the problems is the teaching of scientific management of natural resources in a way that suggests central governments impose uniform regulations that fit textbook solutons: "National governmental agencies are frequently unsuccessful in their efforts to design effective and uniform sets of rules to regulate important common-pool resources across a broad domain."[91] Because alternative, successful institutions might exist, it becomes imperative to understand when centralized control, property rights or contracting, or self-organizing institutions are likely to be successful.

This type of analysis is equally relevant to understanding emerging CPR problems. Three areas where Ostrom's insight into self-enforcing CPR management are potentially valuable are global carbon dioxide emissions, the arctic, and outer space. The melting of the arctic ice cap has opened many potential fossil fuel deposits to extraction in an area where several large and wealthy countries all claim extraction rights. Mineral resources in outer space offer a similar, if currently hypothetical, scenario. More pressing is the problem of global climate change. These situations might seem to be scaled-up versions of a classic CPR. However, the institutional features Ostrom emphasized—such as group cohesion and long-evolved, shared norms—are unlikely to play a large role in governance of the global climate, the arctic, or outer space. Applying the findings of this chapter to these settings, however, reveals essential components of the structure of collective action problems in general, highlighting the need for institutions that perform specific functions (e.g., enforcement, sharing of benefits and costs).

Libecap brings together several empirical examples to illustrate factors that affect the success of collective action in managing CPRs of varying scales.[92] In pointing out the collective action problems inherent in property rights formation, his work points to the fallacy of viewing Ostrom only as a "third-way" alternative to government ownership or privatization. Instead, he applies Ostrom's insights about collective action to the study of the success or failure of private property and government regulation. This chapter offers one example of how researchers can build on Ostrom's legacy by bringing the lessons from her work to new institutional and resource settings by examining resource governance empirically and carefully. As Ostrom suggests,

> As an institutionalist studying empirical phenomena, I presume that individuals try to solve problems as effectively as they can. . . . It is my responsibility as a scientist to ascertain what problem individuals are trying to solve and what factors help or hinder them in these efforts.[93]

This drive to understand how resource users try to solve problems, and when they are successful, is the common thread woven through the work of both Gary Libecap and Elinor Ostrom.

The Environmental Benefits of Long-Distance Trade: Insights from the History of By-Product Development

Pierre Desrochers and Joanna Szurmak

Size (and Scale) Matter: Addressing Ostrom's Critics

In his classic article "The Tragedy of the Commons," Garrett Hardin famously declared that "ruin is the destination toward which all men rush, each pursuing his own best interest in a society that believes in the freedom of the commons."[1] Elinor Ostrom disagreed.[2] She argued that, even in the absence of clearly defined and enforced private property rights or statist regulations, bottom-up arrangements have historically often been sufficient to prevent the overuse and destruction of common-pool resources (CPRs) such as pastureland, fisheries, forests, and irrigation systems.

Ostrom is celebrated for devising and championing the Institutional Analysis and Development framework. By collecting, systematizing, and analyzing numerous case studies, Ostrom paved the way for a more nuanced analysis of how, working collectively, economic actors can sustainably manage activities such as irrigation, fishing, forestry, and grazing outside the contexts provided by either well-defined private property rights or edicts from political or regulatory authorities. Both the supporters and the critics of Ostrom's work generally agree that most of the examples of successful CPR management she gathered and analyzed relate to sparsely populated, remote, and economically stagnant rural or forested areas. These include some of the most economically marginal regions of advanced and developing economies[3] such as those of Japan, Switzerland, Spain, Turkey, and the Philippines.[4] Using fisheries as an example, distinguished Canadian applied ecologist Fikret Berkes demonstrated why the economically more modest CPRs tend to provide cases of spontaneous evolution of Ostromian cooperative frameworks more frequently than their larger counterparts: "While open-ocean, large-scale fisheries usually come under national and international levels of management, the small-scale coastal fisheries often operate outside the framework of measures instituted by central governments."[5]

Ostrom's preference for modest and marginal locations, so convincingly explicated by Berkes, has, nevertheless, supplied some ammunition to critics of her work. For instance, Swiss agricultural economist Philipp Aerni wrote that Ostrom was "fascinated by remote villages in the Swiss Alps that were governing the local commons sustainably without much trade and exchange with the outside world and without relying exclusively on private property rights."[6] Yet, Aerni argued, this "lack of contact with the outside world also prevented these villages from adopting new techniques and innovative practices that would have enhanced their agricultural productivity." He added that "local investment in innovation was also neglected because of the absence of ownership rights," the result being stagnating agricultural productivity. Furthermore, Aerni contended, the equilibrium Ostrom described was historically possible only when the "surplus population (the population that could not be fed with the available resources and traditional techniques) could be exported as mercenaries to foreign armies or as non-farm labourers to lowland industrial centres," in the process contributing remittances that "allowed the villagers to buy food from elsewhere during periods of scarcity."[7]

Taking a broader view of the issue, economist Ted Bergstrom similarly argued that "the real-world commons problems that Ostrom studies usually involve repeated interactions among a relatively small number of players who are able to develop subtle institutions for monitoring and enforcing a degree of cooperation."[8] Bergstrom was skeptical that such a local, polycentric approach can prove useful when dealing with a problem of global scope, such as climate change caused by unmonitored carbon dioxide emissions.

Prominent Marxist geographer David Harvey similarly questioned the scalability of communal solutions, pointing out that "most of [Ostrom's] examples . . . involve as few as a hundred or so appropriators. Anything much larger (her largest case involved fifteen thousand users) required a 'nested hierarchical' structure of decision making, rather than direct negotiations between individuals."[9] Therefore, Harvey argued, there is an "unanalyzed . . . scale problem" in Ostromian solutions for the "possibilities for sensible management of common-property resources that exist on one scale, such as shared water rights between one hundred farmers in a small river basin, do not and cannot carry over to problems such as global warming or even to the regional diffusion of acid deposition from power stations." When attempting to translate a solution to one problem to another at a different scale, however, the "whole nature of the common-property problem and the prospects of finding a solution change dramatically," because what "looks like a good way to resolve problems at one scale does not hold at another scale." "Even worse," Harvey argued, "good solutions at one scale (say, the local) do not necessarily aggregate up, or cascade down, to make for good solutions at another scale (say, the global)."[10] This is ultimately why, in his opinion, "the lessons gained from the collective organization of small-scale solidarity economies along common-property lines cannot translate into global solutions without resort to nested hierarchical forms of decision making."[11] Ostrom would have likely disagreed with Harvey's analysis as her work exposed the over-reliance on the hierarchical governance models she saw as part of the "dichotomous" schema in which the government (coercively) controls public issues and the private sector controls the market.[12]

While Ostrom herself recognized that people evolve economic structures and systems that are multilayered, polycentric, subject to feedback loops, and operating at multiple scales, she rarely drew on examples involving transregional engagement or extended time lines. Our work shows, however, that, given free market institutions and government interventions that amounted to enforcement of private property rights, effective environmental remediation solutions arose spontaneously among individuals separated by continents and industries. Building on Ostrom's emphasis on local, spontaneous, and bottom-up processes, we illustrate how environmental remediation in rapidly developing economies has often been achieved historically through the decentralized and spontaneous development of lucrative by-products out of polluting emissions and residuals. Although such cases were arguably closer to a property rights approach to environmental externalities than to the type of communal management studied by Ostrom, the waste remediation cases we present ultimately relied on voluntary and decentralized processes at the core of Ostrom's work. Unlike the cases she discussed, however, the remediation cases we have studied required from their beginning that local activities be embedded in a broader division of labor, one that included distant markets that could absorb by-products created out of former production residuals.

Our aim in this chapter is to argue that, while critics of Ostrom might have a point in terms of the scalability of communal management solutions, spontaneous bottom-up processes have nonetheless long helped private businesses and local communities address environmental degradation issues such as air, land,

and water pollution in times of rapid economic development. The success of these processes, however, required the (market) participation of economic actors located far from the local communities in question.

The specific class of solutions we address consists of solutions that involve the neutralization of polluting emissions through the development of lucrative by-products out of production or processing residuals. We first discuss past assessments of the polluting emissions problem before addressing the incentives that promoted profitable and environmentally beneficial by-product development. We then illustrate and supplement this discussion with two historical case studies from the late-nineteenth-century United States: the development of valuable by-products out of once-highly-polluting cottonseed and the reuse of petroleum-refining residuals.

As will be illustrated, unlike many of the approaches discussed in the commons literature, the solutions to local environmental problems required the development of increasingly sophisticated and geographically distant markets. We thus present a discussion of the spontaneous emergence of local pollution management through the combination of legislative, communitarian, and market-driven processes at many levels and across large geographical distances. Our conclusion illustrates that, contrary to the arguments made by many sustainable-development theorists, long-distance trade is often critical in the development of "greener" production and processing practices. Because of this, our examples fit in with, but also supplement, Ostrom's observation that "many successful CPR institutions are rich mixtures of 'private-like' and 'public-like' solutions defying classification in a sterile dichotomy."[13]

Increasing Profitability through Pollution Reduction

Do profit-seeking activities necessarily require that processing or manufacturing companies ignore the negative externalities from their activities? Or, to the contrary, can the profit motive provide incentives to generate "eco-innovations"—innovations that have both economic and environmental benefits? Does the profit motive need to resolve into a single incentive instead of a complex matrix of feedback mechanisms that come into play at many levels in an action arena? While Ostrom would likely find cases that allow her to answer the second and third question affirmatively,[14] it is probably fair to say that most contemporary analysts share the perspective of the systems engineering researcher Milena Ristovska that markets are replete with environmental problems and failures of all kinds because of the profitability requirement faced by firms:

> Continuous pressure to cut costs in a competitive market encourages companies to externalize costs as much as possible. Unless restricted by law, companies will seek to maximize their use of the natural environment as a "sink" for waste materials and they have a strong incentive to externalize some costs by exploiting the "free" services of the natural environment. Thus pollution is an inevitable by-product of an economic system in which companies seek to maximize profits and the free market dictates that companies seek to minimize costs in order to maximize profits regardless of any environmental damage that might be caused. Market failure of this kind is very common and results from the

need to stay commercially competitive in the
short term.[15]

This perspective is largely shared by economists and other analysts who believe that firms only have an incentive to eliminate
waste when benefits exceed costs and that corporate social responsibility initiatives, public pressures, and the threat of regulation might play a more significant role in this respect. While the
latter has sometimes been true, much evidence does suggest that
the profit motive was typically the key motivation behind the actions of creative business owners, managers, and technicians who
invested in the development of new ways of doing things in the
hope (often turned to reality) that value can be created out of en
vironmental nuisances.[16]

First, the value of residuals was often initially low or non-exis-
tent, while their disposal or neutralization costs (occasionally triggered by actual or potential property rights–based lawsuits) were
often significant. Second, unlike domestic waste, industrial residuals were uniform in nature and typically available in large quantities. Last, they were often produced in industrialized regions, thus
reducing transportation costs to different industrial plants where
they could be used as inputs (needless to say, additions to existing
plants were often built for that purpose). In this context, several
manufacturers followed a process described by the French engineer Paul Razous at the turn of the twentieth century.[17] Residuals
were first thoroughly analysed and broken into their basic components. If any of these had significant value, it was isolated. If no
component was particularly valuable on its own, the composition
of the residual was compared to the composition of similar products such as fuels, fertilizers, animal food, and building materials.
Two scenarios were then possible. If the residual components were
similar to those of a given commercial input, the residual could
probably be used for the same purpose. If one or a few compo-

nents were missing, it was often possible to add whatever was necessary to turn the residual into a suitable substitute.

Perhaps the best-known historical instance of by-product development out of processing residuals occurred in the meatpacking industry. As the American editor and essayist William George Jordan remarked more than a century ago, "when an ox was slaughtered [in past decades], forty per cent of the animal was wasted." By the late nineteenth century, however, "nothing [was] lost but its dying breath."[18] Among other creative developments, blood was used as an input in sugar refining and papermaking or turned into doorknobs and buttons. Bones were not only the primary material in the manufacture of countless combs, buttons, handles, and various types of jewelry, but the dust created as a result of sawing them became food for cattle and poultry. Even "the undigested food in the stomach, which formerly cost the packers of Chicago thirty thousand dollars a year to remove and destroy," was used to make paper.

An anonymous contributor to the *Illustrated Magazine of Art* had suggested nearly five decades earlier than Jordan's analysis of waste recycling that, "as the best way of destroying an enemy is to make him a friend, so the best way of getting rid of a noxious gas is to find a method by which it may be retained in a useful form."[19] The contributor described how "the operations of chemistry have brought into employment a thousand substances which had otherwise been useless or pernicious."[20] After discussing several examples, he concluded, "Such is the economy of the chemistry of art, which, by the combination of apparently useless elements, produces, as though with the touch of an enchanter's wand, order out of confusion, advantage and beauty from the offensive and injurious."[21]

Arguably the most important chronicler to work on this issue was the Danish-born British writer Peter Lund Simmonds (1814–1897).[22] In the thirty-five chapters of *Waste Products and Underde-*

veloped Substances; or, Hints for Enterprise in Neglected Fields (1862),
he described numerous examples of creating wealth from waste
from various animal, vegetable, and mineral substances. In the
conclusion of the revised edition of his book, Simmonds observed,

> I . . . bring my labours to a close—not because the
> subject is exhausted, since every day furnishes
> new instances of what has become one of the
> most striking features of modern industry—to let
> nothing be lost, and to re-work with profit and
> advantage the residues of former manufactures—
> but for fear I should weary the reader with too
> ponderous a volume.[23]

Numerous contemporaneous writers made similar comments.[24]
For instance, in his *Handbook of Chemical Technology*, German professor of chemistry Johann Rudolf von Wagner wrote that the
"ideal of a chemical manufactory is that there should be no real
waste products at all, but only chief or main, and by-products.
The better, therefore the waste products are applied to good and
advantageous use, the more nearly the manufactory will approach the ideal, and the larger will be the profit."[25] In 1886, an
encyclopedia entry described how "in the earlier days" of many
manufacturing branches, "certain portions of the materials used
have been cast aside as 'waste,'" but over time "first in one branch
and then in another, this 'waste' material has been experimented
upon with a view to finding some profitable use for it; and in most
instances the experiments have had a more or less satisfactory results."[26] A year later, a scientific retrospective highlighted "the utilization of waste materials and by-products" as a "leading feature
of the Victorian epoch."[27]

Writing at the turn of the twentieth century, the American technical writer Leebert Lloyd Lamborn commented that if "there is

one aspect more than any other that characterizes modern commercial and industrial development," it is "the utilization of substances which in a primitive stage of development of any industry were looked upon as worthless." These were either "secondary products incurred in the manufacture of the main commodity, for which the industrial acumen of the age found no use," or else products for which, "if a use were known, the prejudices and conservatism of society allowed them to languish in the shadow of a similar commodity already strongly intrenched."[28]

Although these analysts sometimes mentioned social, environmental, and (property rights–driven) legal concerns, most of them suggested that the profit motive was the main incentive behind widespread by-product development. Among these was Simmonds, who argued that as "competition becomes sharper, manufacturers have to look more closely to those items which may make the slight difference between profit and loss, and convert useless products into those possessed of commercial value."[29] Even Karl Marx agreed with the notion that waste recovery increases "the rate of profit" because it helps "reduce the cost of the raw material to the extent that [materials recovered from waste] are saleable." After production efficiencies from economies of scale, he viewed industrial waste recovery as "the second great branch of economy in the conditions of production."[30] More than a century ago the editor of the *Boston Journal of Commerce*, Henry J. Kittredge, similarly commented,

> Nothing in the arts of manufacture is more indicative of economic efficiencies than the utilization of products that have been rejected as wastes or residues in the industrial processes. . . . The refuse of to-day is a source of profit to-morrow; and this has been going on for years and probably will be going on for years to come. . . .

New revelations and new uses are constantly being found for substances of all kinds, whether in their original forms, or in their changed forms due to outside agencies. The world's increment of wealth is largely dependent upon finding new and more economical uses for materials, however exalted or humble they may be in the industrial scale.[31]

Two North American Case Studies of How Companies Turned Polluting Waste into Wealth

We will now use two historical case studies to illustrate in more detail the processes of by-product development and its incidental environmental benefits, showing the spontaneous emergence of solutions ameliorated across different industries and in different settings.

Cottonseed By-Products

Cotton is the world's most significant and most industrialized textile crop. *Gossypium hirsutum*, also known as upland or short-staple cotton, typically accounts for between 90 and 96 percent of world cotton production. *Gossypium barbadense*, also known as Egyptian, sea-island, long-staple, or pima cotton, is the second most valuable variety, accounting for between 1 and 6 percent of world cotton production. While pima cotton fibers are strong, long, and fine, and hence ideal for superior products, the variety's yield and resistance to pests and diseases are inferior, making the species less economically advantageous.[32]

The cotton fruit is known as a *boll*; each boll contains three to five *loculi* or compartments in which five to eleven seeds mature. The boll opens halfway through its approximately one-hundred-day growth cycle, allowing the fiber, known as *lint*, to dry. Seeds are 66 percent of the weight of a measure of seed cotton (cotton boll with seeds and lint); they are characterized by a dark brown or ash-colored husk which, particularly in the upland cotton species, is entirely encased in short, compact white fuzz commonly called *linters*. Pima cottonseed husks, much less fuzzy than their upland relatives, appear black and smooth instead of dark brown and rough.

Both upland and pima cotton were cultivated in the United States by the eighteenth century. Until the development and widespread use of the cotton gin in the mid-1790s, the limited volume of cottonseed available in the United States was either replanted (about 10 percent of the total), fed to mature ruminants that could digest the seed,[33] or used as fertilizer once the seeds had been deactivated by fermenting them in compost heaps, keeping them wet in large piles, or covering them in deep furrows. After the advent of the cotton gin and the sudden dramatic increase in the profitability of the cotton crop, however, the land area devoted to cotton soon increased dramatically. As more cotton was grown and harvested, large heaps of cottonseed proved an unmitigated nuisance.

While the seeds could be burned, cottonseed fires were difficult to control because of dangerously flammable oil and linters. Another complaint was that "land where piles of seed had remained for some time refused to bring forth any plants at all."[34] Since cottonseed contains a toxic substance called gossypol, it proved lethal as a feed for most livestock, prompting some farmers to isolate their animals from the harmful seeds. Thus, cottonseeds were often put in pens in "order to protect the hogs, . . . and both cattle and hogs were carefully guarded to see that they did not feed on them."[35] Similar concerns about harming livestock were raised when cottonseed hulls were proposed as animal feed, although the burning of hulls for fuel provided an early, if insufficient, outlet for this residual product. One seemingly widespread disposal method was to dump cottonseeds in flowing streams and let them be washed away,[36] creating large-scale pollution of a CPR. Most planters, however, elected to "dump them into creeks or swamps where the cattle and hogs could not find them,"[37] but the result was "a miasmic stench which was not only very offensive, but was thought to produce malaria and other diseases."[38]

Interestingly, in the early years of the crop's rapid expansion, the problem of cottonseed disposal was so significant that some commentators seriously suggested "that it would be better . . . to discontinue the production of cotton, since the seed were injurious to man, beast, and plant."[39] Some of America's earliest environmental regulations can be traced back to cottonseed disposal. For instance, similarly to the codes of Alabama and Georgia, the *Revised Code of Mississippi* of 1857 included a significant fine for "throw[ing] or permit[ting] to be thrown the cottonseed from [any cotton gin] into any river, creek, or other stream of water which may be used by the inhabitants for drinking or fishing therein."[40] It also contained a provision that prevented ginners from accumulating seed within half a mile of a city, town, or village so as to "not prejudice the health of the inhabitants."[41] We see, thus, an example of state regulation of a rapidly evolving negative agricultural and crop-processing externality.

For the first five decades of the nineteenth century, many innovators tried in vain to create wealth out of the oily and fibrous, yet hazardous, waste that was cottonseed. One problem was the poor fit of existing oil extraction technology to the unique challenges of cottonseed. Most entrepreneurs' reliance on simple oil extraction techniques was vexed by the capacity of upland cottonseed linters to absorb a significant portion of the extracted oil. Other issues with cottonseed use for oil included the abundance and cheapness of competing goods—animal fats and oils in the American market—as well as the consumer prejudice against vegetable oils. Because of its composition, cottonseed oil also proved inadequate for a number of industrial uses, for instance as a lubricant, a wood filler, a leather-treating agent, and a component in paint. In time, however, numerous lucrative uses were developed.[42] As the physician and one of the first analysts of the cottonseed industry, Henry Ogden, put it nearly a century and a half ago, while creating value out of cottonseed was "a discovery of no slight magnitude and importance," it came "as most great discoveries do, accompanied by pecuniary loss, delay and disappointment; and [the industry] was successfully established only after repeated failures."[43]

Writing in 1889, the engineer and author Robert Grimshaw observed that cottonseed was long "considered a refuse for which there was no use; long burned or thrown away," but that "its main and by-products are now very important elements in our national industries. The garbage of 1800 became the fertilizer of 1870, the cattle food of 1880, and is now made to yield table food and useful articles of industrial pursuits." The oil, "more widely known throughout the world and used for a greater variety of purposes than any other oil," was by then most valuable, but the "residuum after [cottonseed oil's]expression" was a valuable fertilizer and the "best cattle food"; the ashes of the hulls delivered "potash of high commercial value"; and the refuse from the refining of crude oil provided a "most excellent stock for laundry and toilet soaps."[44] The only industry where cottonseed oil underperformed was that of illumination. Cottonseed oil pioneers had originally set their eyes on the whale oil market, but by the early 1860s petroleum-derived kerosene proved too formidable a competitor, itself in time eclipsed by electric lighting.

By the 1880s, Luther A. Ransom, an industrialist and former president of the Interstate Cottonseed Crushers' Association, described cottonseed by-product development as the story "of a raw material practically without value" that, within two decades, was converted "into products worth one hundred million dollars" that brought much economic prosperity in regions desperate for it.[45] The seeds had made possible the creation of "edible oil without olives; medicinal oil without codfish; butter without cows;

ice cream without cream; lard without hogs; fertilizers without blood; mattresses without hair; stock feed without corn or oats and explosives without powder," the result being "as good or better articles than the originals."[46] These and later advances are perhaps conveyed most effectively in a 1930 promotional poster produced by the National Cottonseed Products Association and titled "The World's Richest Seed" (see figure 1).

Figure 1. 1930 Promotional Poster, "The World's Richest Seed"

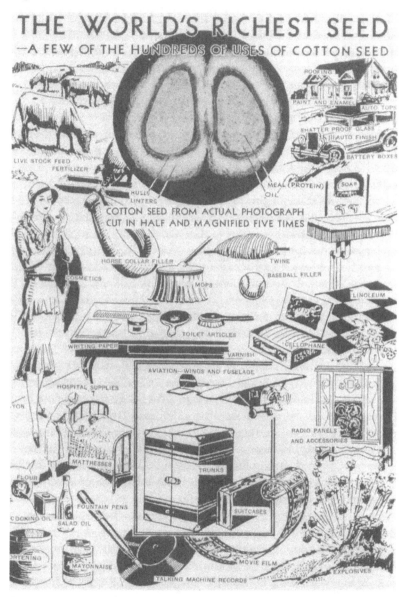

Source: Produced by the National Cottonseed Products Association. (Image reproduced with the permission of the National Cotton Council of America.)

Beginning in the middle of the twentieth century, however, palm-seed oil, soybeans, petroleum by-products, and other alternatives progressively displaced cottonseed and ushered in a decline in the percentage of American cottonseed sent to crushing mills, from a high of nearly 90 percent in 1950 to approximately 45 percent in 2000. Whole cottonseed was not wasted, though: despite being a rather inconvenient feedstuff to handle, it was increasingly added to the diet of certain livestock, primarily lactating dairy cows and beef cattle, a practice once frowned upon. In other words, while the uses of cottonseed might not be as numerous as they once were, market actors have nevertheless found ways to create value out of what would otherwise be an environmental problem.[47]

Petroleum By-Products

Even greater creativity and market complexity can be observed in the history of the petroleum production and refining industries.[48] Petroleum was first sought after in western Pennsylvania in the 1850s, as it proved a more economical source of kerosene (a combustible hydrocarbon used for illumination), which had previously been produced from coal, oil shale, and bitumen. Kerosene was seen as a superior and more reliable alternative to animal and vegetable oils, the best of which were derived from sperm whales.[49] In the early days of the industry much of the raw material was wasted during extraction, storage, and transport. As one traveler reported in 1864,

> At the curves of the bluffs, sometimes at their feet,
> but more frequently on the opposite sides of the
> creeks, wide flats extend. These flats for miles are
> covered with black derricks. . . . The whole aspect
> is as unattractive as any one with a prejudice for
> cleanliness, a nose for sweet smells, and a taste
> for the green of country landscapes can well

imagine. Every thing you see is black. The soil is black, being saturated with waste petroleum. The engine-houses, pumps and tanks are black, with the smoke and soot of the coal-fires which raise the steam to drive the wells. The shanties—for there is scarcely a house in the whole seven miles of oil territory along the creek—are black.[50]

Historical accounts, however, suggest that such environmental damage was then largely deemed an acceptable price to pay for the wealth generated by the industry.[51]

Nevertheless, problems related to the extraction, handling, transportation, and storage of crude oil were soon addressed through advances such as greater recovery at the pump, the development of better barrels (eventually metal drums), and the building of pipelines (at first made out of wood) and railroads (including the development of metal tank cars), among others. The residual matter left after the distillation of petroleum for the extraction of valuable raw materials, however, remained problematic. As the geographers Robert C. Estall and R. Ogilvie later commented, despite the very high quality of Pennsylvania crude oil, these leftover portions "were waste products, and the main problem was how to dispose of them."[52] Petroleum waste disposal typically occurred through dumping or burning, and either way affected the local environment.

By-product development once again allowed wealth to be created out of polluting residuals. In the first quarter of a century after the petroleum industry began, the proportion of waste was reduced from about half of the original material to less than a quarter. The mid-1860s thus saw the creation of lubricating oils, greases, paraffin, petrolatum (or petroleum jelly, better known by the trademark Vaseline), candles, insect repellents, and solvents out of the liquid residue. These new commodities, however, were largely extracted from the "middle of the barrel." By contrast, lighter gasoline and most heavy residuals remained problematic, save for the use of some heavy crude oil and residuum as fuels in refining operations and in buildings in oil-producing regions when alternative fuels (typically coal) were more expensive. As the refining specialist William Leffler put it, "Gasoline and naphtha were mostly considered waste products, often allowed to 'weather,' a euphemism for evaporating into the atmosphere, before the kerosene was recovered. Sometimes refiners just burned the light material in pits or dumped it into nearby streams to get rid of it," much as cotton ginners did with cottonseed.[53] Innovation scholars Newton Copp and Andrew Zanella wrote, somewhat more bluntly, "The typical solution for this problem was to dump the gasoline into adjacent rivers and hope it would evaporate before the river caught on fire!"[54] The problem was that, while gasoline found limited markets by being used in products such as solvents for paint and varnish, it proved too flammable and too volatile to be used for household lighting and heating. Similarly, while some of the heavier components of crude oil had limited uses for road surfacing and roofing, no adequate furnace technology had been developed to burn heavy oil for space heating.

By the mid-1870s, Standard Oil employees began selling paraffin wax for chewing gum and residual oil tar and asphalt for road building. They soon added lubricants (for railroads and machine shops), candles, paints, dyes, and industrial acid. In 1880, Standard Oil acquired the Chesebrough Manufacturing Company of New Jersey in order to strengthen its sales of petroleum jelly.[55] By the end of the nineteenth century, the company sold approximately two hundred petroleum by-products, including "naphtas for local anesthetics, solvents for industry, fuel for stoves and the internal combustion engines, wax for pharmaceuticals and candles, oils and lubricants to free machines from friction, heavy oils for the gas industry."[56]

In his 1908 book *Wealth from Waste*, George Powell Perry attributed much of the success of the Standard Oil corporation to the "wise use of that which was once regarded worthless" rather than to "financial shenanigans and deceptive practices." He supported his contention using a brief account of the development of paraffin out of a "sticky, slimy stuff . . . left over from the refining business":

> At first [the residual] was thrown into the river. But soon the authorities complained because of the pollution it produced. Then it was put into a deep trench and they tried to burn it. It made such a furious flame that the heat became unendurable and the strongest wall could not resist it. In great perplexity the company finally sought the help of some expert chemists to see if some way could not be found to get rid of the nuisance. It was at that time that a process was discovered whereby this disagreeable refuse could be converted into paraffine. Then it was found that this troublesome refuse could be made a good source of revenue.[57]

A few illustrations can illuminate how by-products relieved pressures on flora and fauna. For instance, paraffin was first introduced into the pharmaceutical industry as a substitute for wax, spermaceti (the highest grade of whale oil), almond oil, and lard in cerates and salves.[58] By 1870 it had supplanted spermaceti as the main laundry sizing for both domestic and commercial uses while gaining market shares in textile manufacturing, being used as a wood preservative, and displacing natural rubber for waterproofing tents, boots, and coats.[59] Each product that petroleum waste supplanted allowed animal and plant species to be spared, exerting less pressure on the environment in two interconnected ways: by reusing environmental pollutants and by reducing the harvesting of living species as resources. Once again, as with the development of cottonseed by-products, a number of polycentric efforts by independent producers, innovators, and tinkerers, often initially not affiliated with broader commercial interests, managed to develop the critical mass of failed prototypes from which more successful and, in the case of Standard Oil, more coordinated efforts could emerge.

In his early twentieth-century history and economic analysis of Rockefeller's founding and leadership of Standard Oil, Gilbert Holland Montague wrote that the main complaint voiced by the company's competitors was that the new "improved methods of utilizing by-products" had made these by-products "as remunerative as the refined oil itself," which gave the company a significant competitive advantage. As was widely understood at the time, the main challenge of by-product development was that it required "the greatest specialization of methods, encouragement of invention, investment of capital, and extension of plant," a combination of efforts beyond the capacity of smaller refining operations. In the end, Montague concluded that the large profits Standard Oil derived from by-products was "owing entirely to its superior mechanical efficiency and organization."[60]

The advent of electric lighting in the late nineteenth century turned kerosene into a by-product of gasoline refining. Writing in 1920, the journalist Frederick A. Talbot observed, somewhat carelessly but colorfully, that the development of the internal combustion engine ensured that the

> volatile spirit which hitherto had been spurned and burned wastefully by the refineries was immediately discovered to be invested with a value which had heretofore escaped attention. It formed the ideal fuel for the new motor.

Forthwith wanton destruction of the volatile spirit was abandoned. Every drop was carefully collected, and, as time went on and the demand for the light liquid fuel increased, the refiners put forth great effort to wring every possible dram of [gasoline] from the crude petroleum.[61]

Talbot also commented that "forty years ago the boring of [an oil] well was followed with mixed feelings," because a successful strike would unavoidably "crash through the roof of an underground reservoir of petroleum gas" that might then blow up and cost the lives of the crew. "Ignorant of the value of this product, though painfully aware of its danger," Talbot wrote, "the early seekers for oil led this gas through a pipe to a point some distance away" where it was ignited and "allowed to burn merrily in the open air." It was only when "the flame flickered and expired" that the "boring for the precious liquid" would proceed. In time, however, the flaring of natural gas was recognized for what it was: the waste of a valuable resource. As Talbot observed, "with passing years and progress came enlightenment. The gas is no longer wasted; it is trapped. In some instances, it is led through piping for hundreds of miles to feed hungry furnaces engaged in the making of steel and other products."[62] This passage illustrates the positive feedback loops that spontaneously arose to take advantage of the versatility and potency of petroleum by-products.

In time, diesel became the dominant fuel for ships, locomotives, and heavy-duty vehicles such as buses and trucks, while the development of jet and turbo-jet aircraft eventually provided a new large-scale market for kerosene.[63] To mention but one later instance of by-product development, the boom in plastics production can be traced back to the development of the cracking of crude oil to produce high-quality gasoline, a process that generated residual gases that were first burned as waste, but that eventually became a cheap feedstock for the production of polymers.[64]

After writing that more than five thousand different products had been developed from crude oil, the geographer Joseph Russell Smith and his collaborators observed in 1961, "The meat-packing industry has long boasted that it uses all parts of a pig except the squeal. The petroleum industry sometimes adds the odor of oil to odorless gas to help detect leaks in pipelines. The petroleum industry claims that it uses everything in crude oil, including the smell."[65]

Long-Distance Trade and Win-Win Innovations

The successful by-product development in the cotton and petroleum industries described in the previous section would have never taken place without a division of labor and markets that went much beyond the local scale. This section will discuss and illustrate these prerequisites in more detail.

Petroleum Markets and Refining Operations

As discussed earlier, in time the interplay between the pursuit of economic self-interest and broader community and environmental interests resulted in improved production technologies and by-product development that neutralized problems at the source. From the beginning in the second half of the nineteenth century these solutions relied on a broader division of labor and long-distance trade, both in terms of final markets[66] and of more distant location of processing operations. For instance, in the 1860s and 1870s refining activities relocated from production sites in western Pennsylvania to larger metropolitan centers such as Pittsburgh, Cleveland, Philadelphia, and New York. The rationale behind these moves included the high cost of refining near pumping sites because of heavy charges there for shipping machinery and inputs (e.g., sulfuric acid), along with the high value of local land. A location like Pittsburgh, by contrast, provided access to well-developed transportation networks both by land and by water, along with a cheap supply of coal, labor, and other inputs.[67]

Business historians Ralph and Muriel Hidy explain the location of refineries from the 1860s to the turn of the twentieth century: "Proximity to producing wells was a factor but not the primary one. Transportation costs on finished products to markets as well as on supplies to refineries were important considerations. The location of markets, therefore, assumed primary significance." Key factors thus included the "availability of fuel and labor, ground space for expansion of the plant, water supply, taxes, state and municipal regulatory provisions, and available fire protection."[68] Another consideration for large and expensive operations was keeping an eye on "continuous changes in sources of supply and rapid exhaustion of producing areas" that favored the potential staying powers of oil fields and room for expansion of existing operations. In time, too, the emergence of significant new production areas near growing markets pulled some refining operations toward them. In the end, if there were "two chief determinants in selecting the exact spot for a refinery, they were the location of the market and available facilities for transporting finished products."[69]

Needless to say, the location of profitable refineries since these early days has remained dependent on the access to feedstocks and the ability to distribute refined products. As the Deutsche Bank research analyst Lucas Herrmann and his coauthors observed, apart from configuration and crude supply, "location is probably the third most important determinant of a refinery's ability to capture profit" because it ultimately determines likely competition and affects crude freight and product dispatch costs, as well as other factors such as labor and environmental regulation compliance costs.[70] In terms of geography and logistics, petroleum refineries have often been classified on the basis of their proximity to resources, markets, or transit points, such as, for instance,

- *Resource refineries*. Located near and supplied from local deposits, resource refineries deliver products locally and elsewhere. Export-oriented refineries typically face higher construction and refined product transportation costs than other refineries.

- *Seaboard export refineries.* Supplied from local or distant oilfields, seaboard export refineries deliver refined products to local and distant markets. Easy access to water and shipping routes minimizes transport and logistical costs, in terms of both imports and exports.

- *Market refineries.* Market refineries are located in regions without significant oil resources but with important local markets. They are supplied from distant crude oil deposits and have little incentive or capability to sell beyond the local market.[71]

Another factor that historically has explained the further development or persistence of some refineries was the building of adjacent and symbiotic petrochemical complexes that depend on large and constant supplies of bulky refinery materials that do not travel well (e.g., naphtha), but that could also profitably supply various essential inputs to refining operations.

Refinery complexity and the state of transportation at any given time have thus typically trumped geographical proximity to production sites. In other words, the fact that a particular crude oil was (or is) pumped out of the ground in relatively close proximity to a refinery might be of no practical consequence if

- the crude oil cannot be delivered to the refinery because of a lack of infrastructure connecting it to the oil wells,
- the refinery is not equipped to handle the type of crude oil produced, or
- the refinery cannot profitably deliver its refined products to suitable markets.

Refinery location dynamics changed over time as a result of new supply sources, improved refining and transportation technologies (that often mandated increased economies of scale), and growing or declining markets. For instance, in post–World War II Europe, seaports were the logical locations for refineries that depended on overseas crude oil, and from there refined products could be conveniently conveyed to inland customers. As inland markets grew and became more diversified, however, crude oil was increasingly moved by pipelines to new inland refineries while coastal refineries became more oriented toward local and spot markets (to balance overall supply and demand in other regions).[72] The same processes have since been playing out on a worldwide scale.

The locational dynamics of refining operations have also shown a few recurring patterns over time. For instance, because moving crude oil is always cheaper than moving a similar volume of different refined products,[73] there is (1) a more direct correlation between the refinery-and places where refined goods are sold to consumers in terms of transportation costs than between oil wells and refineries, and (2) a more limited area for refined products than for crude oils. Other considerations, however, such as the fact that the molecular composition of available crude oils often makes it economically impossible to perfectly match refinery output and consumer demand, will always create the need for inter-regional trade in refined petroleum products.

Another pattern in the locational dynamics of refining is the relaxation of locational constraints on the production of niche specialty products. Finally, any technological advance or infrastructure development that makes it more convenient or cheaper to ship refined petroleum products and refining operation inputs relaxes the geographical constraints that benefit market refineries. Although some landlocked refineries have fewer options, they can be very profitable because of (quasi)regional monopolies and sudden increases in local crude oil production that lower crude oil prices. When there are opportunities to take advantage of significant price differences between two or more markets (what economists refer to as *arbitrage*), creative businesspeople tend to find a way around logistical bottlenecks.

In the end, while some landlocked refineries that rely on fewer crude oil options have proved very profitable because of regional monopolies,[74] in most cases the most profitable—and therefore the more efficient—creation of refined petroleum products has long required long-distance trade in terms of both feedstock and refined products.

Cottonseed Markets and Processing Operations

As with petroleum refining, the development of by-products out of cottonseed involved numerous steps through which a complex raw material was broken down into components that were often (re)combined with other materials.[75] Because of the insufficient size of the market and the initial reluctance of domestic consumers, finding profitable markets for cottonseed further implied moving large quantities of material over long distances. The result, in the words of Wiliam C. Mullendore, an economics education promoter and president of California utility companies, was that "cottonseed must go through an unusually large number of steps in its passage from the producer to the consumer" and that "each step of manufacture and distribution represents a separate and distinct phase of the industry, in many instances as to both location and ownership."[76] Most of these steps or phases arose spontaneously in response to demand, opportunity, and profitability—as Ostromian ground-up interactions, not planned interventions.

From its early days, the cottonseed value chain was built around the interactions between numerous market actors that were often physically distant from each other:

- *Cotton producers* (both large ones that employed seasonal cotton pickers or tenant farmers and smaller, independent ones) produced field cotton and might have historically taken a portion of cottonseed back home. Producers had the option to use the seeds for planting, to sell them to an intermediary, or to sell them directly to a cottonseed oil mill.

- *Ginners* separated the fiber from the cottonseed. They acted as intermediaries between cotton producers and cottonseed processors.
- *Cottonseed buyers*, also known as dealers, brokers, or wholesalers, traded in cottonseed.
- *Crushing mill operators*, also known as cottonseed oil mill operators, collected and stored cottonseed, then produced crude cottonseed oil, protein-rich cottonseed cake and meal made from the pressed seed meat remaining in the press after oil extraction, and finally, empty seed hulls, as well as linters, the latter shaved from the seeds before the crushing process.
- *Refiners* refined the crude oil and often created other by-products in the process.
- *Manufacturers of cottonseed products* (including livestock feed and a wide range of consumer and industrial products) derived their products wholly or partly from the output of crushing mills and oil refineries.
- *Wholesalers* distributed finished products to consumer retail outlets or industrial customers.

From the origins of the American cottonseed value chain in the relatively small-scale shipments of pima cottonseed cake from the US Atlantic coast to British mills, distant markets proved extremely significant in its development. In an age when unpaved land transportation was at best slow, ineffective, and extremely costly— prominent American geographer George Deasy described the roads of the time as being "little more than trails"[77]—and warehouses lacked climate control machinery, much of the movement of cottonseed between plantations, ginning operations, and crushing operations first proceeded along waterways, especially around the Mississippi River and its navigable tributaries. It proved profitable only over relatively short distances because of the perishability of the cottonseed. Herman Nixon, an American political scientist, thus observed that, for a couple of decades after the industry took off, cottonseed-oil operations "hug[ged] the lines or points of water transportation" and the mills were concentrated in locations such as New Orleans; Memphis and Nashville, Tennessee; Natchez, Mississippi; Savannah, Georgia; and Charleston, South Carolina.[78]

Some early processing operations, however, were located far from cotton fields because their owners had first gained experience with crushing materials such as flaxseed (before gradually moving away from those materials), and had taken advantage of the transportation routes of the time. As the American educator and author Lynette Wrenn observed, "For several decades flax cultivation had been declining in the United States because of the widespread availability of inexpensive, easy-to-clean cotton textiles. Linseed-oil mills began to experiment with various oil seeds in their search for additional raw materials."[79] Once the extant oil mills could be retrofitted with efficient hullers to handle upland cottonseed, little stood in the way of retooling an oilseed mill for cottonseed processing. Notably, shifting processing from one type of seed to another took ample advantage of other industrial links established for the trade in flax, sesame, or castor bean oil, such as warehousing logistics, mill workforce contracting, by-product sales, and the all-important transportation to and from the mills via the waterways. For instance, in New Orleans the entrepreneur A. A. Maginnis switched from manufacturing linseed oil (from flaxseed) to cottonseed crushing in 1856, and a St. Louis producer of linseed and castor oils followed suit the next year. In short order, in western Ohio, the center of flax growing up to that time, linseed-oil manufacturers bought cottonseed and had it shipped up the Mississippi and Ohio Rivers in boats that had previously carried goods from Cincinnati to southern ports and plantations. Flaxseed mills in the areas of New York City and Providence, Rhode Island, also switched to cottonseed processing and oil refining at the time, because they could similarly benefit from reasonable freight rates on ships returning from southern ports. In time though, most northern operations either closed or relocated closer to their main input.[80]

As might be expected, much valuable material was left to rot far from navigable waterways. Henry Ogden thus insisted at the time that the claim that there was a large surplus of cottonseed available for processing was "true in the abstract [but] false in the concrete" because the surplus owed its existence to "the lack of transportation facilities and their unequal distribution over the broad area of cotton culture." He was nonetheless confident that "sooner or later this difficulty [would] be remedied [when] the South [became] netted and fretted with railroads" and that, when this was the case, "every tonne of surplus seed will be utilized and help to swell the tide of general prosperity."[81]

In time the railroad came and new cottonseed mills were built at railroad centers in order to gather cottonseed from a wider area served by the new communications network. Interestingly, Eugene Brooks, the director of the American Correspondents' School of Textiles, observed that in the early years of the industry "river cotton seed produces a little more oil than railroad seed, and there is often a corresponding difference in their values."[82] He added that while seed could be shipped by rail in bulk, bags were required for river shipping, which added to the costs of this mode of transportation.

The financial arrangements between cotton growers and ginners varied over time. Luther A. Ransom observed that in the early stages of the industry the mill operator would return "to the farmer the products of his seed, after deducting an amount sufficient to cover the cost of production and a reasonable profit."[83] Three decades later, Deasy wrote that cotton producers would usually get bales of lint back upon the completion of ginning operations to dispose of as they wished, while the bulk of the seed was bought on the premises by the ginner. Seed would then be purchased from many other small operations, gathered until one or more railroad cars were filled, and shipped in bulk to crushing mills. From there crude oil was barreled and shipped to more distant refineries.[84]

In the early twentieth century demand for cottonseed was sufficiently strong that, for a time, "many small mills [were] erected near the cotton fields, and these [got] their seed from the neighboring producers."[85] Ransom believed that smaller operations would prove viable on account of their proximity to cotton fields, which would allow them to market their seed locally. He wrote: "small mills, by reason of their nearness to the cotton fields, are able not only to market their seed without freights, but can dispose of their by-products at home, where they are needed by the farmers, stock-raisers and dairymen, at less expense than their larger competitors."

Advantages of proximity, Ransom thought, would "probably be sufficient to sustain these small mills in any competition coming from the larger interests."[86] This being said, many "operating refineries at centrally located points" controlled crude oil plants "located at the sources of the seed supply"[87] and, as American geographer Albert Carlson observed a few decades later, "like all new industries, cottonseed processing appears to have attracted many who expected to make quick fortunes" but ignored broader logistical and commercial considerations.[88] Over time a number of these small mills did not survive the consolidation that followed changing market demand, improved processing technologies, and the advent of trucking. By the early 1950s, all processing plants in the cotton belt states were distributed on the basis of the local volume of seed production. As a result of the low density, bulkiness, and perishability of cottonseed, it was then typically uneconomical to ship the seeds "for crushing purposes more than 200 to 300 miles as a maximum."[89]

If whole cottonseeds did not travel far, their by-products typically did. From an early date, cottonseed cake and meal not only found ready markets both in the South and in other sections of the United States, but also in much of Western Europe. Brooks thus observed that "much of the Chicago and Kansas City dressed beef shipped to all parts of America in refrigerator cars is simply concentrated cotton seed meal and hulls," while "many farmers near enough to the mills" fed cottonseed products to dairy cows near southern US cities.[90] Additionally, many early purchasers of cottonseed meal were located in northern European countries such as Denmark, England, and the Netherlands, where cheap American livestock feed (which included both cottonseed products and other cereals), combined with other animal feed from Eastern Europe, profoundly altered local agricultural production.

The case of Denmark is illustrative in this respect. In the second half of the nineteenth century, Danish farmers reacted to the availability of cheap animal feed imports by specializing in more lucrative livestock and dairy production. In the latter case, imported feedstuff proved absolutely essential to expanding production from summer to year-round dairying. Although limited quantities of American cottonseed meal had been bought before, Danish imports took off after a near failure of the Russian sunflower crop and a drastic reduction in the availability of sunflower cake. Ransom wrote admiringly that in the "famous Trifolium dairy in Denmark," at the time the largest in the world, "15,000 head of milk cows are fed on cottonseed meal."[91]

As a result of this open-trade policy, between the mid-1870s and the mid-1920s the Danish cattle herd doubled, the pig herd increased sixfold, and the chicken flock fourfold. By 1938, the British and German markets absorbed more than 76 percent of Danish exports (56 percent and 20 percent, respectively), then mostly consisting of butter, eggs, lard, and bacon. By embracing free trade, Danish farmers not only discovered "the fields of production in which they had the best opportunity to compete successfully with the farmers of the world, but they also were able to develop their own abilities, their agricultural production and marketing plants to almost functional perfection." According to agricultural economist Karl Brandt, the result was "a most remarkable degree of culture and the art of decent living."[92]

Foreign markets played an even more significant role than local markets described by Ransom in providing early outlets for cottonseed oil, because American consumers were originally not fond of vegetable oils. On the plus side, upland cottonseed oil had many advantages over alternatives (including pima cottonseed oil) available to European mills and consumers between the late 1800s and the early decades of the twentieth century. Furthermore, parts of Europe were then struggling with a shortage of vegetable oils and dairy products. As Ransom put it, a "butter shortage, almost a famine, already exists, and it is said that in some parts of Europe the people have not seen real butter in twenty years."[93] As a result, "during the early years of its manufacture cottonseed-oil was almost entirely exported to foreign countries, and export figures for those years represent very nearly the production of the country."[94] Despite increased home consumption of cottonseed products (more than made up for by the increased domestic supply), the offerings of the briskly developing cottonseed industry had, as Ransom observed, "invaded the great olive groves of Europe and Asia" and were then "competing on equal terms" with the production of the traditional vegetable oil industries of those regions.[95] Brooks added that the best grade of upland cottonseed oil, "summer yellow," was used in many European countries (at first mostly the Netherlands) in the preparation of dairy and lard substitutes and in salad oil, while the inferior grades were converted into soap (at first mostly in France).[96]

Although the evidence presented in this section gives but a glimpse of the rich history of the development of the cottonseed by-product industry, access to distant markets provided consumers in many locations with superior products that would not have been available to them if recovery links had remained local. Long-distance trade also made food production and provisioning more resilient overall and lessened the environmental impact of residual materials, which would otherwise have been destroyed locally.

Conclusion

Elinor Ostrom's case on behalf of spontaneous and bottom-up communal polycentric governance has been criticized on the grounds that it is not scalable. While her critics have a point, their (typical) fondness for more direct and comprehensive government interventions in more complex cases of environmental degradation can be challenged through a better understanding of the circumstances that historically led to the development of complex value chains created around the development of by-products out of once problematic production residuals. As has been discussed in this chapter, both petroleum and cotton residuals were once the sources of significant local pollution. To many of Ostrom's critics, the solutions to such problems would have revolved around the need for a top-down regulatory environment in which government legislation, monitoring, fines, and perhaps a cessation of operations would have played a significant role. An Ostromian analysis, on the other hand, would arguably start with an "it depends" perspective and proceed to characterize the entire action arena comprising the impacted commons and the human participants we have described. As the British political scientist Mark Pennington observed, "Ostrom's work represents a direct challenge to [traditional 'tragedy of the commons'] theorising because, while recognising that incentives matter, she argues that incentive structures are more varied and complex than conventional analysis assumes."[97] In the cases we presented, however, it seems doubtful that either the authoritarian "stick" of the government or the decentralist "local solutions for local people" would have delivered better results than the drive to innovate and to make better products—and profits—out of production residuals. While these developments were asynchronous, polycentric, and spontaneous, they nonetheless required a very large geographical scale—indeed, one that quickly became much larger than that covered by the American federal government—to allow the development of the required coordination of various economic actors that eventually made it possible to solve local problems.

What is important is that polycentric profit, creativity, and property rights–driven processes required free trade and global markets to satisfy complex production schedules and needs. While our case studies do differ from those covered by Ostrom, they bear out one of her big-picture insights into all aspects of the development of governance solutions: "'One-size-fits-all' policies are not effective."[98] On the basis of these historical studies of spontaneous yet profit-driven environmental commons remediation, the key policy recommendation should repeat Ostrom's warning that a dichotomous system is not sufficiently nuanced to provide optimal solutions for disposing of externalities. Ostrom described as dichotomous a system in which institutions and enforcement strategies are dictated either solely by the state (in the case of non-private goods such as security) or by the private sector (in the case of the market for private goods), and, according to her, such a division does not "adequately deal with the wide diversity of institutional arrangements that humans craft to govern, provide, and manage public goods and common-pool resources."[99] Analysts such as Milena Ristovska, who believe in a fundamental opposition between the search for increased profitability and environmental remediation, may find it both distasteful and odd that privately owned and privately managed businesses undertook the task of finding efficient ways to repurpose environmentally noxious waste.[100] But Ostrom's Institutional Analysis and Development framework provides one necessary—although in our opinion insufficient—perspective that allows us to tease out the value that these diverse participants, each in their own way, found in not having to dump an externality in sensitive local environments. In the end, oversimplifications about the result of traditional business incentives, along with a reliance on poorly fitting assumptions, have the potential to result in top-down political approaches that are likely to prevent the spontaneous development of economically, environmentally, and socially beneficial solutions.

Contributors

Shane Day, Author
Shane Day is an Assistant Professor in the Mark O. Hatfield School of Government at Portland State University, and Affiliated Faculty in the Ostrom Workshop at Indiana University – Bloomington. His research interests include comparative indigenous group policy; environmental policy and natural resource management, particularly in the areas of fisheries, forestry, water, and protected lands; economic development; international relations; agricultural policy; comparative federalism and intergovernmental relations; and collaborative policy.

Pierre Desrochers, Author
Pierre Desrochers is an Associate Professor of Geography at the University of Toronto Mississauga. His main research interests are economic development and energy, environmental and food policy. He has published or co-authored three books, including the 2018-19 Donner Prize short-listed *Population Bombed! Exploding the Link Between Overpopulation and Climate Change*, over fifty academic articles and over 200 columns on these and other topics. Professor Desrochers is affiliated with numerous think tanks in Canada,

the United States, and France. His work has been awarded or has been short-listed for a variety of academic and policy prizes.

Eric C. Edwards, Author

Dr. Edwards is an assistant professor in the Department of Agricultural and Resource Economics at North Carolina State University. His work is focused on the economics of water resource management, and the management of natural resources generally. Applications in the water realm have included conservation, markets, groundwater management, urban water pricing, climate change, irrigation, and ecosystem services. His research has been funded by the USDA and National Science Foundation and included interdisciplinary collaborations with scientists, engineers, and legal scholars. His work has been conducted in a number of locations including California, Kansas, Alaska, Chile, and Australia. He holds a Ph.D. in economics and environmental science from the University of California, Santa Barbara, as well as an MBA from the University of Rochester and a B.S. in mathematics from the University of Idaho.

Peter J. Hill, Author

Peter J. Hill is professor of economics emeritus at Wheaton College in Wheaton, Illinois, and a senior fellow at the Property and Environment Research Center (PERC) in Bozeman, Montana, where he currently resides. He is the co-author of several books, including *Growth and Welfare in the American Past* with Terry L. Anderson and Douglass North, *The Birth of a Transfer Society* with Terry Anderson, and *The Not So Wild, Wild West: Property Rights on the Frontier* with Terry Anderson. He has also authored numerous articles on the theory of property rights and institutional change and has edited six books on environmental economics. His undergraduate degree is from Montana State and his Ph.D. from the University of Chicago. P.J. grew up on a cattle ranch in eastern

Montana, which he operated with his family until 1992, when he sold the ranch and bought a smaller ranch in western Montana, which he operated until 2012.

Megan E. Jenkins, Co-Editor

Megan E. Jenkins is the Research Director at the Center for Growth and Opportunity where she manages the Center's portfolio of policy-relevant research while ensuring student fellows receive quality mentorship and hands-on research experience. Megan's research on environmental policy explores how incentives and bottom-up approaches can help achieve better conservation outcomes. Her research and opinion commentary have been published in state and national outlets including USA Today, The Salt Lake Tribune, and The Hill. Megan received a master's degree in economics from Utah State University in 2016

Bryan Leonard, Author

Bryan Leonard's work focuses on the design of institutions to resolve collective action problems associated with sustainable resource management, focusing on land, water, and other resources in the Western United States. He uses a combination of formal theory, historical research, and econometric methods to study the evolution and performance of institutions that are crafted to solve resource challenges at a particular point in time. By studying the contemporary legacy of past policies, his research helps provide context for modern policy challenges while also informing the design of more sustainable institutions for the future. Bryan holds a Ph.D. in Economics from the University of California-Santa Barbara.

Jordan K. Lofthouse, Author

Jordan Lofthouse received a Ph.D. in economics from George Mason University in spring 2020. He also received the William P. Snavely Award for Outstanding Achievement in Graduate Studies in Economics. While working on his doctorate degree, Jordan was a Ph.D. Fellow with the Mercatus Center at George Mason University and a Graduate Fellow with the F.A. Hayek Program for Advanced Study in Philosophy, Politics, and Economics. Prior to his doctoral program, he received a B.S. in geography and an M.S. in economics, both from Utah State University. His primary research areas are environmental economics and Native American economic development.

Shawn Regan, Author
Shawn Regan is the vice president of research at the Property and Environment Research Center (PERC). He is also the executive editor of *PERC Reports*, the magazine for free-market environmentalism. His writing has appeared in the *Wall Street Journal*, *Los Angeles Times*, *Outside*, *High Country News*, *National Review*, *Reason*, and *Regulation*, and his research has been published in academic journals such as the *Natural Resources Journal*, *Journal of Energy Law & Resources*, and *Breakthrough Journal*. He holds an M.S. in Applied Economics from Montana State University and degrees in economics and environmental science from Berry College. He is also a former backcountry ranger for the National Park Service.

Randy T Simmons, Co-Editor
Randy T. Simmons received his Ph.D. from the University of Oregon in 1980. He is Professor of Political Economy and Director of the Institute of Political Economy in the department of economics and finance at Utah State University. Previously he was head of the department of political science at Utah State University. Simmons offers a unique view of the political economy having been trained in political economy and having spent ten years in city government, four of them as mayor. Simmons is a Senior Fellow

at the Property and Environment Research Center as well as the Independent Institute. His book, *Beyond Politics: The Roots of Government Failure* (2nd edition, 2012) is a primer on public choice theory and practice. His 2012 co-authored book *Green vs. Green* examines how local green activists use green ordinances to stop green energy development—a kind of green government failure. His co-edited book *Aquanomics: Water Markets and the Environment* (2011) shows how water markets are far superior to government water regulations and controls. His most recent book is *Nature Unbound: Bureaucracy vs. the Environment* (2016), an analysis of the politics of ecology and the ecology of politics.

Joanna Szurmak, Author

Joanna Szurmak is a Ph.D. candidate in the Science and Technology Studies program at York University in Toronto and a research librarian at the University of Toronto Mississauga. She has earned graduate degrees in electrical engineering and information studies from the University of Toronto and has worked in research labs, the telecommunications industry, and university libraries in the United States and Canada. Szurmak is the co-author of the 2018-2019 Donner Prize short-listed book *Population Bombed! Exploding the Link Between Overpopulation and Climate Change* (2018) and has authored academic and popular publications.

Camille H. Wardle, Co-Editor

Camille Wardle holds a master's degree in economics from Utah State University. Her past work includes research on endangered species, wildfire policy, renewable energy, and federal revenue sharing programs. She is interested in the practical implications of Elinor Ostrom's work and loves seeing textbook economics in the real world. Camille is also a former graduate research fellow at the Center for Growth and Opportunity at Utah State University.

Endnotes

INTRODUCTION

1   Ostrom, Elinor, "Beyond Markets and States. Polycentric governance of complex economic systems," *American Economic Review* 100, no. 3 (June 2010): 643.

2   Elinor Ostrom, "Beyond Markets and States: Polycentric Governance of Complex Economic Systems," *American Economic Review* 100, no. 3 (June 2010): p. 641. (This piece was originally presented as Ostrom's Nobel prize lecture at Stockholm University on December 8, 2009.)

3   Garrett Hardin, "The Tragedy of the Commons," *Science* 162, no. 3859 (December 1968): 1244.

4   Ostrom, "Beyond Markets and States," p. 659.

5   Ostrom, "Beyond Markets and States," p. 664.

6   Ostrom, "Beyond Markets and States," p. 665.

CHAPTER 1. "RESOURCE GOVERNANCE IN THE AMERICAN WEST: INSTITUTIONS, INFORMATION, AND INCENTIVES"

1   See Carol Hardy Vincent, Laura A. Hanson, and Carla N. Argueta, "Federal Land Ownership: Overview and Data," Congressional Research Service, March 3, 2017, https://fas.org/sgp/crs/misc/R42346.pdf. The eleven coterminous western states are Arizona, California, Colorado, Idaho, Montana, Nevada, New Mexico, Oregon, Utah, Washington, and Wyoming.

2   Elinor Ostrom, *Governing the Commons: The Evolution of Institutions for Collective Action* (Cambridge: Cambridge University Press, 1990), 14. We are relying on Ostrom's work for our theoretical model. Our model could be expanded using the work of political scientists on collaborative governance, but owing to space constraints, we are not referencing any of that research. For examples of that work, see Chris Ansell and Alison Gash, "Collaborative Governance in Theory and Practice," *Journal of Public Administration Research and Theory* 18, no. 4 (2007): 543–71; Kirk Emerson and Tina Nabatchi, *Collaborative Governance Regimes* (Washington, DC: Georgetown University Press, 2015).

3   Ostrom, *Governing the Commons*, 14.

4   Ostrom, 14.

5   Ashutosh Sarker and William Blomquist explain that Ostrom's work was not anti-statist or anti-privatization, noting that "Ostrom was not an advocate against statist solutions or privatization provisions, nor was she even in blind favor of community-based management; instead, she was against any of these responses being viewed as a panacea." Moreover, they explain, "Ostrom also emphasized that the appearance of some successful cases of user self-governance of the commons should not be misunderstood as demonstrating that user self-governance is a necessary condition for commons management." Ashutosh Sarker and William Blomquist, "Addressing Misperceptions of Governing the Commons," *Journal of Institutional Economics* 15, no. 2 (2019): 281-301.

6   Elinor Ostrom, "Beyond Markets and States: Polycentric Governance of Complex Economic Systems," *American Economic Review* 100, no. 3 (June 2010): 648.

7   The *Historical Atlas of the American West* (Beck and Haase 1989) uses the 100th meridian as the beginning of the West. Some authors, notably Walter Prescott Webb, instead use the 98th meridian. Walter Prescott Webb, *The Great Plains* (1931; repr., New York: Ginn, 1971). For the purposes of this chapter, we follow the most generally accepted convention and use the 100th meridian.

8   David J. Wishart, ed., *Encyclopedia of the Great Plains* (Lincoln: University of Nebraska Press, 2004), David A. Wilhite, Drought, 852.

9   Edward R. Cook et al., "North American Drought: Reconstructions, Causes, and Consequences," *Earth-Science Reviews* 81 (2007): 93–134; Glen M. MacDonald, "Severe and Sustained Drought in Southern California and the West: Present Conditions and Insights from

the Past on Causes and Impacts," *Quaternary International* 173–74 (2007): 87–100.

10   Gary D. Libecap and Zeynep Kocabiyik Hansen, "'Rain Follows the Plow' and Dryfarming Doctrine: The Climate Information Problem and Homestead Failure in the Upper Great Plains, 1890–1925," *Journal of Economic History* 62, no. 1 (2002): 86-120.

11   Beck and Haase, *Historical Atlas*, 6.

12   Two major tragedies occurred as settlers tried to cross the mountain ranges. In 1846, the Donner party attempted to cross the Sierra Nevada mountains too late in the year and was trapped by heavy snowfall. Of the eighty-seven members of the party, only forty-eight survived, and it seems cannibalism aided the survivors. Another group of travelers argued over the correct trails to follow as they traveled from Utah to California in 1849. The rugged trail they chose limited the party to six miles of travel over ninety-seven days, resulting in substantial loss of life and property. Beck and Haase, 33.

13   Webb, *Great Plains*, 8–9. Italics in original.

14   For a detailed description of the Progressive Era origins of natural resource governance that led to centralized control of western resources, see Robert H. Nelson, *Public Lands and Private Rights: The Failure of Scientific Management* (Lanah, MD: Rowman & Littlefield, 1995).

15   Ostrom, *Governing the Commons*; Ostrom, "Beyond Markets and States." See also Elinor Ostrom, Roy Gardner, and James Walker, *Rules, Games, and Common Pool Resources* (Ann Arbor: University of Michigan Press, 1994).

16   Included in our concept of resources is one's own abilities and personality.

17   For a more complete discussion of the processes and levels of decision making, see Thomas Sowell, *Knowledge and Decisions* (New York: Basic Books, 1980), chapter 2.

18   Ostrom, *Governing the Commons*, 88–102.

19   Friedrich A. Hayek, "The Use of Knowledge in Society," *American Economic Review* 35, no. 4 (September 1945): 521.

20   Nelson, *Public Lands and Private Rights*.

21   Robert Nelson notes that many aspects of federal land management in the West in effect function as "a virtual planning and zoning board" for large areas of the rural West, a function that in other parts of the United States is typically left to local governments and municipalities. Nelson, *Public Lands and Private Rights*, 304.

22 Hayek, "Use of Knowledge in Society," 519.

23 Wishart, *Encyclopedia of the Great Plains*, M. Jean Ferrill, Rainfall Follows the Plow, 395.

24 Wishart, 395.

25 Wishart, 398.

26 Libecap and Hansen, "Rain Follows the Plow."

27 Walter Prescott Webb, *The Great Frontier* (1951; repr., Lincoln: University of Nebraska Press, 1986), 239.

28 Webb, *Great Frontier*, 239.

29 Gary D. Libecap, "The Assignment of Property Rights on the Western Frontier: Lessons for Contemporary Environmental and Resource Policy," *Journal of Economic History* 67, no. 2 (2007): 259.

30 Paul W. Gates, *History of Public Land Law Development* (Washington, DC: Public Land Law Review Commission, 1968), 64–65.

31 Robert C. Ellickson, "Property in Land," *Yale Law Journal* 102 (1993): 1315–400.

32 For a discussion of land claims clubs as local "Ostrom-type organizations," see Ilia Murtazashvili, *The Political Economy of the American Frontier* (New York: Cambridge University Press, 2013).

33 The act also required a $10 entry fee. If a homesteader resided on the plot for six months, the land could be purchased for $1.25 per acre.

34 For a more complete discussion of rent dissipation through early entry, see Terry L. Anderson and Peter J. Hill, "Privatizing the Commons: An Improvement?," *Southern Economic Journal* 50, no. 2 (1983): 438–49; Terry L. Anderson and Peter J. Hill, "The Race for Property Rights," *Journal of Law and Economics* 33 (April 1990): 177–97.

35 Dan Fulton, *Failure on the Plains: A Rancher's View of the Public Lands Problem* (Bozeman: Big Sky Books, Montana State University, 1982), 66.

36 Gates, *History of Public Land Law Development*, 505.

37 Gates, 502.

38 Zeynep Kocabiyik Hansen and Gary D. Libecap, "Small Farms, Externalities, and the Dust Bowl of the 1930s," *Journal of Political Economy* 112, no. 3 (2004): 665–94.

39 There were several modifications to the 1862 Homestead Act that allowed for larger claims under certain conditions, but the basic size did not change until 1909. In 1873, the Timber Culture Act gave

the settler an additional 160 acres if trees were planted on 40 acres. The 1877 Desert Land Act allowed a homestead of 640 acres if it was irrigated within three years. In 1878, the Timber and Stone Act allowed the sale of land in parcels of 160 acres or fewer for land that was unfit for farming but could be logged or mined.

40   Douglas Allen argues that homesteading was an efficient way for the federal government to enforce property rights to US public lands in the face of simultaneous, competing claims by American Indians, as a substitute for direct military force. Douglas W. Allen, "Homesteading and Property Rights; or, 'How the West Was Really Won,'" *Journal of Law and Economics* 24 (April 1991): 1-23.

41   Aldon S. Lang and Christopher Long, "Land Grants," Texas State Historical Association, last modified January 29, 2016, https://tsha-online.org/handbook/online/articles/mpl01.

42   The Texas state capital was financed by a syndicate that received three million acres in return for the construction. This was the foundation of the XIT Ranch. J. Evetts Haley, *The XIT Ranch of Texas* (1929; repr., Norman: University of Oklahoma Press, 1951), 5.

43   Nelson, *Public Lands and Private Rights*, 26.

44   Samuel P. Hays, *Conservation and the Gospel of Efficiency: The Progressive Conservation Movement, 1890–1920* (Cambridge, MA: Harvard University Press, 1959), 271.

45   See Nelson, *Public Lands and Private Rights*.

46   Alfred R. Golze, *Reclamation in the United States* (New York: McGraw Hill, 1952), 14. By 1950 there were 5.7 million acres irrigated by the government (primarily under the Bureau of Reclamation) and 19.0 million acres irrigated by private development. Golze, 4.

47   Richard W. Wahl, *Markets for Federal Water: Subsidies, Property Rights, and the Bureau of Reclamation* (Washington, DC: Resources for the Future, 1989), chapter 2.

48   Stephen P. Holland and Michael R. Moore, "Cadillac Desert Revisited: Property Rights, Public Policy, and Water-Resource Depletion," *Journal of Environmental Economics and Management* 46, no. 1 (July 2003): 131–55.

49   Quoted in Marc Reisner, *Cadillac Desert: The American West and Its Disappearing Water* (New York: Penguin, 1993), 292. Not only did reclamation projects not meet benefit-cost tests in terms of the value of the water delivered, there were also significant environmental damages. The Central Valley Project in California diverted the entire flow of the San Joaquin River for agriculture, with no thought given to changes in the ecosystem or in fish habitats. Harrison C.

Dunning, "Confronting the Environmental Legacy of Irrigated Agriculture in the West: The Case of the Central Valley Project," *Environmental Law* 23 (1993): 943–69.

50 The first economic use by Euro-Americans was fur trapping, but some of the earliest agriculture was established by wagon train settlers who went to the Willamette Valley. Terry L. Anderson and Peter J. Hill, *The Not So Wild, Wild West: Property Rights on the Frontier* (Stanford, CA: Stanford University Press, 2004).

51 Douglas W. Allen and Dean Lueck, *The Nature of the Farm: Contracts, Risk, and Organization in Agriculture*, (Cambridge, MA: MIT Press, 2002, 23–24). There were early attempts to apply the techniques of industrial production to farming. In the 1870s and 1880s, at the eastern edge of the Great Plains, entrepreneurs created vary large wheat farms of thirty thousand acres or more with one thousand workers. These farms used factory techniques, assigning a large group of workers to specific tasks under a system of hierarchical management. By 1910 such farms had ceased to exist, largely because of the problems of monitoring costs. Allen and Lueck, 185–87.

52 Allen and Lueck, 95–120.

53 Robert H. Fletcher, *Free Grass to Fences* (New York: University Publishers, 1960), 139.

54 Anderson and Hill, *Not So Wild, Wild West*, 181.

55 Bryan Leonard and Gary D. Libecap, "Collective Action by Contract: Prior Appropriation and the Development of Irrigation in the Western United States," *Journal of Law and Economics* 62, no. 1 (2019): 67–115.

56 Golze, *Reclamation in the United States*, 14.

57 Rodney T. Smith, "The Economic Determinants and Consequences of Private and Public Ownership of Local Irrigation Facilities," in *Water Rights: Scarce Resource Allocation, Bureaucracy, and the Environment*, ed. Terry L. Anderson (San Francisco: Pacific Institute for Public Policy Research, 1983).

58 Donald J. Pisani, *To Reclaim a Divided West: Water, Law, and Public Policy, 1848–1902* (Albuquerque: University of New Mexico Press, 1992), 102.

59 Edward Paul McDevitt, "The Evolution of Irrigation Districts in California: The Rise of the Irrigation District" (PhD diss., Department of Economics, University of California, Los Angeles, 1994), table 3.4.

60 Pisani, *To Reclaim a Divided West*, 103.

61 Wahl, *Markets for Federal Water*, 13.

62 Leonard J. Arrington, *Great Basin Kingdom: An Economic History of the Latter-Day Saints, 1830–1900* (Cambridge, MA: Harvard University Press, 1958), 53.

63 Anderson and Hill, *Not So Wild, Wild West*, 104–12.

64 Richard O. Zerbe Jr. and C. Leigh Anderson, "Culture and Fairness in the Development of Institutions in the California Gold Fields," *Journal of Economic History* 61, no. 1 (2001): 114–43.

65 More than six million acres had been illegally fenced. Proceedings were started to remove fences on two million acres and forced removal occurred on one million acres. Anderson and Hill, *Not So Wild, Wild West*, 170.

66 Anderson and Hill, 153–54.

67 Robert C. Ellickson, *Order without Law: How Neighbors Settle Disputes* (Cambridge, MA: Harvard University Press, 1991).

68 See Bryan Leonard and Shawn Regan, "Legal and Institutional Barriers to Establishing Non-use Rights to Natural Resources," *Natural Resources Journal* 59, no. 1 (2019): 135–79.

69 Douglas C. North, *Institutions, Institutional Change, and Economic Performance* (Cambridge: Cambridge University Press, 1990).

70 Ronald Coase, "The Problem of Social Cost," *Journal of Law and Economics* 3 (October 1960): 1–44.

71 Bryan Leonard, Christopher Costello, and Gary D. Libecap, "Expanding Water Markets in the Western United States: Barriers and Lessons from Other Natural Resource Markets," *Review of Environmental Economics and Policy* 13, no. 1 (2019): 43–61.

72 Terry L. Anderson and Ronald N. Johnson, "The Problem of Instream Flows," *Economic Inquiry* 24, no. 4 (1986): 535–54.

73 Brandon Scarborough, "Environmental Water Markets: Restoring Streams through Trade" (PERC Policy Series 46, Property and Environment Research Center, Bozeman, MT, 2010).

74 Zachary Donohew, "Property Rights and Western United States Water Markets," *Austrian Journal of Agricultural and Resource Economics* 53, no. 1 (2009): 85–103. Donahew also reports that between 1987 and 2007, agricultural-to-environment water trades composed 9 percent of all trades and 22 percent of annual flows.

75 Leonard and Regan, "Legal and Institutional Barriers."

76 See Leonard and Regan, "Legal and Institutional Barriers," 144–59; Shawn Regan, "Where the Buffalo Roam," *Breakthrough Journal*, no. 10 (Winter 2019): 66–82.

77 Under certain conditions, grazing allotments can be "rested" for short periods, but permittees generally cannot end grazing altogether on their permitted allotments. For a more detailed discussion of these relevant factors, see Leonard and Regan, "Legal and Institutional Barriers."

78 An armed standoff between the Bureau of Land Management and the Bundy family in Bunkerville, Nevada, during the spring of 2014 gained national media attention, as did a dramatic forty-one-day occupation of the Malheur National Wildlife Refuge in eastern Oregon in 2016 by a group protesting various aspects of federal land policy.

79 Shawn Regan, "Managing Conflicts over Western Rangelands" (PERC Policy Series 54, Property and Environment Research Center, Bozeman, MT, 2016).

80 One of us (Shawn Regan) explores several case studies of environmental groups seeking to acquire grazing permits for non-use conservation purposes and the ways in which federal rangeland policy prevents such exchanges, or significantly increases the costs of making them. Regan, "Managing Conflicts over Western Rangelands."

81 For a detailed exploration of the legal and institutional barriers to establishing conservation-oriented "non-use" rights to federal- and state-managed natural resources, including grazing, timber, energy, and water resources, see Leonard and Regan, "Legal and Institutional Barriers."

82 Leonard and Regan, "Legal and Institutional Barriers," 166–72.

83 Leonard and Regan, 159–66.

84 A recent example illustrates the challenges created by these policies. In 2016, environmental activist and author Terry Tempest Williams purchased a federal oil and gas lease in southern Utah but had no intention of developing the energy resources. The Bureau of Land Management subsequently canceled Williams's lease, arguing she was in violation of the bureau's lease requirements. Leonard and Regan, 162-163.

85 Interestingly, state policies governing natural resources on state-owned lands in the American West are much more likely to allow competing environmental, recreational, or other non-use demands to be resolved directly through the state land institutions. For instance, on state trust lands in the West, many states allow conservation groups to acquire leases on state grazing allotments for non-use conservation purposes. State trust lands also allow groups to bid for timber conservation licenses and other non-use rights on

state-owned lands, allowing demands for environmental or ameni-ty resources to be accommodated directly through the exchange of use rights. See Holly Fretwell, "Trust in Reform: Trust Alternatives for Range Resource Allocation," in *Ranching Realities in the 21st Century*, ed. Holly Fretwell and Mark Milke (Vancouver, British Columbia: Fraser Institute, 2015); Hannah Downey, Holly Fretwell, and Shawn Regan, "Access Divided: State and Federal Recreation Management in the West" (PERC Public Lands Report, Property and Environment Research Center, Bozeman, MT, April 2016).

CHAPTER 2. "SELF-GOVERNANCE, POLYCENTRICITY, AND ENVIRONMENTAL POLICY"

1   Vincent Ostrom, "A Conceptual-Computational Logic for Federal Systems of Governance," in *Constitutional Design and Power-Sharing in the Post-modern Epoch*, ed. Daniel J. Elazar (Lanham, MD: University Press of America, 1979); Elinor Ostrom, "Beyond Markets and States: Polycentric Governance of Complex Economic Systems," *American Economic Review* 100, no. 3 (June 2010): 641–72.

2   Vincent Ostrom, *The Meaning of American Federalism* (San Francisco: ICS Press, 1991), Chapter 9; Vincent Ostrom, *The Meaning of Democracy and the Vulnerability of Democracies: A Response to Tocqueville's Challenge* (Ann Arbor: University of Michigan Press, 1997).

3   Elinor Ostrom, *Governing the Commons: The Evolution of Institutions for Collective Action* (Cambridge: Cambridge University Press, 1990).

4   V. Ostrom, "Conceptual-Computational Logic."

5   Paul Dragos Aligica, *Public Entrepreneurship, Citizenship, and Self-Governance*, Cambridge Studies in Economics, Choice, and Society (Cambridge: Cambridge University Press, 2019), 167–87.

6   E. Ostrom, *Governing the Commons*.

7   E. Ostrom, "Beyond Markets and States."

8   Elinor Ostrom and Vincent Ostrom, "The Quest for Meaning in Public Choice," *American Journal of Economics and Sociology* 63, no. 1 (January 2004): 105–47.

9   Alexis de Tocqueville, *Democracy in America* (New York: G. Dearborn, 1838); Robert L. Bish, "Vincent Ostrom's Contributions to Political Economy," *Publius: The Journal of Federalism* 44, no. 2 (April 2014): 227–48.

10 E. Ostrom and V. Ostrom, "The Quest for Meaning in Public Choice," 111.

11 E. Ostrom, interview by Paul Dragos Aligica, *Rethinking Institutional Analysis: Interviews with Vincent and Elinor Ostrom with Introductions*

by Vernon Smith and Gordon Tullock (Washington, DC: Mercatus Center at George Mason University, 2003), 14.

12 V. Ostrom, *Meaning of Democracy*, 4.

13 Aligica, *Public Entrepreneurship*, 5–11.

14 Aligica, 6.

15 Aligica, 7.

16 V. Ostrom, *Meaning of Democracy*, 271.

17 Aligica, *Public Entrepreneurship*, 6.

18 Aligica, 6.

19 E. Ostrom, *Governing the Commons*; Vincent Ostrom, *The Intellectual Crisis in American Public Administration* (University: University of Alabama Press, 1973); V. Ostrom, *Meaning of Democracy*; Filippo Sabetti and Paul Dragos Aligica, eds., *Choice, Rules and Collective Action: The Ostroms on the Study of Institutions and Governance* (Colchester, UK: ECPR Press, 2014); Theo Toonen, "Resilience in Public Administration: The Work of Elinor and Vincent Ostrom from a Public Administration Perspective," *Public Administration Review* 70, no. 2 (March 2010): 193–202.

20 Garrett Hardin, "The Tragedy of the Commons," *Science* 162, no. 3859 (December 1968): 1243–48.

21 Harry N. Scheiber, "The 'Commons' Discourse on Marine Fisheries Resources: Another Antecedent to Hardin's 'Tragedy,'" *Theoretical Inquiries in Law* 19, no. 2 (2018): 489–505.

22 E. Ostrom, *Governing the Commons*, 9.

23 Vincent Ostrom, interview by Paul Dragos Aligica, *Rethinking Institutional Analysis: Interviews with Vincent and Elinor Ostrom with Introductions by Vernon Smith and Gordon Tullock* (Washington, DC: Mercatus Center at George Mason University, 2003), 6.

24 Elinor Ostrom, "A Behavioral Approach to the Rational Choice Theory of Collective Action: Presidential Address, American Political Science Association, 1997," *American Political Science Review* 92, no. 1 (March 1998): 1–22; Aligica, *Public Entrepreneurship*.

25 E. Ostrom, *Governing the Commons*; Michael Cox, Gwen Arnold, and Sergio Villamayor Tomás, "A Review of Design Principles for Community-Based Natural Resource Management," *Ecology and Society* 15, no. 4 (December 2010).

26 Vlad Tarko, *Elinor Ostrom: An Intellectual Biography* (New York: Rowman and Littlefield, 2017), 16.

27 Elinor Ostrom, *Understanding Institutional Diversity* (Princeton, NJ: Princeton University Press, 2005), 256.

28 E. Ostrom, *Understanding Institutional Diversity*, 284.

29 Aligica, *Public Entrepreneurship*, 25–27.

30 Vincent Ostrom, "Epistemic Choice and Public Choice," *Public Choice* 77, no. 1 (September 1993): 163–76.

31 E. Ostrom, "Beyond Markets and States," 665.

32 Richard E. Wagner, "Self-governance, polycentrism, and federalism: recurring themes in Vincent Ostrom's scholarly oeuvre," *Journal of Economic Behavior & Organization* 57, no. 2 (June 2005): 173-188.

33 Aligica, *Public Entrepreneurship*, 21–39.

34 Tarko, *Elinor Ostrom*, 118.

35 Vincent Ostrom and Elinor Ostrom, "Public Choice: A Different Approach to the Study of Public Administration," *Public Administration Review* 31, no. 2 (1971): 203-16.

36 Vincent Ostrom, Charles M. Tiebout, and Robert Warren, "The Organization of Government in Metropolitan Areas: A Theoretical Inquiry," *The American Political Science Review* 55, no. 4 (December 1961): 831–42.

37 Charles M. Tiebout, "A Pure Theory of Local Expenditures," *Journal of Political Economy* 64, no. 5 (October 1956): 416–24.

38 Aligica, *Public Entrepreneurship*, 25–32.

39 Ostrom, Tiebout, and Warren, "Organization of Government."

40 H. Spencer Banzhaf and Randall P. Walsh, "Do People Vote with Their Feet? An Empirical Test of Tiebout's Mechanism," *American Economic Review* 98, no. 3 (2008): 843–63.

41 Ostrom, Tiebout, and Warren, "Organization of Government."

42 Elinor Ostrom, *The Delivery of Urban Services: Outcomes of Change* (Beverly Hills, CA: Sage, 1976).

43 Ostrom, Tiebout, and Warren, "Organization of Government"; Paul Dragos Aligica, Peter J. Boettke, and Vlad Tarko, *Public Governance and the Classical-Liberal Perspective* (Oxford: Oxford University Press, 2019), 161–63.

44 Jason A. Robison and Lawrence J. MacDonnell, "Arizona v. California & the Colorado River Compact: Fifty Years Ago, Fifty Years Ahead," *Arizona Journal of Environmental Law & Policy* 4, no. 2 (March 2014): 130–59.

45 Ostrom, Tiebout, and Warren, "Organization of Government."

46 V. Ostrom, "Polycentricity."

47 Friedrich A. Hayek, "The Use of Knowledge in Society," *American Economic Review* 35, no. 4 (September 1945): 519–30.

48 Paul Dragos Aligica and Vlad Tarko, "Polycentricity: From Polanyi to Ostrom, and Beyond," *Governance* 25, no. 2 (April 2012): 237–62.

49 Elinor Ostrom, "A Diagnostic Approach for Going beyond Panaceas," *Proceedings of the National Academy of Sciences* 104, no. 39 (September 2007): 15181–87; Elinor Ostrom and Michael Cox, "Moving beyond Panaceas: A Multi-tiered Diagnostic Approach for Social-Ecological Analysis," *Environmental Conservation* 37, no. 4 (December 2010): 451–63; Elinor Ostrom, Marco A. Janssen, and John M. Anderies, "Going beyond Panaceas," *Proceedings of the National Academy of Sciences* 104, no. 39 (September 2007): 15176–78.

50 T. H. Morrison et al., "The Black Box of Power in Polycentric Environmental Governance," *Global Environmental Change* 57 (July 2019): 1–8.

51 Elinor Ostrom, "Polycentric Systems for Coping with Collective Action and Global Environmental Change," *Global Environmental Change* 20, no. 4 (2010): 552.

52 "Greater Sage-Grouse—Species Information," US Fish and Wildlife Service, last modified November 28, 2017, https://www.fws.gov/greatersagegrouse/speciesinfo.php.

53 US Fish and Wildlife Service Endangered Species Program, "Listing a Species as a Threatened or Endangered Species: Section 4 of the Endangered Species Act," August 2016, https://www.fws.gov/endangered/esa-library/pdf/listing.pdf.

54 US Fish and Wildlife Service Endangered Species Program, "Critical Habitat: What Is It?," March 2017, https://www.fws.gov/endangered/esa-library/pdf/critical_habitat.pdf.

55 US Fish and Wildlife Service Endangered Species Program, "Habitat Conservation Plans: Section 10 of the Endangered Species Act," December 2005, https://www.fws.gov/endangered/esa-library/pdf/HCP_Incidental_Take.pdf; US Fish and Wildlife Service Endangered Species Program, "Endangered Species Act | A History of the Endangered Species Act of 1973 | 1982 ESA Amendment," December 2018, https://www.fws.gov/endangered/laws-policies/esa-1982.html; Christopher S. Mills, "Incentives and the ESA: Can Conservation Banking Live Up to Potential?," *Duke Environmental Law & Policy Forum* 14, no. 2 (Spring 2004): 523–62.

56 Endangered and Threatened Wildlife and Plants; 12-Month Finding for Petitions to List the Greater Sage-Grouse as Threatened or Endangered, 70 Fed. Reg. 2244 (January 12, 2005); US Fish and Wildlife Service, "Summary of Sage-Grouse Listing Petitions Submitted to the U.S. Fish and Wildlife Service (USFWS) (as of August 27,

2008)," https://www.fws.gov/nevada/nv_species/documents/
sage_grouse/SG_petition_sum_8_27_2008.pdf.

57 Endangered and Threatened Wildlife and Plants; 12-Month Findings for Petitions to List the Greater Sage-Grouse (*Centrocercus
urophasianus*) as Threatened or Endangered, 75 Fed. Reg. 13909–
4014 (March 23, 2010); US Fish and Wildlife Service, "Summary
of Sage-Grouse Listing Petitions"; Western Watersheds Project v.
United States Forest Service, No. CV-06-277-E-BLW (US District
Court for the District of Idaho 2007).

58 75 Fed. Reg. 13909–4014.

59 US Fish and Wildlife Service Ecological Services Program, "Candidate Species: Section 4 of the Endangered Species Act," October
2017, https://www.fws.gov/endangered/esa-library/pdf/candi-
date_species.pdf.

60 State of Wyoming Executive Department Exec. Order No. 2015-4,
https://wgfd.wyo.gov/WGFD/media/content/PDF/Habitat/
Sage%20Grouse/SG_Executive_Order.pdf; State of Idaho Executive
Department Exec. Order No. 2012-02, https://idfg.idaho.gov/old-
web/docs/wildlife/SGtaskForce/execOrder.pdf; State of Montana
Office of the Governor Exec. Order No. 12-2015, https://governor.
mt.gov/Portals/16/docs/2015EOs/EO_12_2015_Sage_Grouse.pdf.

61 Reid Wilson, "Western States Worry Decision on Bird's Fate Could
Cost Billions in Development," *Washington Post*, May 11, 2014.

62 "Audubon and the Greater Sage-Grouse: A History," in "Greater Sage-Grouse: One Bird, 11 States, 165 Million Acres—How
Audubon Helped Protect the Sagebrush's Most Iconic Resident,"
Audubon website (National Audubon Society), accessed December
2, 2019, https://www.audubon.org/conservation/issues/greater-
sage-grouse; "Greater Sage-Grouse Decision Benefits Elk, Wildlife
Habitat, Sportsmen," Rocky Mountain Elk Foundation, September
23, 2015, http://www.rmef.org/NewsandMedia/PressRoom/
NewsReleases/GreaterSageGrouseDecision2015.aspx.

63 US Department of the Interior, "Bureau of Land Management
National Sage-Grouse Habitat Conservation Strategy," November
2004; Scott Streater, "Western Governors Fret as Zinke Ponders Review of Grouse Plans," *Energy & Environment News*, May 31, 2017;
US Forest Service, "Common Questions & Answers BLM-USFS
Greater Sage-Grouse Conservation Plans," September 22, 2015,
https://www.fs.usda.gov/sites/default/files/common-qa-greater-
sage-grouse.pdf.

64 US Department of the Interior, "Historic Conservation Campaign
Protects Greater Sage-Grouse," press release, September 22, 2015,

https://www.doi.gov/pressreleases/historic-conservation-campaign-protects-greater-sage-grouse.

65 US Fish and Wildlife Service Ecological Services Program, "Candidate Conservation Agreements," October 2017, https://www.fws.gov/endangered/esa-library/pdf/CCAs.pdf.

66 Draft Candidate Conservation Agreement with Assurances, Receipt of Application for an Enhancement of Survival Permit for the Greater Sage-Grouse on Oregon Department of State Lands, and Draft Environmental Assessment, 80 Fed. Reg. 9475 (February 23, 2015); Draft Candidate Conservation Agreement with Assurances, Receipt of Application for an Enhancement of Survival Permit for the Greater Sage-Grouse on Oregon Department of State Lands, and Draft Environmental Assessment; Reopening of Comment Period, 80 Fed. Reg. 19341 (April 10, 2015); Endangered and Threatened Wildlife and Plants; Enhancement of Survival Permit Application; Draft Greater Sage-Grouse Umbrella Candidate Conservation Agreement with Assurances for Wyoming Ranch Management, and Environmental Assessment, 78 Fed. Reg. 9066 (February 7, 2013); Endangered and Threatened Wildlife and Plants; Permit Application; Greater Sage-Grouse; Washington, Adams, Gem, and Payette Counties, Idaho, 74 Fed. Reg. 36502 (July 23, 2009); Leanne Correll, "A Landowner's Approach to Greater Sage-Grouse Umbrella CCAA for Wyoming Ranch Management," Wyoming Stock Growers Association, 2014; Ann Haas, "Farmers and Ranchers in Eastern Oregon Sign On as Partners to Conserve the Sage-Grouse, a Candidate Species," US Fish and Wildlife Service, last updated June 17, 2014, https://www.fws.gov/endangered/map/ESA_success_stories/OR/OR_story4/index.html.

67 US Fish and Wildlife Service, "Frequently Asked Questions: Greater Sage-Grouse Status Review," September 22, 2015, https://www.fs.fed.us/sites/default/files/fws-faqs-greater-sage-grouse.pdf.

68 US Department of the Interior, Bureau of Land Management, Oregon State Office, memorandum, "Greater Sage-Grouse Programmatic Candidate Conservation Agreement for Rangeland Management on Bureau of Land Management Lands in Oregon," OR-IM-2013-034, May 30, 2013, https://www.blm.gov/policy/or-im-2013-034; US Department of the Interior, Bureau of Land Management, Oregon/Washington State Office, "Oregon Greater Sage-Grouse Approved Resource Management Plan Amendment," September 2015, https://www.blm.gov/sites/blm.gov/files/greater_sage-grouse_rmp_amendment.pdf.

69 US Department of the Interior, "Historic Conservation Campaign Protects Greater Sage-Grouse," September 22, 2015, https://

www.doi.gov/pressreleases/historic-conservation-campaign-pro-tects-greater-sage-grouse

70   "Proactive Conservation," Sage Grouse Initiative, National Resources Conservation Service, accessed December 2, 2019, https://www.sagegrouseinitiative.com/our-work/proactive-conservation/.

71   Natural Resources Conservation Service, "Sage Grouse Initiative 2.0 Investment Strategy, FY 2015–2018" (US Department of Agriculture, 2015), http://www.sagegrouseinitiative.com/wp-content/uploads/2015/08/SGI2.0_Final_Report.pdf; Natural Resources Conservation Service, "Greater Sage-Grouse 2015 Progress Report" (US Department of Agriculture, 2015), http://www.sagegrouseinitiative.com/wp-content/uploads/2016/02/GSG_FINAL.pdf.

72   Empowering State Management of Greater Sage Grouse: Oversight Hearing before the Committee on Natural Resources, 114th Cong. Serial No. 114–7 (2015).

73   Wyoming Exec. Order No. 2015-4; Idaho Exec. Order No. 2012-02; Montana Exec. Order No. 12-2015

74   *Empowering State Management*, 114th Cong. Serial No. 114–7; Utah Division of Wildlife Resources, "Final Conservation Plan for Greater Sage-Grouse in Utah," 2013; "Idaho Governor's Sage-Grouse Task Force Recommendations," June 15, 2012, https://idfg.idaho.gov/old-web/docs/wildlife/SGtaskForce/FinalRecommendations.pdf; Christian Hagen, "Greater Sage Grouse Conservation Assessment and Strategy for Oregon: A Plan to Maintain and Enhance Populations and Habitat," Oregon Department of Fish and Wildlife, April 22, 2011, http://www.dfw.state.or.us/wildlife/sagegrouse/docs/20110422_GRSG_April_Final%2052511.pdf.

75   San J. Stiver et al., "Greater Sage-Grouse Comprehensive Conservation Strategy," Western Association of Fish and Wildlife Agencies, December 2006, http://www.sagegrouseinitiative.com/wp-content/uploads/2013/07/WAFWA-comprehensive-strategy.pdf; Western Association of Fish and Wildlife Agencies, "Invasive Plant Management and Greater Sage-Grouse Conservation: A Review and Status Report with Strategic Recommendations for Improvement," 2015, https://www.wafwa.org/Documents%20and%20Settings/37/Site%20Documents/Initiatives/Sage%20Grouse/WAFWA%20Invasive%20Plant%20Management%20and%20Greater%20Sage-Grouse%20Report%20FINAL%203-28-15.pdf.

76   "Partner: Western Association of Fish and Wildlife Agencies," Sage Grouse Initiative, National Resources Conservation Service, accessed December 2, 2019, https://www.sagegrouseinitiative.com/partners_list/western-association-fish-wildlife-agencies/.

77 State of Utah, "Conservation Plan for Greater Sage-Grouse in Utah," February 14, 2013.

78 Terry A. Messmer et al., "Utah's Adaptive Resources Management Greater Sage-Grouse Local Working Groups 2018 Annual Report" (Utah Community-Based Conservation Program, Jack H. Berryman Institute, Department of Wildland Resources, and Utah State University Extension, Logan, UT, 2018), https://utahcbcp.org/publications/2018LWGAnnualReportMarch2019.pdf.

79 Lorien R. Belton, S. Nicole Frey, and David K. Dahlgren, "Participatory Research in Sage-Grouse Local Working Groups: Case Studies from Utah," *Human–Wildlife Interactions* 11, no. 3 (January 2017): 287–301.

80 State of Utah Office of the Governor Exec. Order No. 2015-001, https://rules.utah.gov/execdocs/2015/ExecDoc156016.htm

81 US Department of Agriculture, Natural Resources Conservation Service, Agricultural Wildlife Conservation Center, Utah State University, "Working with Sage-Grouse Local Working Groups: A Practical Guide for NRCS Staff," April 2009, http://digitalcommons.usu.edu/cgi/viewcontent.cgi?article=1092&context=extension_curall; Belton, Frey, and Dahlgren, "Participatory Research."

82 Messmer et al., "Utah's Adaptive Resources Management."

83 Belton, Frey, and Dahlgren, "Participatory Research"; April Reese and Kathryn Sachs, "Utah Sage Grouse Working Groups," Red Lodge Clearinghouse, October 3, 2005, http://www.rlch.org/stories/utah-sage-grouse-working-groups

84 Kurt T. Smith, Jennifer S. Forbey, and Jeffrey L. Beck, "Effects of Mowing and Tebuthiuron on the Nutritional Quality of Wyoming Big Sagebrush," *Rangeland Ecology & Management* 71, no. 4 (July 2018): 417–23.

85 Belton, Frey, and Dahlgren, "Participatory Research."

86 Melissa Chelak and Terry Messmer, "Population dynamics and seasonal movements of translocated and resident greater sage-grouse populations (*Centrocercus urophasianus*), Sheeprock Sage-grouse Management Area," Annual report, Jack H. Berryman Institute, Utah State University, February 2019; Belton, Frey, and Dahlgren, "Participatory Research."

87 Belton, Frey, and Dahlgren, 298.

88 Belton, Frey, and Dahlgren, "Participatory Research."

89 Belton, Frey, and Dahlgren, "Participatory Research."

90 Nick Salafsky, Richard Margoluis, and Kent Redford, "Adaptive Management: A Tool for Conservation Practitioners" (Biodiversity Support Program, World Wildlife Fund, Washington, DC, 2001); Richard A. Lancia et al., "ARM! For the Future: Adaptive Resource Management in the Wildlife Profession," *Wildlife Society Bulletin* 24, no. 3 (September 1996): 436–42.

91 E. Ostrom, "Polycentric Systems."

92 Belton, Frey, and Dahlgren, "Participatory Research," 299.

93 US Fish and Wildlife Service, "Frequently Asked Questions."

94 Georgina M. Mace, Hugh P. Possingham, and Nigel Leader-Williams, "Prioritizing Choices in Conservation," in *Key Topics in Conservation Biology*, ed. David W. Macdonald and Katrina Service (Oxford: Blackwell, 2007).

95 "Partner List," Sage Grouse Initiative, National Resources Conservation Service, 2019.

96 US Forest Service, "USDA Releases Proposed Amendments to Greater Sage Grouse Land Management Plans," August 1, 2019, https://www.fs.fed.us/news/releases/usda-releases-proposed-amendments-greater-sage-grouse-land-management-plans; Bureau of Land Management, "Sage-Grouse Conservation Plan Amendments Supported by Affected States' Governors," press release, March 15, 2019, https://www.blm.gov/press-release/sage-grouse-conservation-plan-amendments-supported-affected-states-governors.

97 US Department of the Interior, "Trump Administration Improves the Implementing Regulations of the Endangered Species Act," press release, August 12, 2019, https://www.doi.gov/pressreleases/endangered-species-act.

98 Elinor Ostrom, 'The Danger of Self-Evident Truths," *PS: Political Science and Politics* 33, no. 1 (2000): 42.

99 Tarko, *Elinor Ostrom*, 172.

100 V. Ostrom, *Meaning of Democracy*, 3.

CHAPTER 3. "PACIFIC SALMON FISHERIES MANAGEMENT: AN (UNUSUAL) EXAMPLE OF POLYCENTRIC GOVERNANCE INVOLVING INDIGENOUS PARTICIPATION AT MULTIPLE SCALES"

1 Elinor Ostrom, Roy Gardner, and James Walker, *Rules, Games, and Common Pool Resources* (Ann Arbor: University of Michigan Press, 1994).

2   North Pacific Anadromous Fish Commission. "Convention for the Conservation of Anadromous Stocks in the North Pacific Ocean". https://npafc.org/convention/.

3   North Pacific Anadromous Fish Commission. "Convention for the Conservation of Anadromous Stocks in the North Pacific Ocean". https://npafc.org/convention/; Edward L. Miles, "The Management of High Seas Salmon in the North Pacific, 1952–1992," in *Environmental Regime Effectiveness: Confronting Theory with Evidence*, ed. Edward L. Miles et al. (Cambridge, MA: MIT Press, 2002).

4   Convention for the Conservation of Anadromous Stocks in the North Pacific Ocean art. 8, § 7 and 10, February 11, 1992, T.I.A.S. No. 11465, https://npafc.org/wp-content/uploads/2017/06/Handbook-3rd-E-Convention-Only-English.pdf.

5   Thomas C. Jensen, "The United States-Canada Pacific Salmon Interception Treaty: An Historical and Legal Overview," *Environmental Law* 16 (1986): 363–422; Joy A. Yanagida, "The Pacific Salmon Treaty," *American Journal of International Law* 81 (1987): 577–92; John F. Roos, *Restoring Fraser River Salmon: A History of the International Pacific Salmon Fisheries Commission* (Vancouver, BC: Pacific Salmon Commission, 1991).

6   "Fisheries and Oceans Canada's Update on the Implementation of the Cohen Commission's Recommendations", Fisheries and Oceans Canada, accessed January 16, 2020, https://www.dfo-mpo.gc.ca/cohen/report-rapport-eng.htm.

7   "About Us: The Pacific Salmon Commission," Pacific Salmon Commission, accessed January 1, 2020, http://www.psc.org/about_role.htm.

8   Treaty Concerning Pacific Salmon art. 2, § 6, U.S.-Can., January 28, 1985, T.I.A.S. No. 11091, https://treaties.un.org/doc/Publication/UNTS/Volume%201469/volume-1469-I-24913-English.pdf.

9   Elinor Ostrom and Sue Crawford, "Classifying Rules," in *Understanding Institutional Diversity*, by Elinor Ostrom (Princeton, NJ: Princeton University Press, 2005), 193.

10   Ostrom and Crawford, "Classifying Rules," 194.

11   Ostrom and Crawford, 200.

12   Ostrom and Crawford, 202.

13   Ostrom and Crawford, 202-203.

14   Treaty Concerning Pacific Salmon art. 2, § 3.

15   Treaty Concerning Pacific Salmon art. 2, § 4.

16   PSC commissioner, interview by the author, December 16, 2009.

17 Treaty Concerning Pacific Salmon art. 2, § 4.

18 Treaty Concerning Pacific Salmon art. 2, § 7.

19 Treaty Concerning Pacific Salmon art. 2, § 8.

20 Treaty Concerning Pacific Salmon art. 2, § 12.

21 Treaty Concerning Pacific Salmon art. 2, § 13.

22 Treaty Concerning Pacific Salmon art. 2, §§ 15–16.

23 Treaty Concerning Pacific Salmon art. 2, §§ 17–18.

24 Sara Singleton, *Constructing Cooperation: The Evolution of Institutions of Comanagement* (Ann Arbor: University of Michigan Press, 1998).

25 "About Us", Northwest Indian Fisheries Commission, accessed January 16, 2020, https://nwifc.org/about-us/.

26 "CRITFC Mission & Vision", Columbia River Inter-Tribal Fish Commission, accessed January 16, 2020, https://www.critfc.org/about-us/mission-vision/.

27 Pub. L. No. 100-581, 102 Stat. 2938 (1988).

28 Pacific Salmon Treaty Act of 1985, 16 U.S.C. § 3632(a) (2012).

29 PSC commissioner, interview by the author, December 16, 2009.

30 NWIFC staff, interview by the author, February 18, 2010.

31 PSC commissioner, interview by the author, December 16, 2009.

32 NWIFC staff, interview by the author, February 18, 2010.

33 PSC commissioner, interview by the author, December 16, 2009.

34 PSC commissioner, interview by the author, December 16, 2009.

35 16 U.S.C. § 3632(h)(1).

36 PSC commissioner, interview by the author, December 16, 2009.

37 16 U.S.C. § 3632(a).

38 PSC commissioner, interview by the author, February 8, 2010; NWIFC staff, interview by the author, February 18, 2010.

39 PSC commissioner, interview by the author, February 8, 2010.

40 Kathleen A. Miller et al., "The 1999 Pacific Salmon Agreement: A Sustainable Solution?," *Canadian-American Public Policy* 47 (2001): 1–57; Ted L. McDorman, "The 1999 Canada-United States Pacific Salmon Agreement: Resolved and Unresolved Issues," *Journal of Environmental Law and Litigation* 15 (2000): 1–20; Robert J. Schmidt, "International Negotiations Paralyzed by Domestic Politics: Two-Level Game Theory and the Problem of the Pacific Salmon Commission," *Environmental Law* 26 (1996): 95–139; PSC commissioner, interview by the author, January 11, 2010; PSC commissioner, interview by the author, March 8, 2010.

41   David E. Smith, "Canada: A Double Federation," in *The Oxford Handbook of Canadian Politics*, ed. John C. Courtney and David E. Smith (New York: Oxford University Press, 2010).

42   Michael Howlett and Sima Joshi-Koop, "Canadian Environmental Politics and Policy," in *Oxford Handbook of Canadian Politics*, 471.

43   Howlett and Joshi-Koop, "Canadian Environmental Politics and Policy."

44   Holly Lake, "Canada Has a New Fisheries Act. How Does It Stack Up?", Hakai Magazine, June 28, 2019. .

45   Fisheries Act, part 1, § 2

46   PSC Enhancement Fund committee member, interview by the author, March 2, 2010; PSC commissioner, interview by the author, March 8, 2010.

47   PSC commissioner, interview by the author, January 11, 2010; DFO staff, interview by the author, March 9, 2010.

48   PSC commissioner, interview by the author, January 11, 2010; former PSC commissioner, interview by the author, March 8, 2010.

49   PSC commissioner, interview by the author, February 9, 2010.

50   PSC commissioner, interview by the author, January 14, 2010; PSC commissioner, interview by the author, February 9, 2010.

51   PSC commissioner, interview by the author, January 14, 2010; former PSC commissioner, interview by the author, March 8, 2010.

52   Former PSC commissioner, interview by the author, March 8, 2010.

53   PSC commissioner, interview by the author, January 11, 2010; DFO staff, interview by the author, January 12, 2010.

54   PSC commissioner, interview by the author, January 14, 2010.

55   PSC commissioner, interview by the author, January 14, 2010; PSC commissioner, interview by the author, March 8, 2010.

56   PSC commissioner, interview by the author, January 14, 2010.

57   DFO staff, interview by the author, January 12, 2010.

58   PSC commissioner, interview by the author, January 11, 2010; former PSC commissioner, interview by the author, March 8, 2010.

59   Fishery Conservation and Management Act of 1976, Pub. L. 94-265, 90 Stat. 331, amended by the Magnuson-Stevens Fishery Conservation and Management Reauthorization Act of 2006, Pub. L. 109-479, 120 Stat. 3575.

60   Pub. L. 109-479, § 302(a)(1)(F).

61 Pacific Fishery Management Council, "Statement of Organization, Practices, and Procedures", http://www.pcouncil.org/wp-content/uploads/Nov_2010_SOPP_FINAL_Jan_2014.pdf

62 North Pacific Fishery Management Council, "Statement of Organization, Practices, and Procedures", https://www.npfmc.org/wp-content/PDFdocuments/membership/Council/NPFMC_SOPP_October2019.pdf

63 Pub. L. 109-479, § 302(a)(1)(G).

64 Washington Department of Fish and Wildlife, accessed January 1, 2020, https://wdfw.wa.gov/fishing/management/north-falcon/faq.

65 "North of Falcon Frequently Asked Questions."

66 "North of Falcon Frequently Asked Questions."

67 "International Law, the Pacific Salmon Treaty, and Infringement of Aboriginal Rights" (Environmental Law Centre, University of Victoria, Victoria, BC, 2009), http://www.elc.uvic.ca/associates/documents/Pacific-Salmon-Treaty-Feb9.09.pdf; PSC commissioner, interview by the author, January 14, 2010.

68 John R. Rich and F. Matthew Kirchner of Ratcliff & Company, memorandum titled "Judgment in Nuu-Chah-Nulth Fisheries Litigation," 2009.

69 Nisga'a Nation Harvest Agreement, Can.-B.C.-Nisga'a Nation, May 11, 2000, https://www.rcaanc-cirnac.gc.ca/DAM/DAM-CIRNAC-RCAANC/DAM-TAG/STAGING/texte-text/har_1100100031748_eng.pdf.

70 DFO representative, interview by the author, January 12, 2010.

71 DFO representative, interview by the author, January 12, 2010.

72 PSC commissioner, interview by the author, January 11, 2010.

73 Fisheries and Oceans Canada (DFO), "2005–2010 Strategic Plan: Our Waters, Our Future," 2008, https://waves-vagues.dfo-mpo.gc.ca/Library/285991_e.pdf.

74 DFO, "2005–2010 Strategic Plan."

75 Singleton, 1998).

76 "The Historic Forests & Fish Law Explained," Forests & Fish website (Washington Forest Protection Association), accessed January 1, 2020, http://www.forestsandfish.com/about.

77 PSC commissioner, interview by the author, January 14, 2010.

78 PSC commissioner, interview by the author, January 14, 2010.

79 PSC commissioner, interview by the author, January 14, 2010; PSC commissioner, interview by the author, January 11, 2010.

80 PSC commissioner, interview by the author, February 8, 2010.

81 PSC commissioner, interview by the author, February 8, 2010.

82 PSC commissioner, interview by the author, February 8, 2010.

83 PSC commissioner, interview by the author, February 8, 2010.

CHAPTER 4. "POPULATION GROWTH AND THE GOVERNANCE OF COMPLEX INSTITUTIONS: PEOPLE ARE MORE THAN MOUTHS TO FEED"

1 For some of the most recent and significant works that discuss Ostrom's output as a challenge to Hardin, see the contributions to the Special Insights section in *Science* 362, no. 6420 (2018), particularly Robert Boyd et al., "Tragedy Revisited," *Science* 362, no. 6429 (2018): 1236–41. See also Brett Frischmann, Alain Marciano, and Giovanni Battista Ramello, "Tragedy of the Commons after 50 Years," *Journal of Economic Perspectives* 33, no. 4 (Fall 2019): 211–28.

2 Garrett Hardin, "The Tragedy of the Commons," *Science* 162, no. 3859 (December 1968): 1243–48.

3 Elinor Ostrom, *Governing the Commons: The Evolution of Institutions for Collective Action* (Cambridge: Cambridge University Press, 1990), 2.

4 Richard Lynn, "Garrett Hardin, Ph.D.—a Retrospective of His Life and Work," Garrett Hardin Society, updated December 11, 2003, https://www.garretthardinsociety.org/tributes/tr_lynn_2001.html; Fabien Locher, "Cold War Pastures: Garrett Hardin and the 'Tragedy of the Commons," trans. Cadenza Academic Translations, Cairn. info, originally published as "Les pâturages de la guerre froide: Garrett Hardin et la 'Tragédie des communs,'" *Revue d'histoire moderne et contemporaine* 60, no. 1 (2013): 7–36; Frischmann, Marciano, and Ramello, "Tragedy of the Commons."

5 Hardin, "Tragedy of the Commons," 1244.

6 Boyd et al., "Tragedy Revisited."

7 Boyd et al., 1236.

8 Frischmann, Marciano, and Ramello, "Tragedy of the Commons," 212.

9 See, for example, a study released on the thirtieth anniversary of TC's publication: Joanna Burger and Michael Gochfeld, "The Tragedy of the Commons: 30 Years Later," *Environment* 40, no. 10 (1998): 4–27.

10 "Hardin's famous sheepherder allegory failed to make two key conceptual distinctions: the allegory conflated the idea of a scarce resource with the governance of that resource, and it further conflated open access with commons." Frischmann, Marciano, and Ramello, "Tragedy of the Commons," 212.

11 Hardin, "Tragedy of the Commons," 1243.

12 David Harvey, "The Future of the Commons," *Radical History Review* 109 (2011): 101.

13 David Correia, "The Future of the Commons, Part I: Elinor Ostrom, Garrett Hardin, and the Politics of Population," *La Jicarita*, June 18, 2012, https://lajicarita.wordpress.com/2012/06/18/the-future-of-the-commons-part-i-elinor-ostrom-garret-hardin-and-the-logic-of-population/.

14 Ostrom, *Governing the Commons*, 3.

15 Ostrom, 7.

16 Hardin, "Tragedy of the Commons."

17 Frischmann, Marciano, and Ramello, "Tragedy of the Commons."

18 The term "Malthusian" invokes the views on human demographic trends promulgated by the Rev. Thomas Robert Malthus (1766–1834), particularly in the first edition of his *Essay on the Principle of Population* (1798). The Malthusian view is that while food availability increases arithmetically (linearly in proportion to inputs), people multiply geometrically (exponentially, doubling their numbers roughly every twenty-five years). Thus, in a classic Malthusian scenario of no technological change, the human population will outstrip the ability of the environment to sustain it, and will hence suffer a catastrophic crash. Malthus, particularly in the later editions of his work, allowed that people might be able to develop either moral or intellectual crash-avoidance mechanisms. Neo-Malthusians—modern adherents to the pessimistic Malthusian doctrine—on the other hand, see no mitigating circumstances to cushion the impending population crash. Some, like biologist Paul R. Ehrlich, have been predicting it for decades with clockwork regularity. The only solution to the population crash neo-Malthusians see as legitimate is top-down population control accomplished through government-imposed measures such as China's former one-child policy or India's forced sterilization programs of the 1960s.

19 Jason Oakes, "Garrett Hardin's Tragic Sense of Life," *Endeavour* 40, no. 4 (2016): 238–48. Numerous scientists, particularly from the 1950s to the 1970s, were trained to view what they studied accord-

ing to the systems school of thought. The world, as seen by systems science, was composed of "complex, hierarchic systems defined more by their structures than by their components." The aim of science was "to construct formal models of system behavior." Hunter Heyck, *Age of System: Understanding the Development of Modern Social Science* (Baltimore: Johns Hopkins University Press, 2015), 1. The structure such a model provided—and the control over the whole it implied—was more important to systems thinking than the identity or attributes of the parts, and it was this feature of the systems paradigm that was attractive to Hardin as he sought a way to direct human behavior rationally on a global scale. Oakes, "Garrett Hardin's Tragic Sense of Life," 246.

20 "Collection Guide: Guide to the Garrett Hardin Papers," Online Archive of California, accessed January 4, 2020, https://oac.cdlib.org/findaid/ark:/13030/kt267nd7tr/. For a compendium of Hardin's writings and a video interview, see the home page of the Garrett Hardin Society, http://www.garretthardinsociety.org/index.html. The journal *Science*, in which TC was originally published, has created a web page devoted to pieces written by Hardin in *Science* and reactions to them: "'The Tragedy of the Commons,' and Beyond," https://www.sciencemag.org/site/feature/misc/webfeat/sotp/commons.xhtml. For a more detailed list of links, including reactions to Hardin's writings, see "Links," Garrett Hardin Society, updated June 28, 2013, https://www.garretthardinsociety.org/info/links.html.

21 The term *carrying capacity*, in ecology, refers to the maximum number of individuals of a certain species that the environment can sustain, without degradation or resource depletion, indefinitely. The exact origin of the expression is not known but its earliest uses in the mid-nineteenth century spanned such fields as range management, engineering, international shipping, and agriculture, where the term did not relate to population. By the early to mid-twentieth century, neo-Malthusian researchers had adopted the term in the context of population biology and demography. For more details on the limitations of the term for assessing the impacts of human population on the environment, see Nathan F. Sayre, "The Genesis, History, and Limits of Carrying Capacity," *Annals of the Association of American Geographers* 98, no. 1 (2008): 120–34; Nathan F. Sayre, "Carrying Capacity," in *The Berkshire Encyclopedia of Sustainability*, vol. 5, *Ecosystem Management and Sustainability* (Great Barrington, MA: Berkshire Publishing Group, 2012).

22 Lifeboat ethics is a metaphor dating back to Hardin's essay on resource distribution bearing the same title. Garrett Hardin, "Lifeboat

Ethics: The Case against Helping the Poor," *Psychology Today*, September 1974. In the metaphor, poor nations are swimmers stranded in the water whereas developed nations are in lifeboats. Obviously, if all the swimmers are helped into the lifeboats, everyone will drown. According to Hardin, such will be the fate of humanity if individuals are allowed to indiscriminately impinge on the scarce resources the planet offers everyone as a commons. Only with firm guidance from authority can such resources be used wisely: Those (few) in charge of the lifeboats must decide what is right for all on the basis of crisis-time lifeboat ethics, not the idealized vision of human harmony and cooperation on Spaceship Earth. For more detail see Hardin, "Lifeboat Ethics" and Garrett Hardin, "Living on a Lifeboat," *BioScience* 24, no. 10 (1974): 561–68.

23   Pierre Desrochers and Christine Hoffbauer, "The Post War Intellectual Roots of the Population Bomb: Fairfield Osborn's *Our Plundered Planet* and William Vogt's *Road to Survival* in Retrospect," *Electronic Journal of Sustainable Development* 1, no. 3 (2009): 73–97; Locher, "Cold War Pastures"; Sebastian Normandin and Sean A. Valles, "How a Network of Conservationists and Population Control Activists Created the Contemporary US Anti-Immigration Movement," *Endeavour* 39, no. 2 (2015): 95–106; Oakes, "Garrett Hardin's Tragic Sense of Life"; Leon Kolankiewicz, "Garrett Hardin—Thinking without Limits about Living within Limits," *Social Contract* 29, no. 3 (2019): 3–23. Hardin's eugenicist roots are more obvious in his discussion of work by Kingsley Davis and of human reproduction. For a recent discussion of Hardin's life and work from the perspective of supportive neo-Malthusian writers, see the spring 2019 special issue of the *Social Contract* journal, "Living within Limits: The Enduring Relevance of Garrett Hardin," https://www.thesocialcontract.com/artman2/publish/tsc_29_3/index.shtml. For the broader intellectual context in which he wrote, see Pierre Desrochers and Vincent Geloso, "Snatching the Wrong Conclusions from the Jaws of Defeat: A Historical/Resourceship Perspective on Paul Sabin's *The Bet: Paul Ehrlich, Julian Simon, and Our Gamble over Earth's Future* (Yale University Press, 2013), Part 2: The Wager: Protagonists and Lessons," *New Perspectives on Political Economy* 12, no. 1–2 (2016): 42–64; Pierre Desrochers and Vincent Geloso, "Snatching the Wrong Conclusions from the Jaws of Defeat: A Historical/Resourceship Perspective on Paul Sabin's *The Bet: Paul Ehrlich, Julian Simon, and Our Gamble over Earth's Future* (Yale University Press, 2013), Part 1: The Missing History of Thought: Depletionism vs Resourceship," *New Perspectives on Political Economy* 12, no. 1–2 (2016): 5–41; Pierre Desrochers and Joanna Szurmak, *Population Bombed! Exploding the Link between Overpopulation and Cli-*

mate Change (Global Warming Policy Foundation, 2018). Sebastian Normandin and Sean Valles also develop the neo-Malthusian roots of Hardin's ideology around the "neo-Malthusian emergence" year of 1968. Normandin and Valles, "Network of Conservationists," 97. They document Hardin's connection to anti-immigration and neo-eugenicist groups through John Tanton, creator of the *Social Contract* journal and, during the 1970s, president of the organization Zero Population Growth (now Population Connection). Energy scholar Vaclav Smil presents a thought-provoking and personal analysis of Hardin's output in "Garrett James Hardin (Dallas 1915–Santa Barbara 2003)," *American Scientist* 92 (January–February 2004): 8–10.

24 Oakes, "Garrett Hardin's Tragic Sense of Life," 238.

25 Oakes, 238.

26 Locher, "Cold War Pastures," v.

27 Oakes, "Garrett Hardin's Tragic Sense of Life."

28 Garrett Hardin, *Biology: Its Human Implications* (San Francisco: W. H. Freeman, 1949). Hardin was still discussing, or perhaps more accurately restating, his key arguments in his last book, *Creative Altruism: An Ecologist Questions Motives* (Petoskey, MI: Social Contract Press, 1999).

29 Hardin, "Tragedy of the Commons," 1244.

30 Hardin, 1244.

31 Garrett Hardin, "Extensions of 'The Tragedy of the Commons,'" *Science* 280, no. 5364 (1998): 682.

32 Garrett Hardin, "The Feast of Malthus: Living within Limits," *Social Contract* (Spring 1998): 181. Italics in original.

33 William Forster Lloyd, *Two Lectures on the Checks to Population, Delivered before the University of Oxford in Michaelmas Term, 1832* (Oxford: Oxford University, 1833), 30–33, available at https://archive.org/details/twolecturesonch00lloygoog/page/n6.

34 Ostrom, *Governing the Commons.*

35 Hardin, "Extensions," 683. For a more detailed historical perspective on the limitations of carrying capacity as a theoretical construct in the context of the human ability to change the environment, see Sayre, "Genesis, History, and Limits"; Sayre, "Carrying Capacity."

36 Hardin is more explicit on this point in *The Concise Encyclopedia of Economics*, s.v. "Tragedy of the Commons," by Garrett Hardin, accessed January 4, 2020, http://www.econlib.org/library/Enc/TragedyoftheCommons.html.

37 Garrett Hardin, "The Tragedy of the Unmanaged Commons," *Trends in Ecology and Evolution* 9, no. 5 (1994): 199. Italics in original.

38 Oakes, "Garrett Hardin's Tragic Sense of Life," 238.

39 Hardin, "Tragedy of the Commons," 1245.

40 Normandin and Valles, "Network of Conservationists," 99.

41 Hardin, "Living on a Lifeboat," 561.

42 Hardin, 561.

43 Normandin and Valles, "Network of Conservationists," 99.

44 John S. Dryzek, *The Politics of the Earth: Environmental Discourses,* 2nd ed. (Oxford: Oxford University Press, 2005), 29.

45 Thomas Burnett, "What Is Scientism?," American Association for the Advancement of Science, accessed January 5, 2020, https://www.aaas.org/programs/dialogue-science-ethics-and-religion/what-scientism.

46 Normandin and Valles, "Network of Conservationists," 99.

47 Normandin and Valles, 99.

48 Hardin, "Tragedy of the Commons," 1248.

49 Hardin, "Extensions," 683.

50 For instance, in a 1990 interview Hardin acknowledged that feeding the world was not a pressing issue, but that negative environmental externalities and the capacity of nature to absorb polluting emissions was. Garrett Hardin, "An Interview with Garrett Hardin on Overpopulation, Carrying Capacity, and Quality of Life," interview by Nancy Pearlman, Educational Communications, Program 802, 1990, available at https://www.youtube.com/watch?v=MyD4x-RQo05s.

51 Hardin, "Extensions," 683.

52 Smil, "Garrett James Hardin," 10.

53 See, for example, Hardin, "Tragedy of the Commons," 1247; Hardin, "Extensions," 683.

54 Amy Poteete, "Elinor Ostrom, Governing the Commons: The Evolution of Institutions for Collective Action," in *The Oxford Handbook of Classics in Public Policy and Administration*, edited by Martin Lodge, Edward C. Page, and Steven J. Balla, (Oxford University Press, 2016), available in Oxford Handbooks Online, doi: 10.1093/oxfordhb/9780199646135.013.29 , page 2 of 13..

55 Gerald Gaus, *The Order of Public Reason: A Theory of Freedom and Morality in a Diverse and Bounded World* (Cambridge: Cambridge University Press, 2011). See also Paul D. Aligica, *Institutional Diversity*

and Political Economy, (Oxford, UK: Oxford University Press, 2013). Needless to say, the true nature of mutual coercion in this context has long been controversial. For an accessible critical take on the issue, see Jonathan Adler, "Property Rights and the Tragedy of the Commons," *Atlantic,* May 22, 2012, https://www.theatlantic.com/business/archive/2012/05/property-rights-and-the-tragedy-of-the-commons/257549/. For a relatively recent call for coercive population control that laments the demise of China's one-child policy, see Sarah Conly, "Here's Why China's One-Child Policy Was a Good Thing," *Boston Globe,* October 31, 2015, https://www.bostonglobe.com/opinion/2015/10/31/here-why-china-one-child-policy-was-good-thing/GY4XiQLeYfAZ8e8Y7yFycI/story.html.

56 The Garrett Hardin Society's website describes him as an "agent provocateur": "Video Interviews with Garrett Hardin," updated June 28, 2013, http://www.garretthardinsociety.org/videos/videos.html.

57 Diana Hull, "CAPS Grieves Deaths of Ecologist and Author Garrett Hardin and His Wife, Population Activist Jane Hardin," Garrett Hardin Society, September 19, 2003, https://www.garretthardinsociety.org/tributes/obit_caps_2003sep19.html.

58 Ostrom recalled that, during a lecture Hardin gave at Indiana University Bloomington after the 1968 publication of TC, he "indicated that every man and every woman should be sterilized after they have one child. He was very serious about it." Margaret Levi, "An Interview with Elinor Ostrom," *Annual Reviews Conversations* (2010), https://www.annualreviews.org/userimages/ContentEditor/1326999553977/ElinorOstromTranscript.pdf, 8. When asked how many children and grandchildren he had, Hardin reportedly said he had four of each: "My children paid attention to what I said, not what I did." Garrett Hardin, interview by Cathy Spencer, *Omni* 14, no. 9 (June 1992): 56.

59 For Hardin's most engaged and sustained critique of economic growth and optimist views on population, see Hardin, "Feast of Malthus," 183. Here he ridiculed Henry George, the best-selling nineteenth-century American economist whose key insights are discussed in section 3; Theodore Schultz; and Julian Simon (the last two anonymously): "Though not considered great, George was an economist of sorts. Sadly, his message is still repeated in our own time by many poorly trained economists [Simon]. . . . Few things are pleasanter to committed capitalists than being assured that more people are always and forever better. Grow! Grow! Grow! The belittling of the seriousness of overpopulation is not restricted to

the quack-economists [Simon] of our time: it is even found among a few of the leaders of the profession [Schultz]."

60 Needless to say, much empirical work was done documenting the changes, and, indeed, the marked improvements in the material conditions and life expectancy of people around the world in the post–World War II era. Desrochers and Geloso, "Snatching the Wrong Conclusions, Part 1." But as optimist economist Julian Simon hinted while discussing the history of thought on both population growth and material conditions of human life, a number of valuable insights on the relationship between a growing population and the availability of resources were arguably lost in mathematical translation at the time. Julian L. Simon, "Economic Thought about Population Consequences: Some Reflections," *Journal of Population Economics* 6, no. 2 (1993): 137–52.

61 Hardin did support and admire China's one-child policy as an exemplary authoritarian reproductive-rights-curtailing measure, although in his own works he did not mention it extensively. The evidence for his admiration, and on-the-record regret that the policy was not enforced in the Chinese countryside, can be found in Lynn, "Garrett Hardin, Ph.D."; and Hardin, interview by Spencer.

62 Garrett Hardin, *Population, Evolution and Birth Control: A Collage of Controversial Readings* (San Francisco: W. H. Freeman, 1964).

63 Niccolò Machiavelli, *Discourses on the First Decade of Titus Livius* (1531), trans. Ninian Hill Thomson (1883), chapter 5, available at the Literature Network, http://www.online-literature.com/machiavelli/titus-livius/66/.

64 Quoted in Arild Saether, "Otto Diederich Lütken—40 Years before Malthus?," *Population Studies* 47, no. 3 (1993): 511. The English translation of the title of the original 1758 Danish article is "An Enquiry into the Proposition that the Number of People is the Happiness of the Realm, or the Greater the Number of Subjects, the More Flourishing the State." It was published in the *Danmarks og Norges Oeconomiske Magazin* 2 (1758) pp. 187ff.

65 Joseph Symes, "The Plain Truth about Malthusianism," *Malthusian* 8, no. 6 (1886): 47.

66 Edward Isaacson, *The Malthusian Limit: A Theory of a Possible Static Condition for the Human Race* (London: Methuen, 1912), xxvi–xxvii, available at https://archive.org/details/malthusianlimitt00isaa/page/n8.

67 Isaacson, *Malthusian Limit*.

68 Thomas Robert Malthus, *An Essay on the Principle of Population, or a View of Its Past and Present Effects on Human Happiness; with an Inquiry into Our Prospects Respecting the Future Removal or Mitigation of the Evils Which It Occasions*, 6th ed. (London: John Murray, 1826), book 3, chapter 14, available at http://www.econlib.org/library/Malthus/malPlong.html.

69 Quoted in "Lord Derby on Emigration and the Land Question," *Malthusian* 1, no. 1 (1879): 6.

70 William Vogt, *Road to Survival* (New York: William Sloane Associates, 1948), 285.

71 Vogt, *Road to Survival*, 285.

72 Malthus, *Essay on the Principle of Population*, book 1, chapter 1.

73 John Stuart Mill, *Principles of Political Economy with Some of Their Applications to Social Philosophy*, ed. William James Ashley (1848; repr., London: Longmans, Green, 1909), chapter 13, available at http://oll.libertyfund.org/titles/mill-principles-of-political-economy-ashley-ed.

74 Edward Murray East, *Mankind at the Crossroads* (1923; repr., New York: Charles Scribner's Sons, 1928), 345.

75 Robert Carter Cook, *Human Fertility: The Modern Dilemma* (New York: Sloane, 1951), 321.

76 William Stanley Jevons, *The Coal Question: An Inquiry Concerning the Progress of the Nation, and the Probable Exhaustion of Our Coal-Mines* (1865; repr., London: MacMillan, 1866), chapters 1 and 2, available at http://www.econlib.org/library/YPDBooks/Jevons/jvnCQ.html.

77 Hardin, "Feast of Malthus," 183.

78 Hardin, 183.

79 Henry Fairfield Osborn Jr., *Our Plundered Planet* (Boston: Little, Brown, 1948), 199, available at https://digital.library.cornell.edu/catalog/chla2932687?c=chla;idno=2932687.

80 Osborn, *Our Plundered Planet*, 68.

81 Vogt, *Road to Survival*, 147.

82 Vogt, 147.

83 Pierre-Joseph Proudhon, *The Malthusians*, trans. (1848; repr., International Publishing Company, 1886), available at https://theanarchistlibrary.org/library/pierre-joseph-proudhon-the-malthusians. Benjamin Tucker translated the essay for the May 31, 1884 issue of *Liberty*. It was reprinted two years later by the International Publishing Company.

84 Charles Stanton Devas, *Political Economy*, 3rd ed. (1907; repr., London: Longmans, Green, 1919), 198, available at https://archive.org/details/politicalecon00deva.

85 Vogt, *Road to Survival*, 257, 13.

86 Bernard Katz, "Archibald Vivian Hill: 26 September 1886–3 June 1977," *Biographical Memoirs of Fellows of the Royal Society* 24 (1978): 71–149.

87 Phillip Magness and Sean Hernandez, "The Economic Eugenicism of John Maynard Keynes," *Journal of Markets and Morality* 20, no. 1 (2017): 79–100.

88 Archibald Vivian Hill, *The Ethical Dilemma of Science and Other Writings* (1962; repr., London: Rockefeller Institute Press in conjunction with Oxford University Press, 1960), 82.

89 Aldous Huxley, *Brave New World Revisited* (New York: Harper & Brothers, 1958), available at https://www.huxley.net/bnw-revisited/.

90 East, *Mankind at the Crossroads*, viii.

91 East, viii.

92 Alfred Marshall, *Principles of Economics*, vol. 1 (New York: MacMillan, 1890), 180, available at https://books.google.ca/books?id=yK-4JAAAAIAAJ.

93 Cook, *Human Fertility*, 319.

94 Harrison Brown, *The Challenge of Man's Future: An Inquiry Concerning the Condition of Man during the Years That Lie Ahead* (New York: Viking, 1954), 6.

95 See Hardin, "Feast of Malthus," and the discussion of his critique of economic growth in footnote As stated earlier, our choice was to use material that predates the publication of TC, material that would therefore have been accessible to Hardin and other post–World War II neo-Malthusian writers. For the most part we will discuss both Hardin and Ostrom within the range of the literature available to them when they wrote the key works in question, such as TC and, in Ostrom's case, works published before her Nobel prize in 2009. There will be exceptions to this material selection constraint in the final section and in the conclusion, but the majority of such exceptions will illustrate points about Hardin's or Ostrom's views, not new empirical or theoretical insights on the topic of population growth and resource management. To provide an example of this exclusion, this chapter does not engage with the population implications of China's one-child policy or of its repeal at the end of

2015, because neither Ostrom nor Hardin addressed the former in great detail, and they had no opportunity to learn of the latter..

96 Hardin, "Feast of Malthus," 183.

97 Oded Galor and David N. Weil, "Population, Technology, and Growth: From Malthusian Stagnation to the Demographic Transition and Beyond," *American Economic Review* 90, no. 4 (2000): 806.

98 Galor and Weil, "Population, Technology, and Growth."

99 Galor and Weil, "Population, Technology, and Growth."

100 Galor and Weil, 806.

101 Galor and Weil, "Population, Technology, and Growth."

102 Galor and Weil, 808.

103 Galor and Weil, 809.

104 Brown, *Challenge of Man's Future*.

105 Galor and Weil, "Population, Technology, and Growth," 809.

106 Galor and Weil, "Population, Technology, and Growth."

107 Galor and Weil, 811.

108 Galor and Weil, "Population, Technology, and Growth."

109 Stephen Davies, *The Wealth Explosion: The Nature and Origins of Modernity* (Brighton, UK: Edward Everett Root, 2019); Deirdre Nansen McCloskey, *The Bourgeois Virtues: Ethics for an Age of Commerce* (Chicago: University of Chicago Press, 2006); Deirdre Nansen McCloskey, *Bourgeois Dignity: Why Economics Can't Explain the Modern World* (Chicago: University of Chicago Press, 2010); Deirdre Nansen McCloskey, *Bourgeois Equality: How Ideas, Not Capital or Institutions, Enriched the World* (Chicago: University of Chicago Press, 2016).

110 Jean-Baptiste Say, *Letters to Mr. Malthus, and a Catechism of Political Economy*, trans. John Richter (London: Sherwood, Neely, and Jones, 1821), available at https://oll.libertyfund.org/titles/say-letters-to-mr-malthus-and-a-catechism-of-political-economy.

111 Say, *Letters to Mr. Malthus*.

112 Galor and Weil, "Population, Technology, and Growth."

113 Henry George, *Progress and Poverty: An Inquiry into the Cause of Industrial Depressions and of Increase of Want with Increase of Wealth; The Remedy* (1879; repr., Garden City, NY: Doubleday, Page, 1912), book 2, chapter 4, available at http://econlib.org/library/YPDBooks/George/grgPP.html.

114 George, *Progress and Poverty*, book 2, chapter 4.

115 George, *Progress and Poverty*, book 2, chapter 4.

116 "Statistics versus Malthus," *Westminster Review* 131, no. 3 (1889): 287, available at https://books.google.ca/books?id=S7WPjYl705k-C&vq=statistics+vs+malthus&source=gbs_navlinks_s.

117 Ostrom, *Governing the Commons*.

118 Harold J. Barnett and Chandler Morse, *Scarcity and Growth: The Economics of Natural Resource Availability* (Washington, DC: Resources for the Future, 1963), 7–8.

119 Herbert Spencer, "Progress: Its Law and Cause," in *Essays: Scientific, Political, and Speculative*, by Herbert Spencer, vol. 1 (1857; repr., London: Williams and Norgate, 1891), available at https://oll.libertyfund.org/titles/spencer-essays-scientific-political-and-speculative-vol-1--5?q=Progress%3A+Its+law#lf0620-01_head_003.

120 Spencer, "Progress."

121 Hardin 1998, "The Feast of Malthus."

122 George, *Progress and Poverty*, book 2, chapter 4.

123 Edward Atkinson, *The Industrial Progress of the Nation: Consumption Limited, Production Unlimited* (1889; repr., New York: G. P. Putnam's Sons, 1890), 160, available at https://archive.org/details/industrialprogre00atki.

124 Atkinson, *Industrial Progress*, 8.

125 Atkinson, 158.

126 Friedrich Engels, "Outlines of a Critique of Political Economy," *Deutsch-Französische Jahrbücher*, 1844, trans. Martin Milligan, available at https://www.marxists.org/archive/marx/works/1844/df-jahrbucher/outlines.htm.

127 David Grigg, "Ester Boserup's Theory of Agrarian Change: A Critical Review," *Progress in Human Geography* 3, no. 1 (1979): 64–84.

128 Vladimir I. Lenin, "The Agrarian Question and the 'Critics of Marx,'" in *Lenin: Collected Works*, ed. Victor Jerome, trans. Joe Fineberg and George Hanna, vol. 5, *May 1901–February 1902* (Moscow: Progress, 1977), available at https://www.marxists.org/archive/lenin/works/1901/agrarian/index.htm.

129 Mao Tse-tung, "The Bankruptcy of the Idealist Conception of History," in *Selected Works of Mao Tse-tung*, trans., vol. 4 (Beijing: Foreign Languages Press, n.d.), available at https://www.marxists.org/reference/archive/mao/selected-works/volume-4/mswv4_70.htm. (This source uses the older Wade-Giles spelling for Mao's name, rather than the now more common Pinyin spelling we have adopted.)

130 Joseph Hansen, *Too Many Babies? A Marxist Answer to Some Frightening Questions* (New York: Pioneer, 1960), available at http://ucf.digital.flvc.org/islandora/object/ucf%3A5107; Frank Furedi, *Population and Development: A Critical Introduction* (Cambridge, UK: Polity, 1997).

131 Edwin Cannan, *Wealth: A Brief Explanation of the Causes of Economic Wealth* (1914; repr., London: P. S. King and Son, 1922), chapter 4, available at http://oll.libertyfund.org/titles/2063.

132 Cannan, *Wealth*, chapter 4.

133 Karl Brandt, "The Marriage of Nutrition and Agriculture," in *Food for the World*, ed. Theodore W. Schultz (Chicago: University of Chicago Press, 1945), 135–36.

134 Alexander H. Everett, *New Ideas on Population: With Remarks on the Theories of Malthus and Godwin* (Boston: Oliver Everett, 1823), 26, available at https://archive.org/details/newideasonpopula00ever.

135 Everett, *New Ideas on Population*, 28.

136 Engels, "Outlines of a Critique."

137 Barnett and Morse, *Scarcity and Growth*, 236.

138 Galor and Weil, "Population, Technology, and Growth."

139 William Petty, *Essays on Mankind and Political Arithmetic* (1682; repr., London: Cassell, 1888), 49, available at http://www.archive.org/details/essaysonmankindp00pettuoft.

140 Cannan, *Wealth*, chapter 4.

141 Clarence E. Ayres, *The Theory of Economic Progress* (Chapel Hill, NC: University of North Carolina Press, 1944), chapter 6. Available at http://cas2.umkc.edu/economics/Institutional/Readings/Ayres/tep/TEP.html

142 Ayres, *Theory of Economic Progress*, chapter 6.

143 Fritz Machlup, "The Supply of Inventors and Inventions," in *The Rate and Direction of Inventive Activity: Economic and Social Factors*, by the National Bureau of Economic Research (Princeton: Princeton University Press, 1962), 156.

144 George, *Progress and Poverty*, book 2, chapter 3.

145 Modern research has since established that the indigenous populations of the Americas were once much more numerous than George believed to have been the case, but this does not invalidate his argument.

146 George, *Progress and Poverty*, book 2, chapter 3.

147 George, book 2, chapter 3.

148 George, book 2, chapter 3.

149 Pyotr Kropotkin, *Fields, Factories and Workshops; or, Industry Combined with Agriculture and Brain Work with Manual Work* (1899; repr., London: Thomas Nelson & Sons, 1912), chapter 2, available at https://theanarchistlibrary.org/library/petr-kropotkin-fields-factories-and-workshops-or-industry-combined-with-agriculture-and-brain-w.

150 Kropotkin, *Fields, Factories and Workshops*, chapter 2.

151 Erich W. Zimmermann, *World Resources and Industries: A Functional Appraisal of the Availability of Agricultural and Industrial Resources* (New York: Harper & Brothers, 1933), 3, available at https://archive.org/details/in.ernet.dli.2015.2623/page/n5.

152 Erich W. Zimmermann, *World Resources and Industries: A Functional Appraisal of the Availability of Agricultural and Industrial Resources*, rev. ed. (New York: Harper & Brothers, 1951), 814–15, available at https://archive.org/details/worldresourcesin0000zimm.

153 Cannan, *Wealth*, chapter 4.

154 Hans H. Landsberg, *Natural Resources for US Growth: A Look Ahead to the Year 2000* (Baltimore. Resources for the Future, 1964), 11–12.

155 Michael Polanyi, *The Logic of Liberty: Reflections and Rejoinders* (London: Routledge, 1951), chapter 3.

156 Polanyi, *Logic of Liberty*, 33.

157 Polanyi, 34.

158 Polanyi, 34.

159 Paul D. Aligica and Vlad Tarko, "Polycentricity: From Polanyi to Ostrom, and Beyond," *Governance: An International Journal of Policy, Administration, and Institutions* 25, no. 2 (2012): 237–62.

160 Aligica and Tarko, "Polycentricity," 238.

161 Polanyi, *Logic of Liberty*, 111–12.

162 Vincent Ostrom, Charles M. Tiebout, and Robert Warren, "The Organization of Government in Metropolitan Areas: A Theoretical Inquiry," *American Political Science Review* 55, no. 4 (1961): 831–42. For more details about the history of the polycentric model and the Ostroms' work at the Bloomington School of Institutional Analysis please see, Paul D. Aligica and Peter Boettke, *Challenging Institutional Analysis and Development: The Bloomington School* (London: Routledge, 2009).

163 Ostrom, Tiebout, and Warren, "Organization of Government," 831.

164 Ostrom, Tiebout, and Warren, 831.

165 Aligica and Tarko, "Polycentricity."

166 Poteete, "Elinor Ostrom."

167 Elinor Ostrom, "Beyond Markets and States: Polycentric Governance of Complex Economic Systems," *American Economic Review* 100, no. 3 (June 2010): 1-12. (This piece was originally presented as Ostrom's Nobel prize lecture at Stockholm University on December 8, 2009.)

168 Ostrom, "Beyond Markets and States," 1.

169 Larry L. Kiser and Elinor Ostrom, "The Three Worlds of Action: A Meta-Theoretical Synthesis of Institutional Approaches," in *Strategies of Political Inquiry*, ed. Elinor Ostrom (Thousand Oaks, CA: Sage, 1982); Elinor Ostrom, *Understanding Institutional Diversity* (Princeton, NJ: Princeton University Press, 2005), 18; Ostrom, "Beyond Markets and States."

170 Ostrom, *Governing the Commons*, 38.

171 Ostrom, *Understanding Institutional Diversity*, 19. Italics in original.

172 Ostrom, 20.

173 Ostrom, 23.

174 Ostrom, 25.

175 Ostrom, 19.

176 Ostrom, 18.

177 Ostrom, 33.

178 Ostrom, 18.

179 Paul A. Samuelson, "The Pure Theory of Public Expenditure," *Review of Economics and Statistics* 36, no. 4 (1954): 387–89.

180 Ostrom, *Understanding Institutional Diversity*, 35.

181 Ostrom called these goods "toll" goods; see discussion in Ostrom, *Understanding Institutional Diversity*, 35–37.

182 Ostrom, *Understanding Institutional Diversity*, 35. A discussion about subtractability of CPRs, and the differences between producers, providers, and resource appropriators and coappropriators can be found in Ostrom, *Governing the Commons*, 31–38.

183 Ostrom, *Understanding Institutional Diversity*, 35.

184 Ostrom, 36.

185 Ostrom, 36..

186 Ostrom, 25.

187 Garrett Hardin and John Baden, eds., *Managing the Commons* (San Francisco, CA: W. H. Freeman, 1977).

188 Hardin, "Feast of Malthus."

189 Hardin, 181.

190 Hardin, 185.

191 Hardin, 183.

192 Levi, "An Interview with Elinor Ostrom."

193 Levi, "An Interview with Elinor Ostrom." 8.

194 Ostrom, *Governing the Commons*, 3.

195 Ostrom, *Governing the Commons*.

196 Ostrom, 4.

197 Ostrom, 5.

198 Ostrom, 6.

199 Ostrom, 7.

200 Ostrom, *Governing the Commons*.

201 Ostrom, 7–8.

202 Ostrom, 8.

203 Ostrom, 8.

204 Garrett Hardin, "Political Requirements for Preserving our Common Heritage," in *Wildlife and America*, ed. H. P. Bokaw (Washington, DC: Council on Environmental Quality, 1978), 310.

205 Hardin, "Political Requirements," 311.

206 Hardin, 314.

207 Ostrom, *Governing the Commons*, 9.

208 Ostrom, 14.

209 Ostrom, 409.

210 Galor and Weil, "Population, Technology, and Growth."

211 "Statistics versus Malthus," 287.

212 Brown, *Challenge of Man's Future*, 5.

213 Ostrom, *Governing the Commons*, 38.

214 Ostrom, 14.

215 Ostrom, "Beyond Markets and States," 2.

216 Mark Pennington, "Elinor Ostrom, Common-Pool Resources and the Classical Liberal Tradition," in *The Future of the Commons: Beyond Market Failure and Government Regulation*, ed. Elinor Ostrom (London, UK: Institute of Economic Affairs, 2012).

217 Pennington, "Elinor Ostrom," 31–32.

218 Pennington, 32.

219 Pennington, 34.

220 Ostrom, *Governing the Commons*.

221 Julian L. Simon, *The Ultimate Resource 2* (1981; repr., Princeton, NJ: Princeton University Press, 1996), available at http://www.juliansi-mon.org/writings/Ultimate_Resource/.

CHAPTER 5. "CONTRACTING AND THE COMMONS: LINKING THE INSIGHTS OF GARY LIBECAP AND ELINOR OSTROM"

1   "Elinor Ostrom: Facts," Nobel Prize (website), accessed December 18, 2019, https://www.nobelprize.org/prizes/economic-scienc-es/2009/ostrom/facts/.

2   Garrett Hardin, "The Tragedy of the Commons," *Science* 162, no. 3859 (December 1968): 1243–48.

3   This is a broad generalization. However, in the ten years since Ostrom won the Nobel prize, we find only a few citations of her work in the *American Economic Review* (21), the *Journal of Political Economy* (4), and the *Quarterly Journal of Economics* (2), and most of these citations are related to her development or behavioral work and not to the management of environmental or natural resource problems. The view that more complex resource problems are beyond Ostrom's framework is summarized by Robert Stavins and Gary Libecap, although both authors argue, as we do here, for the relevance of Ostrom's work in this context. Robert N. Stavins, "The Problem of the Commons: Still Unsettled after 100 Years," *American Economic Review* 101, no. 1 (2011): 81–108; Gary D. Libecap, "Addressing Global Environmental Externalities: Transaction Costs Considerations," *Journal of Economic Literature* 52, no. 2 (2014): 424–79.

4   Elinor Ostrom, *Governing the Commons: The Evolution of Institutions for Collective Action* (Cambridge: Cambridge University Press, 1990); Elinor Ostrom, Marco A. Janssen, and John M. Anderies, "Going beyond Panaceas," *Proceedings of the National Academy of Sciences* 104, no. 39 (2007): 15176–78.

5   Arthur Cecil Pigou, *The Economics of Welfare* (MacMillan and Co: Londo1932).

6   See, for example, Gary D. Libecap and Steven N. Wiggins, "The Influence of Private Contractual Failure on Regulation: The Case of Oil Field Unitization," *Journal of Political Economy* 93, no. 4 (1985): 690–714.

7   Pigou, *Economics of Welfare*.

8   Ostrom, *Governing the Commons*, 21.

9   Ostrom, 14.

10 Ronald N. Johnson and Gary D. Libecap, *The Federal Civil Service System and the Problem of Bureaucracy: The Economics and Politics of Institutional Change* (Chicago: University of Chicago Press, 1994), 163; Gary D. Libecap, *Contracting for Property Rights* (Cambridge: Cambridge University Press, 1989), 22.

11 Libecap, *Contracting for Property Rights*, 27.

12 Mancur Olson, *The Logic of Collective Action: Public Goods and the Theory of Groups* (Cambridge, MA: Harvard University Press, 1965), 2. Italics in original.

13 Libecap, *Contracting for Property Rights*, 74.

14 See, for example, Libecap and Wiggins, "Influence of Private Contractual Failure."

15 Ostrom, Elinor. "Toward a behavioral theory linking trust, reciprocity, and reputation." *Trust and reciprocity: Interdisciplinary lessons from experimental research* 6 (2003): 19-79.

16 Ostrom, 22.

17 See, for example, Elinor Ostrom, Roy Gardner, and James Walker, *Rules, Games, and Common-Pool Resources* (Ann Arbor: University of Michigan Press, 1994), 198.

18 Ostrom, Gardner, and Walker, *Rules, Games, and Common-Pool Resources*, 215.

19 Ostrom, *Governing the Commons*, 35.

20 See, for example, H. Scott Gordon. "The Economic Theory Of A Common-Property Resource: The Fishery'." *The Journal of Political Economy* 62, no. 2 (1954): 124-142; Jonathan M. Karpoff, "Suboptimal Controls in Common Resource Management: The Case of the Fishery," *Journal of Political Economy* 95, no. 1 (1987): 179–94; Frances R. Homans and James E. Wilen, "Markets and Rent Dissipation in Regulated Open Access Fisheries," *Journal of Environmental Economics and Management* 49, no. 2 (2005): 381–404.

21 Elinor Ostrom, "Collective Action and the Evolution of Social Norms," *Journal of Economic Perspectives* 14, no. 3 (2000): 150.

22 Gary D. Libecap and James L. Smith, "The Self-Enforcing Provisions of Oil and Gas Unit Operating Agreements: Theory and Evidence," *Journal of Law, Economics, and Organization* 15, no. 2 (1999): 526–48.

23 Olson, *Logic of Collective Action*; Baland, Jean-Marie, and Jean-Philippe Platteau. *Halting degradation of natural resources: is there a role for rural communities?. Food & Agriculture Org.*, 1996..

24 Andrew B. Ayres, Eric C. Edwards, and Gary D. Libecap, "How Transaction Costs Obstruct Collective Action: The Case of California's Groundwater," *Journal of Environmental Economics and Management* 91 (2018): 46–65; Ostrom 2014.

25 Olson, *Logic of Collective Action*; Gary D. Libecap, "Distributional Issues in Contracting for Property Rights," *Journal of Institutional and Theoretical Economics (JITE) / Zeitschrift für die gesamte Staatswissenschaft* 145, no. 1 (1989): 6–24; Ostrom, *Governing the Commons*; Bhim Adhikari and Jon C. Lovett, "Transaction Costs and Community-Based Natural Resource Management in Nepal," *Journal of Environmental Management* 78, no. 1 (2006): 5–15; Lore M. Ruttan, "Economic Heterogeneity and the Commons: Effects on Collective Action and Collective Goods Provisioning," *World Development* 36, no. 5 (May 2008): 969–85.

26 Arun Agrawal and Sanjeev Goyal, "Group Size and Collective Action: Third-Party Monitoring in Common-Pool Resources," *Comparative Political Studies* 34, no. 1 (2001): 63–93; Arun Agrawal, "Group Size and Successful Collective Action: A Case Study of Forest Management Institutions in the Indian Himalayas" (International Forestry Resources and Institutions Research Program, Indiana University, 1996).

27 Ayres, Edwards, and Libecap, "How Transaction Costs Obstruct Collective Action"; Amy R. Poteete and Elinor Ostrom, "Heterogeneity, Group Size and Collective Action: The Role of Institutions in Forest Management," *Development and Change* 35, no. 3 (2004): 435–61.

28 Libecap, "Distributional Issues," 21.

29 Gary D. Libecap and Steven N. Wiggins, "Contractual Responses to the Common Pool: Prorationing of Crude Oil Production," *American Economic Review* 74, no. 1 (1984): 87–98.

30 Elinor Ostrom, "A Diagnostic Approach for Going beyond Panaceas," *Proceedings of the National Academy of Sciences* 104, no. 39 (2007): 15181–87.

31 Elinor Ostrom, "Reformulating the Commons," *Ambiente & Sociedade* 10 (2002): 13.

32 Poteete and Ostrom, "Heterogeneity, Group Size and Collective Action."

33 Poteete and Ostrom, "Heterogeneity, Group Size and Collective Action."

34 Ostrom, "Reformulating the Commons," 14.

35 A notable exception is Ostrom's study of Spanish *huertas,* which sometimes contained in excess of ten thousand users. However, the *huertas* are still marked by the homogeneity of the participants. Ostrom, *Governing the Commons.*

36 Libecap and Wiggins, "Contractual Responses"; Ostrom, "Reformulating the Commons, " 14.

37 Libecap and Wiggins, "Contractual Responses."

38 Libecap, *Contracting for Property Rights.*

39 Ayres, Edwards, and Libecap, "How Transaction Costs Obstruct Collective Action."

40 Barbara Alexander and Gary D. Libecap, "The Effect of Cost Heterogeneity in the Success and Failure of the New Deal's Agricultural and Industrial Programs," *Explorations in Economic History* 37, no. 4 (2000): 370–400.

41 Gary D. Libecap, "The Conditions for Successful Collective Action," *Journal of Theoretical Politics* 6, no. 4 (1994): 563–92.

42 Libecap, Gary D., and Steven N. Wiggins. "The influence of private contractual failure on regulation: the case of oil field unitization." *Journal of Political Economy* 93, no. 4 (1985): 690-714.

43 Ostrom, "Reformulating the Commons," 14.

44 Ronald N. Johnson and Gary D. Libecap, "Contracting Problems and Regulation: The Case of the Fishery," *American Economic Review* 72, no. 5 (1982): 1005–22.

45 Elinor Ostrom, "Self Governance and Forest Resources," in *Terracotta Reader: A Market Approach to the Environment,* ed. Parth J. Shah and Vidisha Maitra (New Delhi: Academic Foundation, 2005), 9; Marco A. Janssen and Elinor Ostrom, "Adoption of a New Regulation for the Governance of Common-Pool Resources by a Heterogeneous Population," in *Inequality, Cooperation, and Environmental Sustainability,* ed. Jean-Marie Baland, Pranab Bardhan, and Samuel Bowles (New York: Russell Sage Foundation and Princeton University Press, 2007).

46 Varughese, G. and Ostrom, E., 2001. The contested role of heterogeneity in collective action: some evidence from community forestry in Nepal. *World development,* 29(5), pp.747-765.

47 Ostrom, "Diagnostic Approach."

48 Elinor Ostrom et al., "Revisiting the Commons: Local Lessons, Global Challenges," *Science* 284, no. 5412 (1999): 279.

49 Friedrich A. Hayek, "The Use of Knowledge in Society," *American Economic Review* 35, no. 4 (September 1945): 519–30; Agnar Sand-

mo, "Asymmetric Information and Public Economics: The Mirr-lees-Vickrey Nobel Prize," *Journal of Economic Perspectives* 13, no. 1 (1999): 165–80.

50 Elinor Ostrom, Burger, J., Field, C.B., Norgaard, R.B. and Policansky, D., 1999. Revisiting the commons: local lessons, global challenges. *science*, *284*(5412), pp.278-282. Ostrom cites Harold Demsetz, "Toward a Theory of Property Rights," *American Economic Review* 62, (1967); Douglass C. North., 1994. Economic performance through time. *The American economic review, 84*(3), pp.359-368; and others.

51 Thomas Dietz, Elinor Ostrom, and Paul C. Stern, "The Struggle to Govern the Commons," *Science* 302, no. 5652 (2003): 1907–12; Elinor Ostrom, "Beyond markets and states: polycentric governance of complex economic systems." *American economic review* 100, no. 3 (2010): 641-72.

52 Steven N. Wiggins and Gary D. Libecap, "Presence of Imperfect Information," *American Economic Review* 75, no. 3 (1985): 368–85; Johnson and Libecap, "Contracting Problems and Regulation"; Bryan Leonard and Gary D. Libecap, "Collective Action by Contract: Prior Appropriation and the Development of Irrigation in the Western United States," *Journal of Law and Economics* 62, no. 1 (2019): 67–115.

53 Libecap and Wiggins, "Contractual Responses."

54 Wiggins and Libecap, "Presence of Imperfect Information."

55 Wiggins and Libecap, "Presence of Imperfect Information."

56 Wiggins and Libecap, "Presence of Imperfect Information."

57 Ostrom, "Diagnostic Approach."

58 Ostrom, Elinor. "Beyond markets and states: polycentric governance of complex economic systems." *American economic review* 100, no. 3 (2010): 641-72.

59 Libecap and Wiggins, "Influence of Private Contractual Failure."

60 Ostrom, Elinor. "Beyond markets and states: polycentric governance of complex economic systems." *American economic review* 100, no. 3 (2010): 641-72.

61 See, for example, Libecap, "Addressing Global Environmental Externalities."

62 See, for example, Dietz, Ostrom, and Stern, "Struggle to Govern the Commons."

63 Elinor Ostrom and Roy Gardner, "Coping with Asymmetries in the Commons: Self-Governing Irrigation Systems Can Work," *Journal of Economic Perspectives* 7, no. 4 (1993): 93–112.

64   Libecap and Smith, "Self-Enforcing Provisions."

65   Libecap and Smith, "Self-Enforcing Provisions."

66   Ostrom, *Governing the Commons*, 87; Robert Y. Siy Jr., *Community Resource Management: Lessons from the Zanjera* (Rome: Food and Agricultural Organization of the United Nations, 1982).

67   Ostrom and Gardner, "Coping with Asymmetries."

68   Libecap and Smith, "Self-Enforcing Provisions."

69   Gardner, Roy, Andrew Herr, Elinor Ostrom, and James A. Walker. "The power and limitations of proportional cutbacks in common-pool resources." *Journal of Development Economics* 62, no. 2 (2000): 515-533.

70   Coman, Katharine. "Some unsettled problems of irrigation." *The American Economic Review* 1, no. 1 (1911): 1-19; Elinor Ostrom, "Reflections on 'Some Unsettled Problems of Irrigation,'" *American Economic Review* 101, no. 1 (2011): 49–63;
Libecap, Gary D. "Institutional path dependence in climate adaptation: Coman's" Some unsettled problems of irrigation"." *American Economic Review* 101, no. 1 (2011): 64-80;
Hanemann, Michael. "Property rights and sustainable irrigation—A developed world perspective." *Agricultural water management* 145 (2014): 5-22.

71   Hanemann, Sustainable Irrigation.

72   Leonard and Libecap, "Collective Action by Contract."

73   Ostrom and Gardner, "Coping with Asymmetries."

74   Ostrom and Gardner, "Coping with Asymmetries."

75   Ostrom, *Governing the Commons*.

76   Ostrom, "Reflections on 'Some Unsettled Problems.'"

77   Ostrom, *Governing the Commons*; Ostrom, "Reflections on 'Some Unsettled Problems'"; Ostrom and Gardner, "Coping with Asymmetries."

78   Ostrom and Gardner, "Coping with Asymmetries"; Ostrom, "Reflections on 'Some Unsettled Problems.'"

79   Leonard and Libecap, "Collective Action by Contract."

80   Leonard and Libecap, "Collective Action by Contract."

81   Ostrom and Gardner, "Coping with Asymmetries."

82   Ostrom, "Reflections on 'Some Unsettled Problems'"; Leonard and Libecap, "Collective Action by Contract."

83   Ostrom, "Reflections on 'Some Unsettled Problems.'"

84   Ostrom, "Reflections on 'Some Unsettled Problems.'"

85 Leonard and Libecap, "Collective Action by Contract."

86 See, for example, Elinor Ostrom, "Public Entrepreneurship: A Case Study in Ground Water Basin Management" (PhD diss., University of California, Los Angeles, 1965).

87 Eric C. Edwards, "What Lies Beneath? Aquifer Heterogeneity and the Economics of Groundwater Management," *Journal of the Association of Environmental and Resource Economists* 3, no. 2 (2016): 453–91.

88 Steven M. Smith et al., "Responding to a Groundwater Crisis: The Effects of Self-Imposed Economic Incentives," *Journal of the Association of Environmental and Resource Economists* 4, no. 4 (2017): 985–1023.

89 Yusuke Kuwayama and Nicholas Brozović, "The Regulation of a Spatially Heterogeneous Externality: Tradable Groundwater Permits to Protect Streams," *Journal of Environmental Economics and Management* 66, no. 2 (2013): 364–82.

90 Krystal M. Drysdale and Nathan P. Hendricks, "Adaptation to an Irrigation Water Restriction Imposed through Local Governance," *Journal of Environmental Economics and Management* 91 (2018): 150–65.

91 Ostrom, "Coping with Tragedies of the Commons," 495.

92 Libecap, "Addressing Global Environmental Externalities."

93 Ostrom, *Governing the Commons*, 25.

CHAPTER 6. "THE ENVIRONMENTAL BENEFITS OF LONG-DIS-TANCE TRADE: INSIGHTS FROM THE HISTORY OF BY-PRODUCT DEVELOPMENT"

1 Garrett Hardin, "The Tragedy of the Commons," *Science* 162, no. 3859 (December 1968): 1244.

2 Elinor Ostrom, *Governing the Commons: The Evolution of Institutions for Collective Action* (Cambridge: Cambridge University Press, 1990); Elinor Ostrom, *Understanding Institutional Diversity* (Princeton, NJ: Princeton University Press, 2005); Elinor Ostrom, "Beyond Markets and States: Polycentric Governance of Complex Economic Systems," *American Economic Review* 100, no. 3 (June 2010): 641–72.

3 Among the few exceptions to CPR management case studies being confined to economically marginal areas is water management in the context of a rapidly growing population, increased manufacturing, and agricultural demand in the United States. In the US water management case, technological innovations and adaptations moved beyond traditional practices and technologies. Elinor

Ostrom et al., eds., *The Drama of the Commons* (Washington, DC: National Academy Press, 2002), https://doi.org/10.17226/10287.

4   Fikret Berkes, "Local-Level Management and the Commons Problem: A Comparative Study of Turkish Coastal Fisheries," *Marine Policy* 10, no. 3 (1986): 215–29; Ostrom, *Governing the Commons*, chapter 3; Tamara L. Whited, *Forests and Peasant Politics in Modern France* (New Haven, CT: Yale University Press, 2000); Robert M. Schwartz, "Review of 'Forests and Peasant Politics in Modern France,'" *H-France Review* 1 (December 2001): 199–203.

5   Berkes, "Local-Level Management," 216.

6   Philipp Aerni, "Food Sovereignty and Its Discontents," *ATDF Journal* 8, no. 1/2 (2011): 23–40, 24.

7   Aerni, "Food Sovereignty," 24–25.

8   Theodore C. Bergstrom, "The Uncommon Insight of Elinor Ostrom," *The Scandinavian Journal of Economics* 112 (2010): 245-261, https://doi.org/10.1111/j.1467-9442.2010.01608.x, 246.

9   David Harvey, "The Future of the Commons," *Radical History Review* 109 (2011): 102.

10   Harvey, "Future of the Commons," 102. We argue in chapter 4 of this volume that Ostrom brought to the analysis of human governance of CPRs a granular understanding of scale and degree. Hence, she would be the first to admit that at a given scale a solution might be no longer applicable to the problem at hand.

11   Harvey, "Future of the Commons," 102.

12   Elinor Ostrom, *Beyond Markets and States: Polycentric Governance of Complex Economic Systems*, (Nobel Prize Lecture, December 8, 2009), 409, available at https://www.nobelprize.org/uploads/2018/06/ostrom_lecture.pdf.

13   Ostrom, *Governing the Commons*, 14.

14   Ostrom, *Governing the Commons*.

15   Milena Ristovska, "The Role of the Business Sector in Promoting a 'Greener' Future," *International Business & Economics Research Journal* 9, no. 4 (2010): 21.

16   Pierre Desrochers, "Regional Development and Inter-industry Recycling Linkages: Some Historical Perspective," *Entrepreneurship and Regional Development* 14, no. 1 (2002): 49–65; Pierre Desrochers, "Did the Invisible Hand Need a Regulatory Glove to Develop a Green Thumb? Some Historical Perspective on Market Incentives, Win-Win Innovations and the Porter Hypothesis," *Environmental and Resource Economics* 41, no. 4 (2008): 519–39; Pierre Desrochers

and Colleen Haight, "Squandered Profit Opportunities? Some Historical Perspective on Wasteful Industrial Behavior and the Porter Hypothesis," *Resources, Conservation and Recycling* 92 (2014): 179–89; Pierre Desrochers and Samuli Leppälä, "Industrial Symbiosis: Old Wine in Recycled Bottles? Some Perspective from the History of Economic and Geographical Thought," *International Regional Science Review* 33, no. 3 (2010): 338–61.

17   Paul Razous, *Les déchets industriels: Récupération, utilisation* (Paris: Dunod, 1905).

18   William George Jordan, "Wonders of the World's Waste," *Ladies' Home Journal*, October 1897, 8, available at https://books.google.ca/books?id=LKwiAQAAMAAJ&source=gbs_similarbooks.

19   "Curiosities of the Chemistry of Art," *Illustrated Magazine of Art* 1, no. 6 (1853): 359, available at https://www.jstor.org/stable/20538008?seq=1#metadata_info_tab_contents.

20   "Curiosities of the Chemistry of Art," 358.

21   "Curiosities of the Chemistry of Art," 358.

22   Pierre Desrochers, "Promoting Corporate Environmental Sustainability in the Victorian Era: The Bethnal Green Museum Permanent Waste Exhibit (1875–1928)," *V&A Online Journal*, no. 3 (Spring 2011), http://www.vam.ac.uk/content/journals/research-journal/issue-03/promoting-corporate-environmental-sustainability-in-the-victorian-era-the-bethnal-green-museum-permanent-waste-exhibit-1875-1928/.

23   Peter Lund Simmonds, *Waste Products and Underdeveloped Substances; or, Hints for Enterprise in Neglected Fields*, rev. ed. (London: Hardwicke and Bogue, 1876), 477.

24   See Pierre Desrochers, "Freedom versus Coercion in Industrial Ecology: A Reply to Boons," *EconJournalWatch* 9, no. 2 (2012): 78–99.

25   Johann Rudolf von Wagner, *Handbook of Chemical Technology*, translated and edited from the eight German edition by William Crookes. (New York: D. Appleton and Company, 1872), 3.

26   *Hazell's Annual Cyclopædia*, ed. E. D. Price (London: Hazell, Watson, and Viney, 1886), s.v. "The Utilisation of 'Waste Materials,'" available at https://books.google.ca/books?id=dv0BAAAAYAAJ&pg=PA462&source=gbs_toc_r&cad=3#v=onepage&q&f=false.

27   "Her Majesty's Jubilee: A Scientific Retrospect," *Chemical News* 55, no. 1440 (1887): 299, available at http://books.google.ca/books?id=cJwEAAAAYAAJ.

28   Leebert Lloyd Lamborn, *Cottonseed Products: A Manual of the Treatment of Cottonseed for Its Products and Their Utilization in the*

Arts (New York: D. Van Nostrand, 1904), 16, available at https://archive.org/details/cottonseedprodu00lambgoog/page/n13.

29 Quoted in Bethnal Green Branch of the South Kensington Museum, *Descriptive Catalogue of the Collection Illustrating the Utilization of Waste Products* (G.E. Eyre and W. Spottiswoode, 1875), 4.

30 Karl Marx, *Capital*, vol. 3, *The Process of Capitalist Production as a Whole*, trans. (1894; repr., Chicago: Charles H. Kerr, 1909), available at http://www.econlib.org/library/YPDBooks/Marx/mrxCpC.html.

31 Henry G. Kittredge, "The Utilization of Wastes and By-Products in Manufactures with Special Reference to the Decade of 1890–1900," *U.S. Census Bulletin*, no. 190 (June 16, 1902), 3, available at https://www2.census.gov/prod2/decennial/documents/03322287no164-208ch4.pdf.

32 This section borrows from Pierre Desrochers and Joanna Szurmak, "Long Distance Trade, Locational Dynamics and By-Product Development: Insights from the History of the American Cottonseed Industry," *Sustainability* 9, no. 4, art. 579 (2017), https://www.mdpi.com/2071-1050/9/4/579. See that text for additional source material and technical discussions.

33 For a short discussion of cottonseed as a feed for ruminants, see Lawton Stewart and Johnny Rossi, "Using Cotton Byproducts in Beef Cattle Diets" (Bulletin 1311, University of Georgia Cooperative Extension, 2010), http://cotton.tamu.edu/General%20Production/Georgia%20Cotton%20Byproducts%20for%20Beef%20Cattle%20B%201311_2.pdf.

34 Eugene Clyde Brooks, *The Story of Cotton and the Development of the Cotton States* (Chicago: Rand McNally, 1911), 354, available at https://archive.org/details/storyofcottondev00broouoft/page/i.

35 Brooks, *Story of Cotton*, 353.

36 Luther A. Ransom, *The Great Cottonseed Industry of the South* (New York: Oil, Paint and Drug Reporter, 1911), available at https://archive.org/details/greatcottonseedi00ransrich/page/n4.

37 Brooks, *Story of Cotton*, 353.

38 Brooks, 353.

39 Brooks, 354.

40 Rev. Code of the Statute Laws of the State of Miss. (1857), art. 19.

41 Rev. Code of the Statute Laws of the State of Miss., art. 18.

42 Desrochers and Szurmak, "Long Distance Trade."

43 Henry V. Ogden, *Paper on Cotton-Seed Oil and Cotton-Seed Oil Mills* (Atlanta: Constitution Print, 1880), available at https://archive.org/details/paperoncottonsee00ogderich/page/n4.

44 Robert Grimshaw, "Industrial Applications of Cottonseed Oil," *Journal of the Franklin Institute* 127, no. 3 (1889): 191–92.

45 Ransom, *Great Cottonseed Industry*, 9–10.

46 Ransom, 53.

47 Desrochers and Szurmak, "Long Distance Trade."

48 For additional details about the early days of by-product development, see Harold F. Williamson and Arnold R. Daum, *The American Petroleum Industry: The Age of Illumination, 1859–1899* (Evanston, IL: Northwestern University Press, 1959), chapter 10.

49 Dominick T. Armentano, "The Petroleum Industry: A Historical Study in Power," *Cato Journal* 1, no. 1 (1981): 53–85; Brian Black, "Oil Creek as Industrial Apparatus: Re-creating the Industrial Process through the Landscape of Pennsylvania's Oil Boom," *Environmental History* 3, no. 2 (1998): 210–29; Brian Black, *Petrolia: The Landscape of America's First Oil Boom* (Baltimore: Johns Hopkins University Press, 2000).

50 B. Franklin, "After Petroleum," *Harper's New Monthly Magazine* 30 (1864): 59.

51 Franklin, "After Petroleum."

52 Robert C. Estall and R. Ogilvie Buchanan, *Industrial Activity and Economic Geography: A Study of the Forces Behind the Geographical Location of Productive Activity in Manufacturing Industry*, 3rd rev. ed. (London, UK: Hutchinson, 1973), 221.

53 William L. Leffler, *Petroleum Refining in Nontechnical Language*, 4th ed. (Tulsa, OK: PennWell, 2008), 1.

54 Newton Copp and Andrew Zanella, *Discovery, Innovation and Risk* (Cambridge, MA: MIT Press, 1993), 147.

55 Ron Chernow, *Titan: The Life of John D. Rockefeller, Jr.* (New York: Random House, 1998), 181.

56 Copp and Zanella, *Discovery, Innovation and Risk*, 156.

57 George Powell Perry, *Wealth from Waste or Gathering Up the Fragments*, 2nd ed. (New York: Fleming H. Revell, 1908), 73–74.

58 Williamson and Daum, *American Petroleum Industry*, 249.

59 Williamson and Daum, 250.

60   Gilbert Holland Montague, "The Later History of the Standard Oil Company," *Quarterly Journal of Economics* 17, no. 2 (1903): 323–24, available at https://doi.org/10.2307/1883667.

61   Frederick Arthur Ambrose Talbot, *Millions from Waste* (Philadelphia, PA: J.B. Lippincott Company, 1920), 16–17.

62   Talbot, *Millions from Waste*, 15–16.

63   Needless to say, large ships are also powered by bunker fuels.

64   Frans Lox, *Packaging and Ecology* (Leatherhead, UK: Pira International, 1992).

65   Joseph Russell Smith, M. Ogden Phillips, and Thomas R. Smith, *Industrial and Commercial Geography*, 4th ed. (New York: Holt, Rinehart and Winston, 1961), 309.

66   The European market from the mid-1860s onward for several years absorbed approximately 70 percent of the refined crude from the United States. Kim Leonard, "Oil Boom: Pittsburgh Was Nation's First Petroleum Capital," *Trib Live*, October 4, 2009, https://archive.triblive.com/news/oil-boom-pittsburgh-was-nations-first-petroleum-capital/.

67   Armentano, "Petroleum Industry."

68   Ralph W. Hidy and Muriel E. Hidy, *History of the Standard Oil Company (New Jersey): Pioneering in Big Business, 1882–1911* (New York: Harper & Brothers, 1955), 417–18.

69   Hidy and Hidy, *History of the Standard Oil Company*, 419.

70   Lucas Herrmann, Elaine Dunphy, and Jonathan Copus, *Oil and Gas for Beginners: A Guide to the Oil & Gas Industry* (London: Deutsche Bank AG, 2010), 164.

71   Robert B. McNee, "Functional Geography of the Firm, with an Illustrative Case Study from the Petroleum Industry," *Economic Geography* 34, no. 4 (1958): 321–37.

72   Willem Molle and Egbert Wever, "Oil Refineries and Petrochemical Industries in Europe," *GeoJournal* 9, no. 4 (1984): 421–30.

73   Apart from logistical complications, refined petroleum products require either dedicated or "clean" tanks for shipping, and either lose value or require further processing when they are sent in batches through pipelines.

74   Andrew Inkpen and Michael H. Moffett, *The Global Oil and Gas Industry: Management, Strategy and Finance* (Tulsa, OK: PennWell, 2011), 455.

75 This section borrows from Desrochers and Szurmak, "Long Distance Trade." See that text for additional source material and technical discussions.

76 W. C. Mullendore, *History of the United States Food Administration, 1917–1919* (Palo Alto, CA: Stanford University Press, 1941), 282.

77 George F. Deasy, "Geography of the United States Cottonseed Oil Industry," *Economic Geography* 17, no. 4 (1941): 348.

78 H. C. Nixon, "The Rise of the American Cottonseed Oil Industry," *Journal of Political Economy* 38, no. 1 (1930): 81.

79 Lynette Boney Wrenn, *Cinderella of the New South: A History of the Cottonseed Industry, 1855–1955* (Knoxville, TN: University of Tennessee Press, 1995), 8.

80 Wrenn, *Cinderella of the New South*, 8–9.

81 Ogden, *Paper on Cotton-Seed Oil*, 12.

82 Brooks, *Cotton: Its Uses, Varieties, Fibre Structure, Cultivation, and Preparation for the Market and as an Article of Commerce* (New York: Spon & Chamberlain, 1898), 312.

83 Ransom, *Great Cottonseed Industry*, 23.

84 Deasy, "Geography of the United States Cottonseed Oil Industry."

85 Albert Galloway Keller and Avard Longley Bishop, *Commercial and Industrial Geography* (Ginn and Company, 1928), 245.

86 Ransom, *Great Cottonseed Industry*, 19.

87 Lamborn, *Cottonseed Products: A Manual of the Treatment of Cottonseed for Its Products and Their Utilization in the Arts*, 37.

88 Albert S. Carlson, ed., *Economic Geography of Industrial Materials* (New York: Reinhold, 1956), 405.

89 Carlson, *Economic Geography of Industrial Materials*, 405.

90 Brooks, *Cotton: Its Uses, Varieties, Fibre Structure, Cultivation, and Preparation for the Market and as an Article of Commerce*, 330.

91 Ransom, *Great Cottonseed Industry*, 57.

92 Karl Brandt, *The Reconstruction of World Agriculture* (New York: W.W. Norton, 1945), 271–73.

93 Ransom, *Great Cottonseed Industry*, 35.

94 Brooks, *Story of Cotton*, 23.

95 Ransom, *Great Cottonseed Industry*, 10–11.

96 Brooks, *Story of Cotton*, 362.

97 Mark Pennington, "Elinor Ostrom, Common-Pool Resources and the Classical Liberal Tradition," in *The Future of the Commons:*

Beyond Market Failure and Government Regulation, ed. Elinor Ostrom (London: Institute of Economic Affairs, 2012), 23.

98 Ostrom, "Beyond Markets and States," 2.

99 Elinor Ostrom, *Beyond Markets and States: Polycentric Governance of Complex Economic Systems*, (Nobel Prize Lecture, December 8, 2009), 409-10, available at https://www.nobelprize.org/uploads/2018/06/ostrom_lecture.pdf

100 Ristovska, "Role of the Business Sector."